JOANNE JOWELL

I am Ella

A remarkable story of survival,
from Auschwitz to Africa

KWELA BOOKS

Copyright © 2023 Joanne Jowell, Evelyn Kaplan, Ella Blumenthal
Copyright in published edition © 2023 NB Publishers
First edition in 2023 by Kwela Books,
an imprint of NB Publishers,
a division of Media24 Boeke (Pty) Ltd, Heerengracht 40, Cape Town

All rights reserved.
No part of this book may be reproduced or transmitted in any form or by any electronic or mechanical means (including photocopying and recording) or by any other information storage or retrieval system, nor may it be used for the purpose of training artificial intelligence technologies or systems, without written permission from the publisher.

Cover design: Nudge Studio
Typography: Nazli Jacobs
Cover image: Micha Serraf, owned by Sanktuary Films
Editor: Gillian Warren-Brown
Proof reader: Kathleen Sutton
Indexer: Anna Tanneberger

I Am Here (2021 by Sanktuary Films) and *I am Ella* (2023):
The two projects are not associated and the image used on the front cover, for both projects, was shot by Micha Serraf, owned by Sanktuary Films, and used by this book under license.

LSiPOD: 978-0-7957-1129-9 (Second edition, first impression 2025)
ISBN: 978-0-7957-1069-8 (epub)

For my children, grandchildren,
great-grandchildren, and future generations.
– Ella Blumenthal

For Maxx – the Tank, the Moose, the boy with the double kiss.
You already consider Ella a legend. Now go tell your friends.
– Joanne Jowell

Contents

Foreword	1
Author's note	3
Prologue	13
Chapter 1 A Warsaw childhood	15
Chapter 2 Growing up Jewish	29
Chapter 3 Invasion	44
Chapter 4 Ghetto	62
Chapter 5 Mila 19	80
Chapter 6 Majdanek	100
Chapter 7 Auschwitz	110
Chapter 8 Bergen-Belsen	136
Chapter 9 Liberation	144

Chapter 10 Separation	161
Chapter 11 Paris	169
Chapter 12 Palestine	184
Chapter 13 Johannesburg	195
Chapter 14 Cape Town	215
Chapter 15 Grandchildren	230
Chapter 16 No place for hate	262
Chapter 17 Faith and hope	267
Epilogue	272
Acknowledgements	275
Selective glossary	280
Index	283
About the author	288

Foreword

Through my involvement in Holocaust remembrance and education in South Africa over more than two decades, I have read many memoirs and biographies of Holocaust survivors and have heard, first-hand, from survivors themselves. Each story has moved me and astonished me, and taken me on a unique and yet shared journey. Indeed, my interaction and friendships with survivors has been one of the most deeply moving, humbling and gratifying aspects of my work.

Joanne Jowell spent close to 45 hours in conversation with Ella Blumenthal, a remarkable woman whose life now spans more than a hundred years. Over the many hours spent together in Ella's Cape Town home, a special relationship develops, which enables Ella to share her complex life history with Joanne and in turn prompts a journey, for Joanne, of deep reflection. What emerges is a cross between memoir and biography of both women.

While Ella's story, largely in her own words, dominates the narrative, Joanne has masterfully ordered memory into a compelling book, with keen observation, reflection and attention to historical detail. We feel as if we have truly met Ella and have been sitting with Joanne as Ella's story has unfolded. The careful use of footnotes and interjections of Joanne's voice at the start and end of most chapters enriches the text and helps to focus us on important themes that emerge. Intrinsic to both Ella's reflections and those of Joanne are links with the younger generation, which are so important as fewer and fewer eyewitnesses to the Holocaust remain with us. The presence of Ella's children; grandchildren and great-grandchildren permeates the text, as does that of Joanne's children. So much in Ella's story and family relationships raises themes that will resonate with young readers, thus adding a significant and timeous dimension to this book.

Much of Ella's life is impacted by her experiences as a Holocaust survivor, but so much more emerges and the reader is gifted with a portrait of a feisty, compassionate, intelligent and reflective woman. Her sense of humour, strong Jewish religious identity and sense of family transcends tragedy and unimaginable suffering and loss. One might have expected bitterness, trauma and overwhelming sadness as a result of such life experiences, but instead we are left with the joy and celebration of life that Ella conveys.

Joanne Jowell's portrait of Ella Blumenthal leaves us inspired and resonates long after we have read the final words. *I am Ella* makes a strong statement about the human spirit and is a powerful tool in urging us towards the just, kind and compassionate world to which we should aspire.

Richard Freedman,
Chairman of the Board of Trustees of the Cape Town Holocaust & Genocide Centre
November 2022

Author's note

My teenage son stands at the desk in his bedroom and strikes a match.

His curtains are drawn and, until the flame flares, only the pale glow of his computer lights the room. From the screen, an assembly of solemn faces watches.

In front of him stands a *yahrzeit*[1] candle – the long-burning vessel of Jewish commemoration which those with both parents living have no need to light. Yet light it he does.

It is the 21st of April 2020. Yom HaShoah.[2]

We're scaling the heights of the Covid-19 pandemic in South Africa. Today my children have returned to school for the first time in three months, and I am only now able to face a project for which I was engaged in 2017. It has taken my writing two other books, planning a literary festival, and enduring a global pandemic to finally bring my pen to paper in the story of Holocaust survivor Ella Blumenthal. I am instantly struck by the disquieting congruence of writing about a Holocaust past during an apocalyptic present. I wonder how Ella herself will approach these 'unprecedented times', having survived an 'unprecedented time' of her own during World War II. Will her shield of survivorship earn her antibodies against this plague?

---

1   Yiddish: the anniversary of a death.
2   Holocaust Remembrance Day.

My interviews with protagonist Ella were conducted soon after her daughter Evelyn Kaplan approached me to write the story. Although fully immersed in writing a very different book at the time, I was anxious to meet Ella and record her testimony as soon as possible. Whether driven by fear (of losing the sprightly, vital, then-96-year-old Ella), compassion (it is impossible not to drop a gaping jaw when hearing even the bare bones of Ella's story), or personal interest (I have a long-held sensitivity towards the subject of the Holocaust), I immediately set about meeting Ella for regular interviews. She preferred to meet in the afternoons, which was lucky because my other project's protagonist preferred mornings. So I juggled the two, often going from one to the other on the same day and attempting to clear my head in between.

We met often over a period of three months, all 22 interviews except one taking place at her apartment in Sea Point, Cape Town. In total, we spoke for close on 45 hours, mining her memories, recording her testimony, and building a very warm relationship.

* * *

The name 'Ella Blumenthal' is instantly recognisable in the South African Jewish community. Hers is one of the most eloquent and strident voices in the treasured choir of approximately 300 Holocaust survivors who made their way to this *goldene medine*[3] during and after the war.

Silence is a common trait among this cohort, wherever they landed in the world. Many survivors suffered inarticulable guilt that they survived when six million of their brethren did not; most felt that the post-war world could not understand their trauma and that they therefore could not share their experiences, choosing to speak of it only among themselves and filtering what they told their children; often they simply could not find the words to describe their suffering or even their redemption; silence gave some survivors space to

---

[3] Yiddish for 'golden state', because of South Africa's association with the precious metal.

heal by putting the greatest possible psychic distance between themselves and their trauma. Survivor authors and poets often address the issue of how inconceivably difficult it is to adequately express Holocaust experience or pain, and to dare to do so on behalf of fellow victims. Author and Nobel laureate Elie Wiesel said, 'Only those who were there will ever know, and those who were there can never tell.'

The children of Holocaust survivors must themselves reckon with their parents' traumatic past and its impact – conscious or not – on their upbringing. Most will have grown up with their parents sharing little to no detail. Holocaust historian Edna Friedberg writes: 'As a teenager I repeatedly nudged my father, "Why won't you talk about what you went through, Daddy?" . . . My father's reply was blunt. "When people I barely know ask me to tell them what happened to me during the Holocaust, it feels like they are saying 'Nice to meet you. I heard you were gang raped, tell me about it.'" His explanation of his silence left me chastened, silenced myself.'[4]

Growing up with silence was certainly the case for Ella's family in their early years. 'As a child, I would ask my mom what the scar on her arm was and she said it was from a car accident,' recalls Evelyn, the youngest of four siblings. 'It was only when I was about 12 or so that she told me about her experience. She only started actively [publicly] speaking about it in the last ten to fifteen years.' And speak she does, taking every opportunity afforded her to educate, illuminate, commemorate. Together with a handful of fellow survivors in South Africa, Ella's story has filled the compendium of this country's survival stories and her name has become synonymous with Holocaust awareness and education. No longer a silent victim of an unspeakable past, Ella's voice, her name, her story ring out like cymbals. She is, as my sons would say, a legend.

But that is not enough.

It is not enough that we know her name or recognise her voice. It

---

4   Friedberg, E. 9 July 2016. *Elie Wiesel and the Agony of Bearing Witness*. The Atlantic. https://www.theatlantic.com/international/archive/2016/07/elie-wiesel-holocaust/490604/. Last accessed 22/12/2022.

is not enough that Ella the survivor bears the burden of bearing witness. That task falls to us all; it is the moral obligation set upon humanity by inhumanity. It is an obligation that I have felt keenly since I was a young girl, though perhaps did not recognise it as such back then.

I grew up in a traditional Jewish home and attended a Jewish day school from the age of five. Holocaust education was an integral part of the curriculum, presented in as age-appropriate a manner as the school could manage. I don't recall the day or year in which I first learned about the Holocaust; I feel as if it is something I have always known, the way I've always known that I'm Jewish, or female, or brown-eyed. I do, however, recall the moment in which I felt the grip of obligation, the precise minute in which my Holocaust identity went from national to personal.

It was 1990. I was 16. Nelson Mandela was free. South Africa was rebirthing. My adult sense of self was fledgling, but my cultural identity, as a Jewish South African, had never been quite so ardent. I was flush with living and learning in an age of such monumental promise, and finally old enough to appreciate the type of material I was considered too immature to understand before.

It is with this newly opened mind that I found myself staring at an iconic photograph of the Holocaust: the 'Warsaw Ghetto Boy', taken during the 1943 Warsaw Ghetto Uprising, shows a crowd of Jews emerging from a building, hands held up in surrender to submachine gun-wielding Nazi soldiers. Front and centre stands a young boy in a coat, long socks and newsboy cap, his brow and mouth crumpled as if on the verge of tears. A woman carrying a bag and holding her arms aloft turns to look at the soldiers. One soldier, flanked by others, directs a defiant glare at the photographer. The little boy, his fear, and his imminent death, take one's breath away.

Later I would learn that this group of Jews had been forced out of their bunker hiding place during the final liquidation of the ghetto. All were deported to extermination camps at Majdanek or Treblinka. I would learn that this photograph was one of a selection included

Author's note

in the Stroop Report – a collection of the daily communications sent by SS commander Jürgen Stroop (the officer in charge of the liquidation of the Warsaw Ghetto) to his higher-ups. I would learn that, of the identities in the photo, we are certain of only one: the MP 28 submachine gun-wielding soldier Josef Blösche – an SS policeman known for his violence against women and children. Even the name of the boy in the photo is still unclear, though several individuals have claimed to be him. But while we may not know his name, we know his story. It is the story of all child victims of the Holocaust. It is, at once, the story of Jewish resistance and suffering.

As I stare at 'Warsaw Ghetto Boy', I am only dimly aware of the bigger picture reflected by this smaller one. I am struck by the boy, the gun, the horror, yes, but I see something else that grabs my gut. Or rather, I see some*one* else . . .

On the edge of the photo's frame, partially obscured by other victims, stands a little girl, not more than six or seven years old. She holds one hand above her head in surrender, her hair is wrapped in a scarf, which frames her face and tucks beneath her chin in the demure manner of a much older woman. She is clearly not the protagonist of this scene, yet it is this girl who catches, and holds, my eye. Is it because her gaze is so direct? Aside from the SS officer with the gun, she is the only person looking directly at the camera. Is it because, unlike the crowd around her, her demeanour appears absolutely calm? Her perfectly oval face, deep brown eyes and not-unsmiling mouth broadcast a misplaced serenity in this haze of brutal commotion.

She looks out. At me, or so it feels. Our gazes lock and we stare at each other, across the years since her untimely death, over the heads of those who lived, and hid, and died alongside her, beyond the endless questions with no answers, all the way to this moment of our meeting. I see her. I know her. I am her.

There is a photo of me as a six-year-old dressed up as a Romani girl for the Jewish festival of Purim. I had borrowed a brightly coloured skirt with bells at the hem and I felt so exotic as they jingled while I walked. Then there were the obligatory giant gold hoop earrings; I was not allowed to pierce my ears until I was much older, so my mother sourced a pair of clip-on hoops, which I simply adored and swore I would never remove – I couldn't bring myself to admit how painfully they pinched my earlobes and I surely wouldn't have lasted more than the car ride to school wearing them. Which explains why they are not in the portrait taken later that day, why the picture that would freeze that event in time and come crashing back into memory decades later was of a sweet little girl with hair pulled back simply, head covered by a scarf knotted beneath her chin. A girl whose perfectly oval face, deep brown eyes and not-unsmiling mouth broadcast a calm serenity in a haze of happy commotion. A girl whose face would be reflected back at me, with a sense of eerie recognition, through a Nazi lens. Looking at the picture of the girl in the foreground of 'Warsaw Ghetto Boy' I saw none other than myself.

Many of us do, or should, hold an interest in and connection to the Holocaust. I believe it is our moral imperative as humans, regardless of religion or cultural identity. No doubt being Jewish deepens my own connection to the subject; for as long as I can remember, I have been drawn to Holocaust study. In my final years of high school, I pleaded with my parents to allow me to join the March of the Living – an international educational programme that brings thousands to Poland to study the history of the Holocaust, culminating in the three-kilometre march from Auschwitz concentration camp to Birkenau on Holocaust Remembrance Day. My much-revered school principal eventually advised against my going, citing my position as head prefect and the looming matriculation exams as 'too much to juggle'. In retrospect, I'm glad he put paid to the idea back then because he simply stoked a flame that was far better tended years later when I got the chance to visit Poland as an adult, older and wiser, in an intimate group, and accompanied by a Holocaust survivor.

In the intervening years, I read Holocaust books, took a course on the subject while studying for my BA and visited Holocaust museums in any city I travelled to that could boast one. I can hardly call my absorption with the subject academic or professional – it is more of a lay fascination that I put down to my innate interest in psychology and my family's own, one-step-removed connection to the Holocaust. My maternal great-grandparents, uncles and aunts were killed, but my grandma and grandpa never spoke of them (at least not to me) and my closer relatives, including my mother, while surely affected by them, did not seem defined by the family's Holocaust losses. The subconscious effects are doubtless – an issue I explored in a university essay examining survivor guilt and the psychological impact on second/third generations. My late mother was a social history researcher – she was fascinated by the Jewish presence in South Africa and immersed herself in learning and writing about our cultural history in this country. I wondered if that was what stimulated my own particular interest.

These explanations for my connection to this tragic history are reasonable and objective, but the pull of my likeness in the photograph I now refer to, at least in my head, as the 'Warsaw Ghetto Boy *and Me*' – is deeply, deeply personal.

Holocaust history is MY story. It could have been me . . . Perhaps in another incarnation it WAS me. That history is more than mine, more than ours. That history is me.

As I watched my son that Yom HaShoah, I considered his rapt attention on the memorial service and wondered if this ritual might light a similar spark in him – a deeply felt interest in a history fast receding. It strikes me that his is the last generation that will be able to reflect on the Holocaust as 'recent history', a past that shaped people loved and known to them as grandparents or living legends. He is still fortunate enough to be able to meet or hear from living Holocaust survivors, to grow up with an intrinsic connection to Holocaust history. He joined me to listen to Ella recounting her experiences during the 2020 Zikaron BaSalon (Memories in the living room) – an annual event that commemorates Yom HaShoah with small gatherings of survivors and their children as guests in private homes; the idea is to give ordinary people direct access to an extraordinary history and the people who lived through it. Of course the unspoken sense of urgency that hangs over such events, and over all Holocaust conversation these days, is the impending survivor extinction. Even those who were born during the war, or were very young at the time, are now in their 80s. So such experiences – much like mine in writing this book – are tinged with both privilege and pressure.

Since it is the time of Coronavirus, Zikaron BaSalon is happening online the world over. Curled up on the couch, my son and I log on to Zoom and watch Ella's face close-up on screen, feeling as if she is talking to us alone. To the Generation Z sitting next to me, so used to consuming his information via screen, it makes a difference that this event is live. My son doesn't feel he can look away, or answer texts or play digital games at the same time as watching a real live survivor tell her real live story. I watch him watching her and hope that this might be his hook – his moment of connection, of obligation, of personal interest.

It's hard to hook the Gen Zs. Even though Ella quite literally walked free of a gas chamber and faced down monsters, can her story resonate with children whose virtual worlds know no graphic limits? I am an author so my first inclination is towards the written word; but reading is not how Gen Z goes about its business, let alone the hefty task of remembering to never forget. While the obligation to educate future generations on the Holocaust and its survivors obviously does not fall to me alone, I can't help hoping to harness the uniqueness of Ella's story for a broader purpose, and to have it claim a place in the canon of Holocaust material that immortalises memory. I want Ella's story, the Holocaust history, to talk to my children as it does to me, to be a story they can absorb and disseminate further still. So, if I'm to bring Ella's experience to my children through longform writing, then perhaps the key is to include characters to whom they can more easily relate, such as one of Ella's grandchildren.

Author's note

I am reminded of Yom HaShoah 2018 – the community's commemorative event at Cape Town's Pinelands cemetery. Four generations shared their thoughts: Ella, her daughter Evelyn, her granddaughter Jade and her great-granddaughter Deena. Each spoke in their own way about the effect of Ella's experiences on their life. Each unpacked and expressed them in words most befitting their age group. I can still hear then-15-year-old Deena's opening lines: 'My great granny sleeps with the curtains open. She wants to be able to see the sun rise every single day.' Deena did not need to explain Ella's reasoning; cause and effect clearly implied, imagery sufficiently charged . . . we instantly understood the significance. By virtue of her position as descendant and all that went before, we understood. And so did I: Ella must tell her story, and keep telling it as long as she is able; but her progeny must tell it too, in language that reaches their friends, touches their peers, and transcends generations from X, to Y, to Z and beyond. We must hear from Ella, but we must hear *about* Ella too. We must find ourselves in the story of the Holocaust – if not in its survivor-protagonists then in its extensive support cast whose ranks swell every time we remember not to forget.

If there is, indeed, 'nothing new under the sun' then no times are truly unprecedented, no circumstance is entirely unrelatable. There is loss, and pain, and survival and triumph in all our histories – national and personal. There is an Ella Blumenthal in every family. There is a 'Warsaw Ghetto Boy *and Me*' for each one of us. It's out there. Our duty is never to forget. Our duty is to find it.

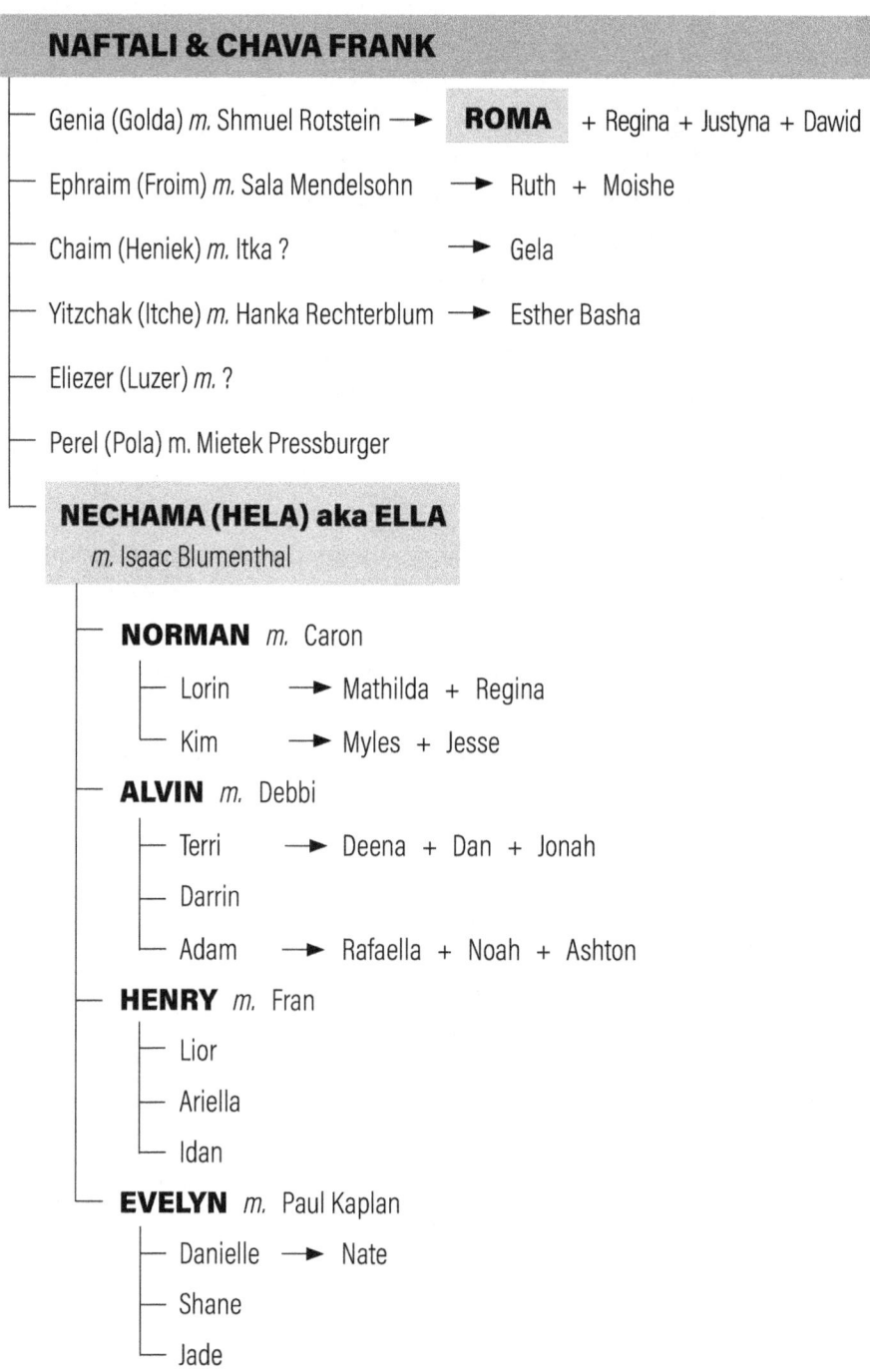

Ella Blumenthal's family tree as at February 2023.

Prologue

ELLA:
I survived the Holocaust with my niece, Roma.

She was my sister Golda's eldest daughter. Golda had four children and we grew up like brothers and sisters. Between Roma and I there was not much difference – only five years. My sister's children, including Roma, were not like my nieces or nephews; they were like my very own siblings.

When the Germans invaded and bombarded Warszawa – in English Warsaw – Roma's apartment was damaged: shrapnel went through the front wall, the balcony came down. So they all came to live with us. We lived like one family. I call all those members of my family 'immediate'. That is how we were with each other.

Twenty-three members of my family died in the Holocaust. Twenty-three. Only Roma and I survived. Out of my parents, my six siblings, their spouses and my nieces and nephews, only Roma and I survived.

I can call them all out to you, the names of my lost family. I've written their names at the back of my *machzor*[5], otherwise I can't manage when it's *Yizkor*[6], which is usually so quick here in South Africa. That way I will always remember each one of them.

I don't like counting. I usually hate to count, ever since the war. But this one time . . .

---

5   The prayer book used on some special Jewish holidays (plural: *machzorim*).
6   Jewish memorial service.

It was just a few years ago. I was celebrating a milestone birthday with a Shabbat feast at my son Henry's place in Johannesburg. My children, grandchildren and great-grandchildren came to be with me. Sitting at that Shabbat table, I looked around at all the beautiful faces of my family and counted twenty-three of us – exactly the number of family members that I lost in the Holocaust. I realised then that *HaShem*[7] had given them back to me.

I have four children, eleven grandchildren and eleven great-grandchildren, bless them. Hopefully I'll still live to see more.

Not only did I survive, but my children and grandchildren are the greatest victory over those who sought to destroy our people.

---

[7] Literally 'The Name'; a way of referring to God in contexts other than prayer and scripture reading because the name itself is considered too holy for such use.

Chapter 1

A Warsaw childhood

Ella lives in Bordeaux – the grande dame of apartment blocks on Sea Point's Beach Road.

Bordeaux spans almost an entire city block and its origins are set firmly in the heritage of both Cape Town and its Jewish community – the former because, in its various guises, it has occupied this particular piece of real estate since the late 1800s, and the latter because it would not be inaccurate to claim that most Cape Jewish families have taken up residence in Bordeaux at some or other point. And if not resided, then at least attended Shabbat dinners here. There is even a particular smell that has pervaded the block on so many Friday afternoons that it is now surely baked into its walls – fried kingklip + baked challah[8] + Estée Lauder – a singular mix evoked instantly by the simple phrase 'it smells like Bordeaux flats'. It is a phrase so laden with idiosyncrasy and nostalgia that it requires no explanation, prompts immediate recognition, and could well be used as a lineage screening question.

So the fact that Ella lives here is not unexpected. I actually find it quite comforting because visiting her takes me back: to my early childhood when my grandparents lived in a big, sea-facing Bordeaux apartment similar to Ella's; to my high school days, when my then-widowed granny moved into a smaller Bordeaux flat with direct sight-

---

8   A plaited loaf, also known in South Africa as a kitke; traditionally eaten when celebrating Shabbat (Sabbath) and major Jewish holidays.

and-sound lines to Marais Road synagogue below; to my university days when my boyfriend (now husband) shared an apartment here with his sister and provided happy refuge from my own digs in university residence.

These days, entry into Bordeaux is strictly monitored by security and I must buzz through two doors, sign in at the reception desk, and wait for the security guard to call up to Ella to confirm that she's expecting me.

I ring the doorbell and wait outside the quintessential Bordeaux front door: a dark mahogany panel inlaid with pimpled opaque glass. I can see the shadows of movement just beyond. Joan, Ella's carer, opens the door with Ella not far behind. They usher me down the passage, past side tables heavy with framed photographs, into the lounge-dining room where the sliding windows are thrown open to the sea breeze and a tea table is freshly laid. Ella's home-baked cookies are piled high on the tray; my children will soon start to look forward to these as a sweet takeaway from my afternoons with Ella.

It is 2017. Ella is 96 years old.

Yeah right.

You may approximate her age from the creases that etch her life's journey across her face, but from the spring in her step and the twinkle in her eye, you'd be forgiven for assuming she is a much younger vintage. Ella is lively and busy and naughty. Her voice is strong, even strident at times, and even though her daughter maintains that Ella has never been interested in the superficial trappings of cosmetics or make-up, I notice that her nails are beautifully polished in an unblemished coat of shining burgundy. Undoubtedly, the fiery nails, the straight teeth, the big bold voice and the arched eyebrows only add to the unexpected air of mischief about Ella, overlaying an indelible youthfulness to the deeply traumatic nature of her past.

She sits me down at the table but not before giving me a full once-over, followed by a warm hug and kiss on the cheek. She notices my necklace – an intricate monogram of my children's initials – and *comments that it looks like one of Gary Nathan's. She is correct. I assume she recognises his jewellery design because Gary is a member of the Camps Bay Shul where Ella's daughter is also a member and where Ella attends many Shabbat and holiday services. But her reply is a curveball: 'No no,' she says, examining the pendant closely, 'I saw them on Facebook.' On Facebook? She is 96!*

For me, and I guess most people, Ella's public recognition is so wholly and inherently tied to her identity as a Holocaust survivor that her aptitude for modern technology is a curious surprise. As I get to know her, I realise how entirely fitting this technophilia is for one who is nothing if not adaptable. She follows the Facebook comment with a housekeeping question about whether I have her phone number (all my communication with her thus far has been through her daughter Evelyn). As I pull out my phone to punch it in, she peers at the Samsung logo and sighs. 'What a pity . . . It's not an iPhone so you can't FaceTime me.'

Best we fasten our seatbelts.

ELLA:

I was born on the 15th of August 1921 in Warsaw, the capital of Poland. Running through the city is a river called in English Vistula and in Polish Wisla; just like in London you have the Thames or in Paris the Seine. I was living in the smaller portion of Warsaw called Praga.

My parents were very religious; my late father, Naftali Frank, was a Chasid[9], actually an Amshinov Chasid – part of a Chasidic dynasty with *rabonim*[10] from generation to generation – like a small caste. He used to travel often to the main rabbi – the Amshinover Rebbe – who lived in Otwock, about an hour by train from Warsaw.

---

9   Chasidism/Hasidism is a strictly Orthodox Jewish sect that was founded as a spiritual revival movement in eastern Europe during the 18th century.
10 Yiddish variation on the Hebrew plural of 'rabbi'.

My father looked like pictures you might have seen of Polish Jews then, with the cap and the *kappotas* (coat) and a *girtel* (belt) – ordinary during the week and satin for Shabbos[11]. During the week he used to wear a black waistcoat where he kept a small brush for his beard and moustache. His beard never grew very long but he kept this little brush in his pocket. For the special holidays like Rosh Hashanah, Yom Kippur and I think Pesach, he wore a white waistcoat and of course a *kittel*[12] and white socks. On weekdays, he wore normal black socks. A woman came once a week to collect all the washed socks for darning – with four men in the house there were so many pairs. You know I could also do beautiful darning once – not any more; nowadays I just throw the socks out if they get a hole! Back then, the woman used to come and collect the folded-up socks, darn them, bring them the following week and collect the next lot. Holes appeared often and my mother had no time to sit and darn them, and you couldn't keep buying new ones – so the woman got paid for darning so many socks every week.

My father was the owner of a store on Targowa Street, a very busy business that supplied tailors with everything from buttons to the cloth of a suit. There wasn't such a thing then that you went to a shop and bought a suit or a coat. There were tailors, Jewish tailors, because Jewish people had to use kosher linen: you can't mix wool and linen – the law is called *shatnes* in Hebrew. My father used to go to suppliers across the river where there were streets lined with wholesalers selling everything you needed for the shop. The outer cloth he would buy from Lodz, which was known for manufacturing it. Friday afternoons were so busy because the tailors were rushing to get the last things to finish off a suit for Shabbos. Their customer would pay only when the suit was ready and the tailor's wife was waiting to buy food for Shabbos, so she would stand and wait until he got the money.

---

11 An Ashkenazi/Eastern European variation on 'Shabbat'; Ella uses the words interchangeably.

12 A white linen or cotton robe worn by religious Jewish men on certain occasions.

We had a telephone in the business. Not many people had that but we had one in the corner. Once, thieves broke into the store; they got into the building around the corner and found the cellar. They dug at night and at the last minute broke through the wood behind the counter and carried out a lot of stuff. There were plenty of thieves then because there were a lot of poor people.

My father wasn't an educated man. He must have gone to *yeshiva*[13] school but he definitely did not go to high school or university. But he checked the books and he had beautiful handwriting – that's what I remember. My brothers, who worked in the shop, used to keep the books, and Sundays my father would look through, see what's happened, and sometimes lend money to the tailors who asked.

We had a neighbour in the business who I now realise was very famous. Rav Menachem Ziemba[14]. When I tell religious Jewish people that I knew him, their eyes go wide and they can't believe it. I didn't know that he was such a famous rabbi. His family's business was ironmongery. He was not often in the shop – he was always studying or writing – but his son Luzer ran the shop and I recall seeing the rabbi sometimes. In fact the corner where the businesses were was a valuable corner – our tailoring business, Rav Ziemba's ironmonger business, and my sister had a clothing business near there too.

I was the youngest in a family of seven children. There was my eldest sister Genia – it's a hard 'g' for Genia in Polish, but in Hebrew it was Golda. Then it was my brother Ephraim – we called him Froim. Then there was Chaim and we called him Heniek. He called himself Henry; he was the only one who was not religious. Then there was Yitzchak – Avraham Yitzchak was his proper Hebrew name

---

13 An Orthodox Jewish college or seminary (plural: *yeshivot*).
14 A distinguished rabbi (thus the title Rav), who was fluent in all of Talmud, the central text of Rabbinic Judaism. Born in 1883 in Praga; shot by the Nazis in 1943 in the aftermath of the Warsaw Ghetto Uprising. Despite the danger, his followers buried him in the courtyard of no 4 Kupiecka Street. His grave was later located and his body exhumed and flown to Israel, where he was finally laid to rest.

but we called him Itche. And then there was Eliezer in Hebrew but we called him Luzer – my children laugh when I tell them what he was called!

After Golda and the four boys came my sister Perel (in Hebrew) and in Polish we called her Pola. She was exactly two years older than me, born in 1919. Golda, the eldest, must have been about thirteen or fourteen years older than me because I was four or five when she got married.

And then there was me. My Hebrew name was Nechama and my father used to call me Chumele – little Chuma, *kleine* Chumele. As a big girl, I tried to change my name to Natalie – it sounded closer to Nechama – but it didn't work *[laughs]*. In Polish they just called me Hela. Hela Frank.

There is a long story to my name, and other names by which I am known – a story that comes from just after the war. But that takes us to the end of my story, after my survival. As far as the name Hela is concerned, that changed when I was coming to South Africa. My late husband told me that in South Africa there is no such name as Hela, 'so we're going to call you Ella'. In Hebrew, I have always been Nechama – I am 'Nechama bat Naftali haKohen[15]'. I was born on *Shabbat Nachamu* – the Sabbath of Consolation, the first Shabbat after the 24-hour fast of Tisha B'Av[16] – the saddest day in the Hebrew calendar. *Nechama* means 'comfort'.

I'm not sure how much comfort I brought though because I was a very naughty child. I don't know if it's because I was the youngest of seven, but it's just how I always was. And I mean very naughty!

---

15 Kohen refers to a Jewish male descendant of the priestly class in Temple times. Religious naming convention is patronymic: first name (Nechama) followed by *ben/bat* (son/daughter of), followed by the father's name (Naftali) and the father's priestly status (in this case haKohen – the priest).

16 A solemn annual 25-hour fast day on the Jewish calendar commemorating numerous disasters that occurred on this day, most notably the destruction of the first and second temples in Jerusalem.

At first I went to a public school and then Bais Yaakov[17] opened and I asked my father to please send me there; I wanted to be like all Jewish women. So I went to Bais Yaakov but it was a very small class because the school was expensive. It wasn't in a normal school building – it was in a flat inside a building.

I used to arrange pranks with the girls. In one of them, there was a little podium with a chair for the teacher on it and we were sitting in front. I arranged that one of us girls would put off the light and then we'd pull off the teacher's *sheitel*[18] *[chuckles]*. Nowadays, women who wear *sheitels* have got short hair underneath, but in my day married women shaved their hair very short like a man. Can you imagine? You've got to have guts to do something like this!

I must have been around 10 or 11 at the time. There was a Purim party and the school arranged for us to put on a play in a theatre. My father had never been to a theatre before, but he came to watch me. Not my mom, not my sister, but my father came to watch me. I was playing the part of Queen Esther.

When the play was finished, we put on a gymnastics display. Remember, we were girls only. And I was always in the front. Whatever we did, I was in the front. I was wearing a white T-shirt and a black skirt in shining material – a full skirt that went quite a bit over the knees and had slits on the side so we could do gymnastics. Of course we couldn't have bare legs, so we were wearing white stockings. They weren't pantyhose, like today, only stockings with garters to keep them up. But when I was getting dressed, I couldn't find one of my garters. Everyone was searching for it, but we had to go on, so they pushed me out with one garter missing. For years, my father used to talk about it – about how *kleine* Chumele's stocking kept falling down, so I had to keep pulling it up. I ran off the stage in the middle of the show.

---

17   Ultra-Orthodox elementary and secondary schools for Jewish girls throughout the world.
18   Married Orthodox Jewish women are obligated to cover their hair. Many do this with a wig called a *sheitel*.

That reminds me of one more case when I ran off. I was trying to help in the shop when it was very busy. Once, maybe more, I had to work out how much the customer had to pay me, but I couldn't. So I ran off and left the customer standing.

I was a busy little thing. And I absolutely loved ice-skating. Not far from us was a skating rink, next to the church. After school I used to go there, sometimes with friends, sometimes alone. Our shoes were not just ordinary shoes: they were lace-up boots and the shoemaker would cut a hole out from the heel as a place to fit a skating blade. I used to skate beautifully. Two or three of us would make a row holding on to each other's shoulders, one knee bent with the bum down low and one leg extended straight out. It was beautiful, a lovely sport every winter. And of course you could walk around in the same lace-up boots and just clip on the blade for skating. I walked all over in those boots; I even walked to high school, which was over the bridge in Warsaw.

I would get tram money from my mom but I often used to pocket it and walk instead. The bridge was three quarters of a kilometre long, a cold walk in winter but I preferred to collect the money and deposit it into my account. I must have been 11 years old when I opened my own account; the post office had a division like a bank and you could save your money there. I've even got a copy of my father's records from the account he also had there. You see, even as a young girl, I had *sechel*[19]! My mother too, Chava Frank. She was a businesswoman. She worked in the shop, and at home we had a maid who cooked for us, a Jewish maid named Sala.

On Friday mornings my mother and Sala used to make challahs; they'd put the mound of dough at my feet in the bed under the duvet. To grow. They needed a warm spot because the climate in Warsaw was very cold. We had double duvets and double windows for the winter. In summer, the extra windows stayed in the cellar, but

---

19 Yiddish and Hebrew for 'wit', 'intelligence', 'common sense'.

in winter they needed to be brought up and fitted on. That was my father's job. There were also long strips of cotton wool, and my father used to tuck it in tight so the cold air shouldn't get through.

Let me tell you about an incident where I used my *sechel* and my savings.

It was my brother Froim's wedding, a few years before the outbreak of the war. He got married to Sala who was from a rabbinical family in a little town outside Lodz called Zgierz. Of course, they met through a matchmaker – a *shadchan* – who came to my parents on a Saturday afternoon and sat next to my father at the head of the table, bringing different *shidduchim*, different matches. Sala came from a very religious family, her father was Rabbi Noach Mendelsohn. She was an intelligent girl, I think she may even have had a degree. Actually, I don't know whether she went to university because the whole family were very, very religious, very *frum*, so maybe she didn't go and study. Anyway, the wedding was in Zgierz and my parents wouldn't take me because they already had my sisters-in-law (my other brothers had to stay in the business), mother-in-law, father-in-law, and children. I must have been 12 because I was at the age where I couldn't have a half-ticket; I had to have a full-price ticket and that was expensive.

We were at our flat and there were *bachorim*, young men, sitting around, singing *zemirot*[20], eating. It was a bachelor's party. My sister's father-in-law was sitting on a couch at the back of the room, watching the young men; I can picture it now. I sat next to him and I was crying.

'Why are you crying Chumele?'

'They won't take me to the wedding. I wanted to go so much. But I have to have a full ticket.'

'Let me think. Maybe they can buy a half-ticket.'

---

20 Jewish hymns and songs, most famously those sung around the table during Shabbat and holidays.

'Well I've got some money in the post office savings division.'

'How much?'

I couldn't remember how much so I brought him the savings booklet to show him.

'You know,' he said, 'It's just enough for a half-ticket – let's take a chance, I'll help you organise it. You'll give your parents a surprise.' When I presented my half-ticket to my parents, what could they do? I went along.

The train compartment was full; I was wearing my sister's coat because my parents wouldn't buy me a new one. I was sitting at the door and the conductor came to check the tickets. I sat like this *[curls herself up]* – huddled, trying to make myself small.

The conductor checked all the tickets and said, 'Who is here with a half-ticket?'

They said, 'This child.'

So he says, in Polish of course: 'This is not a child, this is a full woman.' At 12 years old, and by his rules, I was no longer a child. I remember those exact words in Polish: 'It's not a child, it's a full woman.'

So what did we do? My parents fixed him; they gave him a bribe. And I attended the wedding!

So yes, I was a naughty child and I didn't pay much attention in school. I passed but not with flying colours. I wasn't one of the best scholars. I did like business though, so I joined a course called *Kursi Pirka*, where I learned some basic bookkeeping and typing. It became useful later in my life.

On top of helping in the shop, I wanted to do more accounting. My mother had a cousin or an aunt who was an old widow, a religious woman, who used to sell fodder for horses and cattle. And she was deaf. Once every two or three weeks, she came and I would do her bookkeeping. She couldn't write, so I used to write for her; she memorised the customer's name, date, how much they bought, how much they owed. I gave her pieces of paper for each of them. She passed away in that time and I think her funeral was the first time

A Warsaw childhood

I went to the cemetery. As young children, we were not allowed to go; children who still had living parents were not allowed to go to the cemetery. She must have passed away after the start of the German occupation because it wasn't natural causes. Anyway, I remember how she used to come in the evenings and how I loved to sit and do the accounting. It was just in me. I was a natural. And after the war, when I got married, it came up again. I was in business for years. I think it's because I grew up in a home where we had a business, and each one of us children took part. There were no strangers who worked in the business. It was very busy but only family worked there.

At first we lived in a large flat in Szeroka Street. There is a small hotel in its place now, though the next-door building is still there. There were lots of rooms, some facing the courtyard so we could see who was coming up, and some facing the street behind. My sister Golda and her husband lived with us for seven years. At that time there was a custom that, when children got married, they stayed at whichever in-laws were the most capable or well-to-do, so the couple had free board and lodging until they could sustain themselves; children got married young then. My brother-in-law was a journalist and he often came home late because they'd work until three or four in the morning. Golda had three children while she was living with us: my niece Roma and two more girls. When she was pregnant with the fourth child, they moved out into a beautiful flat of their own where they lived until the outbreak of the war.

The last few years before the war, my father had a problem with the landlord and we moved out of our lovely large flat and into a place on Brukowa Street, closer to our business. It was a terrible place, small and cold. But it was central.

I don't remember any pictures or decorations on the walls but there was a big cupboard – a *shenkele* – like a wardrobe except that it was filled with *sefarim*[21]. There were big ones, like you might see at

---

21 Hebrew for 'books', in this case referring to religious texts.

the back of a shul, and small ones. It had fancy doors with glass inlay and dark lilac curtains. It was there that we kept our own *sefer* Torah[22]. My late father used to *daven*[23] in a *shtiebel*[24] and he donated a *sefer* Torah. I remember it as a small Torah with a suede cover saying it was donated by Naftali and Chava Frank, and a beautiful silver ornament on top. That was our family Torah.

Later, when we were ordered to move to the ghetto at the end of 1940, we managed to take that beautiful, sacred *sefer* Torah with us. But, like most things, it did not survive the war. Since then, I've always wanted to donate a Torah in my parents' name. I asked my son-in-law how much a *sefer* Torah costs and he says about R100 000! Really, I should have done it. But it's very, very expensive.

Anyway, back to our flat on Brukowa Street.

In this small, horrible flat, I shared a bed with my sister Pola. It wasn't like Szeroka Street where we had our own rooms. There was a writing desk behind our bed with drawers where we kept our books. Just before the outbreak of the war, we begged our parents to buy a radio. They bought us a big Telefunken. It stood behind the bed, on top of the desk, and it looked as if it had a green eye – the knob was green, and it was always, always on. And you know what? When the German army occupied Warsaw, one of the orders was that we hand in our radios. Ours was so big that my sister and I had to carry it together. So that was the end of this radio.

My two unmarried brothers who were still at home shared a big sofa-bed. And my parents had their own bedroom. There was no bathroom, but there was a toilet, a proper toilet with a tank on top and a chain to pull. If we looked down into the courtyard, we could see a big square with staircases for different entrances. We could see people coming and going in the yard. Poor people carrying bags

---

22 A handwritten Torah scroll (the five books of Moses).
23 Yiddish for 'pray'.
24 Yiddish for 'little house' or 'little room'; used for communal Jewish prayer and gathering, more informal than a synagogue.

used to come and sing, call for food, 'send down what you've got, whatever you don't need throw it down, throw it down'.

My parents worked hard and they were good people. We were considered well-off, but my father had some distant relations who were cobblers and very poor. They lived on the same street where our business was but much further down, almost at the end of the city. I have this memory of them sitting on very low stools, repairing shoes, two or three men. My father always wanted to help them, to give them work. So when we were sleeping, he would look under our beds and check the shoes – to see if they needed to be soled, heeled or repaired in any way.

The flat had a very big basin in the kitchen, so if we wanted to wash, we used that. There was a coal stove for cooking and a gas one with two plates. For Shabbat there was a samovar. We used to prepare the tea essence in a small pot; you couldn't make tea the normal way on Shabbos, you could just use a bit of the essence and boiling water.

How did we do the washing, the linen, in those times? There were no laundries and the maid was cooking or doing the house or washing up dishes. Very few people could have a maid anyway. So for the laundry, once a month or once every two months, a strong, hefty Polish woman came to do it. She had a daughter named Helena, who I was very friendly with; we played together as children.

There was a big wooden tub with iron around it, higher on one side than the other. Attached to the higher spot was this frame that had two rollers covered with sponges and a handle on the side; it was called a *mengel*. When the washing was rinsed, it went between the two rollers; the handle was turned and the water dripped into the basin. Oh, and there was a board with steel strips inside that basin, and place for a big piece of soap. The Polish woman stood and rubbed the washing with this gadget in the basin.

I can't remember where it was stored – must have been in our cellar – and the machine squeezed so tight that the sheets would come out almost dry, they didn't need wringing. Then the washing went up to the attic just under the roof, with big wooden beams – warm in summer but cold in winter. You hung your laundry on the lines there and then you locked up; I suppose each tenant had a different day because you couldn't put laundry up together with somebody else or it would be stolen. Sometimes the dry washing was taken to be pressed, to a place with a big wooden press.

It was a lot of linen and we didn't change every week, every two weeks possibly – maybe in winter even longer because there were a lot of duvets. There were no blankets; we had proper down duvets. We also had a sort of under-duvet on top of the mattress and beneath the sheet, so you were warm even from below.

This was the way we lived – if it's interesting for anybody to know how it was in Warsaw at that time. I don't know about the small towns but that's how it was at home.

Chapter 2

Growing up Jewish

To say that every interview with Ella starts and ends with talk of tea, biscuits, snacks or even whole meals would not be an overstatement. Even when she is impatient to get on with her story, Ella will never let our work stand in the way of a good fress[25].

Of course Jewish food has a long and varied history, with influences stretching as far as biblical times and as wide as the countries across the globe where Jews have settled. The laws of keeping kosher have played an important role in shaping Jewish cuisine, certainly in the case of Eastern European Jews like Ella. Food preparation on Shabbat in particular is carefully governed, giving rise to such fare as cholent[26], *chopped herring and* gefilte fish[27], *which remain as Shabbat staples in traditional communities.*

ELLA:
Shabbat was special. The food was beautiful; my father sitting at the one head of the table and my mother at the other, children between, singing *zemirot*. Mainly we ate *gefilte* fish. *Upon seeing my mouth turn downwards in an expression of distaste, Ella exclaims:* But not like we make here! Here we call *gefilte* fish which

---

25 Yiddish: to eat voraciously, to gobble up food.
26 Traditional Jewish stew simmered overnight and eaten for lunch on Shabbat, conforming with laws that prohibit cooking on that day.
27 In Yiddish, literally 'stuffed fish' – a traditional Jewish appetiser made from a poached mixture of ground deboned fish.

is not *gefilte* fish. You know? It's like a carp fish. You don't get them here. When you want to make proper *gefilte* fish, you clean the scales off the carp, cut off the head, clean up the stomach. Then you slice the fish. Take some of the flesh, chop it with onions, and you make like a dough. Then you fill the fish with the dough – you can even fill the head. That's why it's called *gefilte* fish – because it is filled. Then you cook it with onions, in one pot. I'll make it for you one day.

Have you ever eaten carp in Israel? The best fish is carp in Israel. When I met my husband, Isaac, in Palestine, I knew him for only a few days and my niece Roma invited him to come to her home for Friday night. She served him the head of the fish; it was a privilege – the head was always eaten by the master of the house or a guest. You didn't cook it with the ears of the fish, or the eyes. You took those out and then you filled the openings and the whole head with that *gefilte*. For years Isaac couldn't forgive me. 'How could you give me a head?' he said after we were married, 'I couldn't look at it!' He was South African, you know, and not used to it *[laughs]*. For years he used to pick me out about it. Me, I love the fish prepared like that – I suck up everything. *I shudder and share with Ella a childhood memory of a visiting uncle coming for dinner and sucking what appeared to be the fish's eyeballs from its head. My parents never served* gefilte *fish in the manner of Ella's description, but a whole baked fish was certainly a special menu item and I can still hear the slurping noise my uncle made as he sucked the gelatinous mess from the sockets of that poor creature. Ella laughs again.* I'm glad you know what I'm talking about. Next time you go to Israel, remember to have the carp. It's a beautiful fish.

Chopped herring was another thing, or chopped liver. You didn't buy it ready-made like that, you bought the herring at the market where there were lots of shops – women used to have stands with barrels. As a matter of fact, my late mother's sister was a wealthy woman – she had a place at the market selling herring. She used to put her hand into the barrel and pull out big, beautiful, fat herring. Years and years ago in South Africa you used to get nice herrings;

you don't any more. It's called *schmaltz*[28] herring – solid like fish almost. You clean it and chop it – or we used to slice it and eat it raw with sliced onion. Beautiful. Everybody loved it, including the children. *I think of my own children's penchant for chicken nuggets and French fries and I simply cannot imagine them even tolerating sliced fish and raw onion – one of the many customs I will have trouble transposing onto their (or my) generation.*

We didn't have a fridge or freezer to keep food. We used the windowsill outside. There was no space for a fridge – the maid slept in the kitchen on a narrow bed. It wasn't bad because it never really got too hot, even in summer. In wintertime, we'd leave the food on the windowsill and the gravy would harden into a jelly and then freeze. It's like *ptcha* (that's the Lithuanian word): you cook the leg of a calf and it becomes jellied, then you put it in a dish with pieces of egg. In winter that fat on top would freeze.

One of my sons who lives in Australia, he loves it. I once bought a piece here at Goldies kosher delicatessen in Cape Town. I ordered it. You get the leg even with the hoof and you put it all into a pot with boiling water and it stands there and you take off the hoof first. Then you shave the hair off, clean the leg, cut it and cook it with garlic, carrots and onions. *Ptcha* is rich but nice.

This *ptcha* we used to eat on Shabbos after *cholent*. I must tell you about *cholent*. But I just want to finish about the meals . . . Friday night was fish, challah of course and always chicken soup. Only ever chicken soup. And then there was *lokshen*[29], which you made yourself; *lokshen* or *farfel*[30]. And on Shabbos day – cooked on the Friday, of course – there was that chicken, no not chicken, and not turkey – what looks like a turkey? Blows up like *[puffs out her chest]* . . . *Are you sure it's not a turkey? I ask.* No, not turkey.

---

28 Technically refers to lard or rendered poultry fat; the term is used colloquially to mean 'fat'.
29 Flat egg noodles.
30 Small pellets of egg noodle dough usually baked/toasted and used in soups or as a side dish.

Quail? Peacock?

No, peacock is not right.

Chicken, pheasant?

No, No. I told you they're blowing up like – in Jewish it's an *indik*.

Really not a turkey?

No, we didn't have turkey. I will come to it. It was like a roasted turkey – on Friday night we had the boiled chicken, the soup, and on Shabbat day we had this roasted . . . turkey . . . duck . . . like a big duck!

A swan? Can't be!

No, no, no.

What's a big duck – a goose?

A goose! *Mazeltov!* There we go!

We both laugh, shouting 'Mazeltov!' as if we have just cracked the Enigma code.

It was a goose – every Shabbos day was a roasted goose. Now I tell you about the *cholent*.

The *cholent* was made at home like the ladies make here but inside there was a separate pot with a kind of sweet *lokshen* pudding. A pot inside a pot. Then around that was of course lots of meat, or vegetables for a vegetarian *cholent*, and the whole thing was covered with paper and tied with string. We didn't have facilities to cook it at home on the stove; for *cholent* on Shabbos there was a proper baker with an oven like the modern pizza ovens but very big and deep. We all brought our pots to the baker who tore off a number from his booklet, put the number on top of your pot and gave you the other ticket so you knew which was yours. We paid the baker and carried our pots home when they were done, nice and brown and beautiful.

We were talking about washing ourselves . . . of course there was also the *mikvah*[31], and men used it too. There was one across the road from us, next to the round shul. Mother used to *daven* every Shabbos in that round shul. She didn't go to the *shtiebel* where my

---

31   A bath used for ritual immersion in Judaism.

father went – there were no ladies there, only on Rosh Hashanah and Yom Kippur did the women come. You know, I was just a child then so I don't remember everything, but I don't think the boys went to the *mikvah*; no, the boys didn't go. I don't remember how often we bathed either but I know for sure it wasn't every day. Wintertime was very cold, so definitely not every day. I used to bath in a big basin in the kitchen, using hot water from the coal stove or the samovar. But we had to use that basin for many things. Like if there was a three-day *yom tov*[32] and you had to cook for the following day; with no fridge we used the basin for storage, and the sink, even the entrance hall. Not me of course, I didn't really help with the cooking. I was a wild thing, running around. I used to run around in the kitchen but not cook in it.

That reminds me: early every morning except Shabbat, even in the freezing winter cold, there was a knock at the door. There was no bell, just a knock at the door and a lady with an apron brought hot bagels and rolls. Well they weren't quite bagels because they didn't have a hole, more like a bun but not completely round, they had a design. Crispy outside, so crispy. She carried them in her apron, hot-hot – baked most probably in the middle of the night. So every morning we had fresh baked goods. I used to cut the pastry and put in cheese and butter to take to school.

In the first building we lived were only Jews. But when we moved into that terrible flat, there were some people who were not Jewish, although the neighbourhood was mainly Jewish. There was even a shop in the building selling polony, brisket, sausages . . . There was a place at the back where you could sit down and order boiled sausages with a roll and mustard – not tomato sauce, it was mustard. The whole shop had glazed tiles and there were hooks there for the meat to hang and dry. My brother Luzer loved it there. He often used to bring home sliced brisket or turkey wrapped in paper; he loved the meat with a piece of bread.

---

32 Jewish holiday.

As for milk, we got that from the markets or, at Pesach time, we got it straight from the cow in the yard of a nearby building; the man used to sit on a low seat to milk the animal and would bring the container of fresh kosher milk straight from the cow!

On a regular day, I carried the basket for my mother when she went shopping. There weren't shops like now; it was a big market place with stalls under a roof. A 'bazaar' we called it. My mom used to go shopping practically every day because we couldn't store much food. She worked in my father's business and then she would do the shopping. I remember lying in bed with her and she'd take out from the cupboard special chocolate squares – Domanski was the make – and she would take off the paper and put the chocolate in my mouth. A treat.

She was a hard-working woman, and a wonderful person. Friday nights she never went to shul; the men went to shul and she used to *daven* by the candles. Women didn't go to shul on a Friday night, but it's a custom here in this country today and I don't like to miss Friday nights. *Ella stops and fiddles with her hearing aid, apologising for the interruption.* I must put in a new battery. My hearing is not too bad. I can hear well on the phone and when one person talks at a time. But when there are a lot of people talking I am lost; I sit like a dummy and I can't take part in the conversation. But I've got used to it, and as Evy says, that should be the worst part of my life . . . Evy, she's a wonderful daughter, bless her. Without her I wouldn't have been sitting here talking to you. It's *Ribono Shel Olam*[33] and her that's keeping me.

We digress into talking about children. I have three sons, and Ella often teases me about 'going for the fourth – your little girl'. The subject of daughters – in particular the absence of them – is a poignant one for me, especially considering my close relationship with my own mother who passed away when my first child was one year

---

33 A Hebrew term adopted into Yiddish referring to God; literally translated as 'Master of the Universe'.

old. Reaching a sense of contentment and privilege with my three male blessings has been a process and, though complete, I still reflect on the difference in relationships wrought by gender. Evelyn is so clearly a devoted daughter. She is also the only one of Ella's four children who lives in Cape Town, so she can interact with her mother in daily, practical ways. I ask Ella if she thinks it is Evelyn's sex, personality or location that makes the difference.

I don't know. I've got three sons; each one is different. They're all lovely sons. But children are not alike. They're born to the same parents, the same mother, but they are different. And Evy lives my life you see . . .

Back to my school days.
So I went from the public school to Bais Yaakov to the high school, called Chavatzelet. The public school was mixed but the others were only Jewish. I had a friend in public school who still lives – I hope she's still alive – in Israel. My parents never liked me to associate with her – her family was not very religious, so my parents were not keen on the friendship. She never went to Bais Yaakov with me, she remained in the public school. Her name was Marysia. She was a year younger than me. Even after I left Bais Yaakov, she would come on Saturdays after the meal and whistle in the courtyard for me to come down. We used to go for a stroll while people were resting on Shabbos afternoon. Marysia had a non-Jewish boyfriend in the building where they lived. He passed away when he was young and she took me to see; the coffin was in the flat and people came past to pay respects. It was the first time I saw a dead body.

I used to come home late every day because school was far. In winter I went ice-skating practically every day. And I would do homework and help around the house. Every *yom tov* we children had to help clean the whole flat, every corner . . . not only for Pesach. Everything had to shine. When I was still at Bais Yaakov, on Saturday afternoons we used to have the *oneg Shabbat*[34] at the school. We

---
34 A celebration in honour of the Sabbath, including singing and refreshments.

girls used to meet with the teacher and sing. One song in particular I remember – every Shabbos here in Cape Town, when the *chazzan*[35] at my shul sings it, I am right back in Bais Yaakov. *Ella sings, and I join her because I know this song, and love its boisterous tune and associate it instantly with a joyful Shabbat chorus* – Yismechu v'malchusecha, shomrei shomrei shomrei Shabbos v'korei oneg Shabbos! *The two of us are chanting and laughing, tapping on the table as we sing.* And not only did we sing it: we had two rows of girls, one row swaying this way and the other row swaying that way with criss-crossed hands *[Ella grabs my hands to demonstrate].*

As I told you, the school wasn't big. It was in a large flat and it was just the start of the Bais Yaakov. Afterwards it spread into every country in Europe – Germany, Czechoslovakia, Austria, Hungary, Romania – they all had Bais Yaakov schools. But it started in Poland; Sarah Schenirer started it in Krakow.

The high school, Chavatzelet, was a religious school across the bridge in the city of Warsaw; we wore long sleeves and long skirts and we *davened* every morning. It was only girls there and I remember a teacher rabbi standing on a bench supervising and *davening* with us every morning. We took the normal subjects like maths, history, geography, Latin, and either German or French – I took French. I should have taken German; I would have been much better off during the war in the camps . . . but I survived without it. Of course, Polish was the language of instruction. And we had a lot of religious studies like *Chumash*[36]. You had to write matric also, but I didn't manage because it was just before the war. I went there until the war broke out.

During summertime in August/September, we used to go on holiday to the bush, with trees and fresh air. Outside Warsaw. We had those things made of string where you lie between two trees –

---

35   Hebrew for 'cantor'.
36   The Torah (in book form).

what do you call it? A hammock, yes, a hammock. We had those and we'd lie on them or walk through the forest and pick those black things that you buy here that are so expensive . . . You buy at Woolworths, those black tiny little . . .? *Ella pinches her thumb and forefinger together and scrunches up her nose . . . and here we go with the guessing game again!* 'Mushrooms?' I ask, thinking back to the types of things we found in our garden growing up. No, not mushrooms, sometimes those are poisonous.

A fruit?

Like little black sweets.

Mulberries?

No, no, not mulberries.

Blackberries?

Yes, yes, blackberries, yes. Beautiful and sweet in a forest full of Christmas trees.

The air was good in those fir forests, especially for people who had lung problems. You'd get there by steam train, go all the way to the last stop, to a big place called Otwock. People with tuberculosis (TB) used to go there. Remember, my father's *rebbe* also used to live there.

There were smaller places and stations on the route too. And *pensions*[37] where you could stay and eat. Roma was always a sickly child and she even spent some weeks during wintertime out there. They sent me to visit her. I'd take the train out there by myself and—

'By yourself!' I exclaim, incredulous. 'But you couldn't have been more than 12 or 13 years old! And you were travelling on your own?'

Ha! You don't understand me. I was always the frontrunner, always, everywhere. They sent *me* to visit Roma. They didn't send my sister Pola, two years older; they sent me! The one who will never get lost *[chuckles]*. You know, I had these white spots on my back – soft, not big. And my late father used to say: 'You're going to be very strong physically.' And he was right. I don't have the spots any more –

---

37 European term for a boarding house.

they disappeared when I grew up – but he knew I would be strong enough for all of us. I was a leader not a follower, and when we came to the camps, I needed that strength for myself and for Roma.

In summer, Roma's parents also hired a chalet outside Warsaw. They had four children and once or twice I went with them. Roma's parents used to come for Shabbos the Friday afternoon – they didn't stay during the week because they had to run their business back in Warsaw. But this place wasn't far from the centre, maybe an hour's ride by train. They would take the place for the whole season and a maid would come and cook their meals; she would stay with the children while their parents went back to the city during the week.

I remember this one holiday in particular because I met a Gypsy woman who told my fortune. She looked at the palm of my hand and said: 'You're going to be lucky and you're going to be wealthy.' When I came to this country, all I had was one little suitcase; I didn't even have a sheet to sleep on! *While Ella laughs, I comment that there are many ways to define wealth, right?* Well I certainly wasn't well-off when I got married, but slowly, with *HaShem*'s help, I guess I became wealthy in marriage, wealthy in children, wealthy in my health . . . Speaking of which, I'm very happy because yesterday morning I went back to swimming after two months off. I swim at the exercise centre here – you know the one owned by that famous British man? *I try to work out which exercise centre she is referring to. I giggle as it dawns on me: 'Richard Branson! You swim at the Virgin Active gym.'* That's the one. I've been a member for years. I used to swim every day except Shabbos. Every morning at half-past-five, six, including wintertime. I made friends. Sometimes they used to pick me up to go together in the dark. Every day. But now I can hardly get into the water without help. But once I'm in, I go. These days I swim three times a week only – normally Sunday, Tuesday and Thursday. To get there, I've got my car but I can't drive. And I can't leave the car either because otherwise it just goes flat. There is a chap, an elderly man, who needs the money, I pay him and he drives me there and back in my car.

When I'm getting out the pool, I manage, but on the last step coming up, Joan helps me. Then we go up the stairs and I lie in the steam bath. I put my feet up against the wall and just lie there, relaxing, breathing in and out, for ten to fifteen minutes. I love it. After the steam bath, I don't dry myself. I go to the sauna and cream my whole body while I'm sitting in there. I make friends there too! When I'm ready, Joan helps me to get dressed and we walk downstairs where the driver is waiting. He brings me home and I have a nice breakfast of porridge. I used to go early but now I go at quarter-past-seven in the morning. I'm a bit more lazy these days.

I used to swim 36 lengths. Then I came down to 25. Yesterday I couldn't do more than 18. I tried water aerobics many years ago and hurt my shoulder, so I don't do that. I prefer the swimming; my whole body works. I also love it because I used to go swimming as a youngster. Over the Vistula River in Warsaw there were two very big bridges, not far from each other. One was called Kierbedź Bridge where we used to walk to school from Praga, and the other was Poniatowski Bridge, a very old bridge. Near there were small beaches where you could go to swim or even hire a kayak. My brother Heniek, the one who was not religious, went to a famous ballet dancing school and he loved the stage. There were always problems at home but eventually they married him off nicely to a Jewish girl, a woman who was older than him. He loved to dance; he had music records, and with the family watching (not my father!) he used to pick me up and dance. He even brought different costumes like Turkish, dressed me and danced with me to show off. Golda, Roma's mother, wasn't very tall, and he would put her on the table with her high heels on and make her dance on the table, wearing her beautiful blonde *sheitl* and everything! Everybody laughed and joked.

Anyway, Heniek (or Henry, as he called himself) used to take me to this bridge, Poniatowski, where there was that beach and he bought me the most beautiful, beautiful bathing costume. In those days the costumes were made from wool – did you know that? He bought it from a big store, something like Stuttafords, in Warsaw, a very expensive store. We'd go to this beach and he put me in the front of a kayak. When I see children in boats now it reminds me . . . I loved to row.

As for learning to swim: where we lived, if you walked maybe ten minutes, to the edge of the river, there was a little wooden hut. Inside, there were round wooden seats, a place to hang your clothes and two steps down to a platform beneath the water. You walked down the steps and you were in the water on the platform, you couldn't drown. The water was fresh, beautiful fresh water. And that's where I learned to swim. I just used to throw myself from one corner to the other, again and again, until I could swim. A lot of people could go in at once; it was quite big; enclosed on the sides but mostly open on the top and the sun came in.

This place was for women only. There was the same thing for men. In summertime my father used to go there to *tunkt* – to dip in. It was like a natural *mikvah*, totally kosher, better even than the *mikvah*, but it was only for summer and summer wasn't very long.

There is another place I remember going to on holiday. North of Warsaw there was a health spa called Ciechocinek; my mother used to go every year for a week or two and sometimes I went with her. At this spa you could get a mud bath . . . bags of mud my mother used to get. That you would do in the mornings; in the afternoons there was a beautiful park with an orchestra playing and there were spots where you could drink mineral water. Only wealthy people used to go there on holiday. I think it was only once that my father joined us and we hired a little hut where we cooked our own food. The accommodation was very primitive. And there was a big bridge made entirely of salt! Like when you see frozen ice? That's what it looked like, with drips of solid salt – long, hanging salt. I have a picture where I am lying in a bathing costume – the one my brother bought for me – and the background is that bridge. In September 1938, when I came back from this holiday with my mother, I signed the back of that picture – 'Hela, Warszawa', and the date – and gave it to a friend.

I was always aware of being Jewish and that that made us a bit different.

For one thing, on Sundays *all* businesses were closed in Warsaw – you weren't allowed to trade. But of course for us, the shop was also closed on Saturdays because we would not trade on Shabbat. That would have meant two days not working, which we could not afford . . . and not just us, all our tradesmen and customers too. So everybody worked on Sundays even though it was illegal. The tailors worked at home and when they needed certain things like buttons, cottons or materials, they came to us. Of course our shop was 'closed' but my two brothers sneaked in when there were no police around. My dad never took part in it on Sundays. He was learning or checking the books, I imagine.

They bolted the shop from the outside with my two brothers inside. The door had a small, elongated opening with an iron grill so you could see through and speak. My mother would walk up and down the sidewalk outside the shop. In wintertime, she wore a fur-lined suede jacket with big pockets where she kept keys and money. When a customer came, she used to walk with him and ask what he needed. She'd look around to make sure none of the police were close and she'd call out the order through the door. Then she waited. She knew more or less how long to wait. She'd climb the three steps to the shop, my brothers would slide the inside panel away and hand the order to my mother; she went down to give it to the customer, and put the payment in her pocket. If you were caught trading on a Sunday, you'd get a hefty fine, or maybe worse, so we had to be very careful.

I mentioned that my brother Heniek, the dancer, gave my parents problems because he wasn't religious; on top of that he had friends who were not to my family's liking. He was such a smart guy. He even had business cards made and didn't call himself 'Heniek Frank'; instead he printed 'Henrik Frankowski'. This was very Polish! You know most Polish names have got a 'ski' in them and our name wasn't really very Jewish – it wasn't Rosenblum or Goldberg – but he made it as Polish as he could by adding '-owski'.

Since the war, the surname 'Frank' has become very well known. Not only was there Anne Frank who wrote the diary – no relation to us – but Hans Frank was the SS man in charge of the General Government in Nazi-occupied Poland. But my brother wanted to make his name sound as Polish, not Jewish, as possible.

He was also very elegant: he dressed in the European style, and he had a bamboo cane like an English gentleman – a fashion accessory. He had beautiful black hair, shiny and full, with waves, which were very fashionable. One Saturday he went walking not far from our building, out on the street, without a hat, no cover . . . this elegantly dressed man, twirling his bamboo cane, came up to our flat on the second floor and knocked on the door. My family would not let him in. He knocked and knocked, and they shouted at him, 'How dare you?' It's called in Yiddish or Hebrew *befressieh* – it's when you make an *aveira*[38] in front of people, doing something wrong without trying to hide it. If you do something wrong where nobody sees it, it's half the trouble, but when you do it in public! *Ella's tone and face portray the scandalised horror of her strictly Orthodox, extremely conservative family confronting their maverick child. At the same time, I see the wry smirk of recognition and fondness, because it takes one to know one. I ask Ella which part of it was the problem – the dress, the cane, the lack of head covering?* 'All of it!' she booms. 'Dressed like a European, smart, no hat, the cane . . . Everything!'

So Heniek is knocking, the family is shouting back at him. The neighbours are all listening. So you know what he did? He kicked in the panel at the bottom of the door! Knocked it straight out.

I guess he must have got in after that – they probably opened the door before he bashed the whole thing down. But I remember the *shande*[39]! And I remember that word, *befressieh* – I always think of my brother when I hear it and it makes me both smile and cry.

---

38 Hebrew for 'sin' or 'transgression'.
39 Yiddish for 'scandal' or 'shame'.

Remember I told you that I used to go skating and that the rink was next to the church? St Florian's Cathedral is still there, with two big towers like you see in England. Attached to the skating rink was a long, low building that belonged to the church. I don't know whether somebody lived there but they must have had lectures or something because young people used to go there.

One day as my brother, Luzer, walked past the low building with all its windows, young Poles came out shouting 'Jew! Jew!' and attacked him. He was wearing the type of small, flat cap that the religious Jews wore in Poland. They attacked him with a knife and he came back with his ear hanging; they nearly cut it off! This was just before the war.

I didn't experience much anti-Semitism until after Hitler came to power. Poland was our home, though we knew that the Poles really didn't like us. There were shops, not many, that belonged to non-Jewish people, to Poles, to Christians; at the bottom of the display window of the shop I can still see the notice they put there: 'This is a Christian shop'. I knew we were different, as Jews, mainly because we dressed differently. Golda had a clothing business but her customers were not Jewish. She sold clothes and shoes, not expensive, so railway men used to buy, and people who worked on trams or on buildings. And they used to pay it off. Jewish people didn't wear these clothes. Even the poorest ones had clothes made because then they could be sure the tailor would use kosher linen. That's why our business existed, because there were lots of tailors. The only thing Jews bought readymade was shoes and even those, some men used to order from shoemakers. I think non-Jewish people must have shopped at the markets. So yes, we looked different because we dressed differently. We also sounded a bit different; our Polish was not completely Polish.

I suppose there was always anti-Semitism but never as openly as it became just before the war.

Chapter 3

Invasion

Today is the 15th of November. My late mother's birthday. I tell Ella this as I arrive at her flat for our interview and her eyes water on my behalf. She has the most elastic of facial expressions, making her easy to read. A joyous upturned mouth stretches as far north in a smile as a forlorn downcast mouth droops south in a frown. I wonder whether her face is a mirror – reflecting back what she sees in others – or a projector – radiating outwards what she herself feels. She appears to have an immense capacity for empathy.

That evening is the 2016 launch of then-Western Cape Premier Helen Zille's autobiography, Not Without a Fight, *at Cape Town's Gardens Synagogue. There is actually a close link between Helen and Ella, but I'm unaware of that as I make plans to attend; I am interested in Zille's story and like to support literary events hosted by the Jewish community. In fact, I am surprised by the choice of location for the launch – until I hear her speak that night. Helen Zille's Jewish heritage was little known to most, including herself, until she heard Ella address the community at the 2015 Yom HaShoah Memorial service. 'As she spoke, she peeled away layers of my own life, releasing snippets of memory I am only now, in my mid-sixties, beginning to piece together.' This she says on the first page of the first chapter of her book. Ella is the inspiration for Zille's own journey into her Jewishness. She describes Ella as unsentimental, direct and matter-of-fact when telling her story, yet finds that 'almost everything about her is intimately familiar to me, from her strong accent . . . to her determination to bury the past and keep moving forward'.*[40]

I had not expected to attend the launch of a politician's autobiography and be met, almost immediately, with the subject of the biography I was writing. But I'm also not surprised that Ella had that sort of impact on Zille. She has that sort of impact on everyone she meets and, in particular, on those who hear her speak about the Holocaust. People's experience of her as 'unsentimental, direct and matter-of-fact' is common, and I wonder if the same is true of many survivors. Sentimentality is surely one of the war's many casualties; surviving the Holocaust and even the post-war world would demand the suspension of nostalgia and the crystallisation of an outer shell hard enough to withstand suffering. The survivor's carapace. And beneath, deep within, is the soft nucleus where memory lies in wait.

ELLA:
When the trouble started, we did not realise what was happening. We knew that the Nazi German army had crossed the border of Austria – they just walked in and occupied it – but it sort of didn't affect us. We didn't realise how serious it was. Soon they were given Czechoslovakia on a platter; they thought it would satisfy Adolf Hitler's appetite.[41] Still we said it can't happen to us; we never thought it would happen to Poland.

Nobody warned us. The papers didn't warn us – they only announced what was happening *around* our country. My journalist brother-in-law got the news, but we never realised how serious it was. We didn't *want* to know that it would affect us so terribly. I call it stupid.

That was August 1939; they crossed the border on the 1st of Sep-

---

40 Zille, H. 2016. *Not Without A Fight: The Autobiography.* Penguin Random House: Cape Town. Page 1.
41 In response to Germany's low-intensity undeclared war on Czechoslovakia in 1938, the United Kingdom and France asked Czechoslovakia to cede its mainly German-inhabited Sudetenland territory, hoping to appease German dictator Adolf Hitler and prevent a major war on the continent. The Munich Agreement, signed by Britain, France, Italy and Germany, formalised the cession.

tember, marching towards Warsaw. Then everything woke up! The army was called up, soldiers on leave were called up, even the older people who had already finished the army service were called up. We had trenches dug so that they couldn't get through. Warsaw stood up against them for three weeks. And then fell.

Those were three weeks of bombardment. People were killed, buildings were burning . . . As a matter of fact, during the bombardment, we moved from our home because where we lived was near a big railway station and we feared that they would bomb the railway station, which they normally did. So our family and Roma's family locked up and left – I don't think we took anything with us – and we went to live with my eldest brother Froim in the Jewish Quarter, on Gęsia Ulitsa[42]. He lived at Gęsia 12 and had a linens and upholstery business across the street at Gęsia 7. We slept on the floor, on the tables – there were a lot of us. My brother lived on the second floor of a big block of flats shaped like a *chet*[43]. At the head of the courtyard there was a shul, so that was what you saw when you looked out the window.

The bombardments continued. We often had to run down to the cellar. We'd all stand in the cellar while the bombs fell – it wasn't safe in there either but it was better than sitting upstairs in the flat waiting. The chief of the army, Edward Rydz-Śmigły[44], announced on the radio: 'We will not give in! We won't give up, we're strong,

---

42 Polish for 'Street'.
43 Hebrew letter shaped like an upside-down U.
44 On 18 September 1939, Rydz-Śmigły escaped to Romania and was interned. He escaped on 10 December 1940 and crossed illegally into Hungary. Rumours about his planned return to Poland angered his rival Władysław Sikorski, then Prime Minister (in exile), who sent a telegram to the Polish Underground declaring: 'The Polish Government will regard a sojourn of the Marshal in Poland as a sabotage of its work in the country. The Marshal must as soon as possible move to some country of the British Empire'. However, on 25 October 1941, Rydz-Śmigły returned to Warsaw to participate in the Resistance movement as a common underground soldier. He died of heart failure on 2 December 1941, aged 55, and was buried in Warsaw under his nom de guerre 'Adam Zawisza'. In 1994, a new tombstone bearing the Marshal's full name was placed over his grave by the people of Warsaw. (Source: Richard Freedman, and Wikipedia https://en.wikipedia.org/wiki/Edward_Rydz-%C5%9Amig%C5%82y.)

we won't let them take over our country.' But we didn't realise that the whole government were leaving for England; they formed a small government in exile there.[45] They left us a day or two before the Germans marched into Warsaw, and we remained.

It was Yom Kippur 1939. People were standing and *davening*, praying for the bombardment to stop. Some buildings were burning; some smouldering. People were killed when buildings collapsed and they were buried under the ruins. We prayed to *HaShem* that it should stop. And soon afterwards . . . it did.

On the 1st of September 1939, the Nazis invaded Poland. On the 8th of September, they marched on Warsaw and the city was under siege for three weeks, until the 28th of September, when it finally fell.

By the time the Nazis took Warsaw, life as we knew it had already been destroyed. But that was just the beginning. Right away there were announcements. Laws came out; new proclamations on the walls of the buildings. All Jewish land was requisitioned. All Jewish bank accounts were frozen, closed – we could only take out a small amount, I think. All public gatherings were forbidden. Schools were closed and synagogues were forbidden and closed. Every few days there was something new. A curfew was imposed. Food was rationed. We had to stand in a queue for bread. *Ella's voice drops to a mournful, sensitive tone as she recalls the scene of queuing for bread.* There were Jewish and non-Jewish people in the queue. And there were Nazis, guards, around to see that everything worked well. Some of the Polish people shouted: 'Jew, Jew, there's a Jew in the queue,' and someone would get pulled out and sent to the end. Even education was forbidden to the Jews. Before the war, Jewish youth studied at university along with the Polish students, particularly in medicine and law. Then they put in quotas – only a certain number of students were allowed to study – and eventually they put

---

45   In fact the Polish government-in-exile was based in France during 1939 and 1940, moving to London only after the fall of France in 1940.

the Jewish students on separate benches. But after the occupation, there was no university for Jews at all. For Jews to be denied education was a terrible thing – we prioritise learning, we never want to be left behind.

You could see what was happening. Before too long, the Polish people were showing the ordinary German soldiers where to go and rob. They came to our home and my brothers had to go down to open up the shop. There was one soldier, not high-ranking, who pointed out what he wanted: beautiful suiting. He came once, twice, and again we suited him. I was with my two brothers – you know I was always everywhere – and the soldier said to me, 'You come with me to Lodz.' He must have been a tailor or in the textile business before the war because he knew exactly what to pick. And in front of my brothers, he said: 'I am coming to fetch you and you show me what to buy, which places to go and where to shop.' When he came back the next time, I wasn't there.

When Warsaw fell, we went back to our homes. There was no need to stay in my brother's place so we went home – although my sister, Roma's mother, and her family had to come and stay with us because of bomb damage to their apartment. They stayed with us for a long time.

You remember I mentioned our relatives, the shoemakers? When the Germans marched in, they also ran away from their home and came to stay with us. They were sleeping on the floor because there were no more beds. And then, I don't know what happened . . . they disappeared! And I don't know any more about them. But that was the start of it . . .

Every day there was something else coming out, a new order or a new law. There was a Jewish council formed in Warsaw – I forget the name . . . *I prod gently: 'Do you mean the Judenrat[46]?'* Yes that's

---

46 German for 'Jewish Council', appointed by German occupying forces; responsible for administering Jewish affairs and enforcing Nazi orders.

right. The Judenrat. They had to count how many Jews were living in Warsaw, and gather their names. A census. I volunteered to go with other people from flat to flat to collect the information . . . how many people were living in each flat and their names . . . What was his name, the head of that council? Czerniaków. Adam Czerniaków. I've got his book, his memoirs, in Polish. I've got a lot of literature which we can look at later, and pictures and documents.

As the German army marched into Warsaw, even before, people were leaving, crossing the border to the Russian side. I did not mention that Stalin and Hitler made a pact when they occupied Poland.[47] There's the River Bug which was closer to the east than the Vistula River, closer to the Russian border. People started to move over to the Russian-occupied side of Poland where it was safer, and they had to cross the River Bug to do so. At the border, there was one little town on the Polish side where the Germans were stationed, watching; and on the other side it was the Russians watching. People were moving; sometimes you could see them with backpacks and schlepping children, some on bicycles, others on carts, whatever – pushing belongings, marching, walking. And my two younger brothers who were still single then, decided to go with them. So they packed a bit of food and their *tefillin*[48], said goodbye to us and left. They joined the crowds that were marching, thousands of people! You know many of the Polish Jews who survived the war did so in Russia. *Ella's voice changes to one of dismay.* When my mother realised that her two sons were gone, she collapsed: 'Where are my children, my boys? Get them back, get them back.' We found them in the crowds. They tried the next morning to do the same thing. Again she called – she couldn't live without them: 'Where are they going to go?' There was nowhere to sleep along

---

47 The pact between Hitler and Soviet leader Joseph Stalin (the Nazi-Soviet Pact) paved the way for their joint invasion and occupation of Poland.
48 A set of small black leather boxes with straps, containing scrolls of parchment with Torah verses; worn by adult Jews during weekday morning prayers.

the way, you had to walk. And even if you managed to cross the border over the River Bug, and you got to the Russian side – who is going to let you in? To sleep where?

They came back and never tried again.

The rest of us never thought of leaving. First of all, my parents were not very young. Secondly, and this was the biggest problem: we were not poor people. We had a business. Of course it became difficult to run the store because our goods were worth tenfold what we sold them for, but how else could we live? Everything became very expensive because you couldn't get anything. The same applied to my sister, Roma's mother, with her clothing business. I don't think I mentioned that when Warsaw was occupied and we came out of hiding, we found her business had been ransacked: the door was broken and empty hangers lay on the floor with Polish army clothes lying next to them. Deserters. Polish soldiers were afraid of the Germans so they got themselves dressed in civilian clothes and left the army clothes there. She still had goods though, and by selling one coat or one suit she could live for a month almost. So why didn't we leave? Because to leave something that you worked for all your life, something that you live on, and to go off into the unknown . . . No. We never thought of leaving.

As I told you, the synagogues were closed, so the services were held in private homes. Sometimes it was in our home – we had our own *sefer* Torah which my father brought from the *shtiebel* and we kept it at home so the services could continue. One day – it must have been almost a year into the occupation – they finished *davening* in our home and my brother-in-law who lived with us, Roma's father, said: 'I want to tell you people that we're in the hands of murderers. Try and run; leave and go!' People just said, 'Ach, he's a writer, he's fantasising, don't listen to him.' But he wanted to leave. He realised what was going on. He was the editor of the Jewish daily paper *Dos Judisze Togblat*, which was one of three or four daily Jewish papers in Warsaw. It was affiliated with

Agudas Yisroel[49], which we belonged to. So he felt he knew; he begged my sister to go with him, with the children of course. She was very much against it. 'Where will I go?' she asked, 'Where will I drag myself with four children? Even if we manage to get to the other side . . .' – she meant to the Russian-occupied side; people always tried to get to Bialystok and from there they went further – 'Even if we get over, you will always get a place on a floor to sleep because people know you.' He was indeed a known writer – Samuel Rothstein was his name, Shmuel Rotsztajn in Hebrew and Polish. 'With me, with four children – who will give us a place? How can I? How dare I put them in such danger?' At that moment we were still living – they hadn't started killing us yet; we still had a roof over our heads, even if it was tight, and we had a bit of food. So she refused and he kept on begging her.

Shmuel set a date to leave with two or three of his brothers. And on that date, they came to our home to fetch him. This I remember *[Ella's face crumples and she closes her eyes]:* my brother shaved off each one's beard. Of course they all had beards – they were religious people; but they couldn't go on such a journey with a beard. I couldn't recognise my brother-in-law and his brothers. And so they left. Even when they got to the train, he still begged my sister: 'Give me the little boy . . .' – my sister had three girls and the fourth child was a little boy – but she wouldn't.

He got through.

He got to Bialystok and from there to Vilna, and from there to another city in Lithuania. While he was travelling like this from place to place, he wrote letters to my sister and sent things like small tins of sardines, which she used to change for an egg to feed their little boy David – eggs were as rare as diamonds. At some point Shmuel had an opportunity to apply for a visa. If he applied for an American visa, he'd have to wait five years to get his family out; he still had in mind to get his wife and four children out, not knowing that by then we were already in the ghetto. So he got a visa for himself, a

---

49 In Hebrew, Agudat Yisrael – meaning 'Union of Israel': an ultra-Orthodox Jewish political party in Israel that has its origins representing ultra-Orthodox Jews in Poland.

British visa because Palestine was under the British mandate. Eventually, in 1941, Shmuel managed to get to Turkey and finally to Palestine.

Meanwhile, things were only getting worse at home.

The Nazis were already collecting people in the streets for labour. They used to stop the men. One morning my father was coming back from the morning service at somebody's home and they called him to work. It was for a few days, a week I think. When he came back at night, we didn't recognise him – full of dust and cement on his clothes. His collar was ripped out of his coat. Half his beard was cut off. We should have realised then that we were in the hands of murderers.

It was Friday night, Shabbat, and my father still hadn't come home. My mother went to the wardrobe where all the holy books were and opened the door. All the *sefarim* were on the shelf, and she begged *HaShem* to bring her husband back. It was late; the candles were on the table. Eventually we heard his hurried footsteps. When he came in, he said to Roma's father (who was at that time already talking about leaving, trying to convince my sister to go with him): 'Shmuel, I want you to go with blessings from God.'

My sister said, 'Father do I understand what you said? Do you allow him to leave?'

'Yes. What I saw today, there's no future for us; I don't think we will survive.'

One of the men who was working with my father was sick and did not present himself for work that day. They fetched him from his home and took him to the place where they were working, where they had already dug a hole in the ground. They made him stand on the edge of that hole and shot him; when he fell in, my father was given the task of covering the grave. The man wasn't even dead yet and my father was a Kohen, of the priestly class, who are not allowed to stand near grave-sites or handle the dead.

'Now go,' said my father. And Shmuel did, with his brothers, not long after.

Some weeks later I got very ill with a high temperature. Every occurrence of sickness had to be reported to the authorities. The sick person was sent to hospital and all the people who lived together were sent to the quarantine, where they usually got sick too. The sick person who went to hospital never came out alive. The empty flat was fumigated and, before it was sealed, anything that was there of value was snapped up, stolen, taken by the people who fumigated. And you were powerless to stop it. So when you got sick, you didn't want anybody to know, like neighbours in the building as there were also non-Jews. My sister Pola's boyfriend, Mietek Pressburger – I'll tell you about him later – he managed to get a Jewish doctor to come to Praga from Warsaw. He must have been very well remunerated because it was very dangerous. He was dressed like a tradesman so as not to arouse suspicion. He examined me and pricked my finger to draw blood. He advised my family that it was typhoid fever – not typhus. Typhus is the infection that is spread by rats and lice and fleas; typhoid you get from food that is contaminated and you get big intestinal sores. He brought some medication but everybody moved out of the flat because I was contagious. I don't know where they went. I stayed in the last room, which was empty except for my bed and a stool with a basin. Pola stayed and nursed me to health.

When I recovered, my bones couldn't move easily. My friend Marysia had a boyfriend who used to massage me. I remember lying on the sofa and he would rub my sore bones. For years afterwards I could still feel it because he was so strong.

You know, lying in bed last night, I was thinking about these non-Jews who helped us, and about Jews who converted to Christianity.

When I was about 10 or 11, I had to have my appendix out. I told you I had a sister-in-law who came from Lodz and I got myself to the wedding. When I had to have the operation, she recommended a doctor by the name of Goldman because he had operated on her stepmother. He was practising in Warsaw. A date was arranged when I had to arrive at the hospital and – I remember it like now – it was a hospital of the nuns. My bed was stones, the place was dark, and in every corner was Jesus Christ and his mother – statues of them. The whole thing was full of it. I got such a fright and said, 'I'm not staying here, take me home, I'm not staying here.'

Of course I knew about Christianity – we lived in a Catholic country, there were churches around us, Polish Catholics we knew. But still, this was very different to where I felt comfortable. I didn't stay at the hospital. My sister-in-law spoke to Dr Goldman and he booked me into a private clinic. That's where I had the operation.

I found out afterwards that my mother didn't know the exact hour of the operation and she went with a basket to the bazaar to do daily shopping for food. Only my brother Heniek (Chaim) whom I loved so much – the one who wasn't religious – he was the one who came *[tearful]*. When they came to fetch me from my ward for the operation, he was standing turned away from me, looking out the window. Afterwards I realised why he was facing away: he must have been crying. He didn't even turn around to wish me . . . And I remember that my brother-in-law Shmuel, who later went to Palestine, was the only one who came to see me on a Saturday afternoon. The hospital was in Warsaw, not in Praga where we all lived, and it was two or three hours' walk from home to the hospital. Shmuel walked to come and visit me because it's a big *mitzvah*[50] to visit a sick person – you know that. So my favourite brother, Heniek, he used to visit, but on Shabbat it was just my brother-in-law who walked and walked to come see me. You must understand that we were like one family with Shmuel, even though he was not a blood relation. My father was always so proud of his son-in-law. He did not come from a very wealthy home but my father used to call him 'my *psumboxl*' – that's the silver spice box that you use in the *Havdalah* ceremony at the end of the Shabbat. My father had an ordinary box, but he referred to my brother-in-law as the beautiful

---

50 Hebrew meaning 'commandment' and 'good deed'.

silver kind because Shmuel was a very fine man and he was so proud of him.

We were like this with their children too, with Roma and her siblings – they weren't like my nieces and nephews, more like brothers and sisters. One family. Even when they moved in with us just after they got married, they stayed for seven years. They could have left many years before but they chose to stay with us. One family.

* * *

A few months before the end of 1940, there was a proclamation: all Jews were to move into a ghetto in Warsaw. But where do we go? There were only certain streets that were included in the ghetto. We managed to get a room – to pay, of course – from my brother Itche's future in-laws; my parents were already negotiating the wedding. So we hired a large room from them and we had a little iron coal stove where we cooked the food. We lived together in that one room: my parents, my two younger brothers who weren't married, and me. My sister Golda, Roma's mother, got a place elsewhere, the last room in a five-roomed flat: a religious Jew across the road had I don't know how many children, and my sister's family had to walk through almost all the rooms to get to their room. They also had to pay a handsome fee.

When we were herded into the ghetto, we managed to pack only some of our belongings: our *sefarim*, the *sefer* Torah and some things we knew we could get money for. For a few days after we moved, we used to go up and down to our old flat with sheets and pack things in to take across. The rest of our possessions were looted by the Poles.

We stored our belongings at my brother Froim's place, the one we went to during the bombardment; you remember he lived in Gęsia Street, which was luckily included in the ghetto. In most buildings in Warsaw, each tenant had a cellar: underneath the building was a long passage with small alcoves that could be locked. People would keep coal, and sometimes potatoes, in there for the winters. So we kept our things in that cellar of my brother's. The *sefer* Torah and *sefarim*, the holy books, we gave to some other people we knew, to keep in their cellar.

The ghetto itself was surrounded by high walls with wire on top and broken pieces of glass – you could never jump over to the Polish Christian side. Jewish people built those walls through forced labour. They were caught in the street and had to work. It took a few months, some people working on roads, others building the ghetto, until that proclamation came that we were to move; if there were Poles that happened to live there, in what was now the ghetto, they had to move out. Of course we had to sort out a place for ourselves; we weren't given accommodation. Sometimes we wanted to make an exchange – you take my place, I'll take yours – but to the Poles it was like, 'Why should I take this little home of yours; we'll eventually get the best apartments in the best streets in Warsaw!' There were no houses, only apartment blocks in Warsaw. As a matter of fact, I never knew how a potato or a tomato grew; I always lived in an apartment in the city.

When we moved, we had to close up the shop because it also fell outside the ghetto limits. So there was no work to go to every day. My clearest memory from that single hired room was my father learning. He was very *frum*, I told you, and he was always learning. But he liked to get somebody to learn with him. This used to be my brother-in-law Shmuel, but he had already left. So my father would bring people from the street – old men. They would sit and study Torah with him because there was nothing else to do. You know it's a *mitzvah* to study the Torah – that was his life. We used to warn him not to bring people from the street because there was an epidemic of typhus, and what brought on the typhus was lice and there was an abundance of lice on everybody. Eventually my father did get sick with typhus and he was very ill with complications, but he survived, thank God.

After some time, Itche married the daughter of that family whose room we were hiring and we moved to live with Froim in Gęsia Street.

I can't remember if maybe that first building was cut out of the ghetto at the time we moved; the Nazis used to take out certain streets so you would suddenly discover that the place you were living in was now outside the ghetto and you had to move. In this way, they crowded us into a smaller and smaller space. Anyway we moved again, to Froim's, deeper inside the ghetto.

You remember I told you the first time I went to the cemetery was for the funeral of the woman I used to help by doing her books? Well that time I didn't see the actual corpse because it was wrapped and covered. At a Jewish funeral, you don't see the corpse. But here, in the ghetto, it was completely different . . .

Every morning when you got up and went out into the street, you could see corpses. They were put out during the night by their families who couldn't even give them a funeral. They were picked up on carts. Sometimes the bodies were covered with newspaper held down by bricks; the bodies were naked underneath because the family needed the clothes they had been wearing. Eventually, when there was no paper, they were lying naked. And they weren't corpses, they were skeletons – so thin were they. At first it was terrible to see, but eventually it became the order of the day.

This didn't happen right away in the ghetto; over time it just got progressively worse. When you walked in the street you couldn't carry any food because desperate people would grab it out of your hands. Kids were sitting and begging in the street with hardly any clothes on them, just in rags, begging for food. Grown-up people would beg too, but mainly little children, trying to get something to take to their parents and siblings.

Of course there was typhus; it was terrible. We had to watch our clothes, especially in the seams; the lice eggs used to sit there and develop with the warmth of the body. As soon as we came into the flat from the street we had to stand at the door and check our clothes.

There was a tap, and a toilet in the flat, yes. And a kitchen – just a shortage of food to cook on the stove. Yet we were lucky, we could afford to buy a bit of food. Other people were starving, begging in the street, almost skeletons.

There was a short man named Rubenstein, who used to beg. We called him the *meshuggenah*[51] Rubinstein, but in fact he wasn't crazy. He was just poor and desperate. I remember him clearly, in his broken clothing with his outstretched hands, singing while begging: '*Alle gleich, urm un reich*' *[Ella emphasises the rolling r's and deepened gutturals of the Polish Jewish dialect over the Lithuanian]* – it means 'Everybody alike, rich and poor'. He used to sing it all the time *[Ella mimics Rubinstein in a plaintive, sing-song voice]* and he would hobble around like this *[she gets up to imitate him]*. It doesn't matter if you are poor or rich, we are all the same – *Alle gleich, urm un reich* . . .

He also used to sing: '*Giv avek de bona en zog ein guten tog*' – the '*bona*' was the food ration card. 'Give away the *bona* and say good day'. He meant that we should donate our ration cards because they were not valid or useful once you were dead; when people were falling at that rate that they fell in the ghetto, what was the point in them hanging on to their *bona*? Give it away and goodbye.

That was Rubinstein. He was a known personality. Anybody who lived through the ghetto will tell you about Rubenstein.

There was not much to do in the ghetto every day.

There were schools, but of course I did not attend as I had finished school by the time the war broke out. I was 19. But the children were sitting doing nothing and there were teachers who had to buy bread, so they made schools in private homes. Everybody who sent their child contributed so that the teacher could earn a bit of something. Roma went. Her teachers lectured them at different homes. In some of the buildings, people like myself and others organised small kids – we played with them, we danced, we sang with them to take up time. There were also secret *yeshivot*, focusing on the study of religious texts.

---

51 Yiddish for 'crazy person'.

There were musicians playing in the streets: desperate, talented people – you'd find a maestro of the violin just lying there, hoping for money to be thrown in the case. *Ella's voice stumbles over the tears unhooked by music, or the memory of music.* These were famous musicians, not only from Warsaw. Many people came from surrounding villages; they thought it may be safer than in a small village, that the Nazis wouldn't kill such a lot of people in one place.

There were also horse-drawn trams in the ghetto, called *kohnhellerki*. They were actually nicknamed after the owners Kohn and Heller – two Jewish magnates, really rich people, who had the licence from the Germans to run the trams. They were of course in the service of the Germans, otherwise they wouldn't have been able to have such a thing. Originally, the ghetto was big, and the tram was flourishing – it would go all around.

Day by day we walked around and gathered news by listening to other people talking. When the Germans attacked Russia in 1941, we heard it all from the Underground news. There was a curfew so you couldn't stay away late in the afternoon.

We'd go out with our coupons to get our food rations – which was bread – and try to pick up a bit of food on the black market. Most of the time we ate watery soup. You couldn't get protein like an egg or milk . . . well, you could but it was so expensive – and there was no sugar, only saccharin for tea. It was a miracle that we could survive from day to day. The Judenrat weren't well-off but they were safe; they had food and they didn't have to stand in line.

There was a kitchen for journalists, where they could get a bit of soup cheaper. Roma's mother went once or twice; they would ask her what she hears from her husband.

There were cafeterias and what I suppose you could call 'restaurants' where the wealthier people went – fat men who somehow did business with Germans, and smartly dressed women who were their wives or lovers. As you walked past, you could smell the food.

I heard that some SS men arrived at one of these restaurants and they had tables put outside set with white tablecloths, plates and cutlery. They ordered some people to sit and the restaurant owner to put nice food on the plates, and they photographed it. This was to show how well off the Jewish people are in the ghetto. Propaganda. I didn't see it but they got some people to dance for them – one who was missing a leg and one who was old – and they filmed it while laughing. It was just a joke to them.

Ella reaches over to the side table and grabs a book from a pile of Holocaust literature. It is A History of the Holocaust (Revised Edition) *by renowned historian Yehuda Bauer and the front cover is a deeply unsettling image of young concentration camp victims, dressed in rags, staring out from behind a barbed wire fence which extends, graphically, beyond the rough edges of the photograph; the barbed wire wraps around the book's spine and dust jacket, so realistic in its portrayal that I feel it might tear my skin.*
  Ella flips pages, showing me pictures that illustrate the ghetto life she is describing: There's the wall of the ghetto, those are the trams and there were also rickshaws – see, like here? – run by people who were trying to make a living. You can see here how everybody was wearing armbands on the right arm; you couldn't go out into the street without them. In other parts of Poland they wore yellow stars on the breast, attached to their clothing, but in Warsaw we wore white armbands.

Life could change in an instant in the ghetto. Overnight, the street where you lived could be cut out of the ghetto limits and you had to move. Or one day you could be walking in the street and suddenly you were blocked off and caught in the middle. That is how they got people. Streets were selected, guards stood at all the adjoining streets to block the openings, and anybody who happened to be in the area was caught and sent off to the *Umschlagplatz*[52]. What

---

52 German for 'collection point', referring to the holding areas next to the railway stations where Jews from the ghettos were assembled and sent to the camps. The *Umschlagplatz* in Warsaw was the largest.

did they say? 'You are being sent to work, to workshops' but actually they were sent to Treblinka[53]. We just didn't know at first.

The next stage, after people were caught in the street, were the raids on flats – this the Nazis did with the help of Ukrainians or Latvians and unfortunately Jewish Police. The Judenrat were ordered to have Jüdischer Ordnungsdienst – Jewish Police[54] – as one of their departments. I can't judge them. I knew somebody who was in the police there. When they climbed up to a flat, and the whole family was there – the parents, grandparents, young people, children, babies with the mothers – everybody was ordered to come down. Doesn't matter if they were pleading, 'Leave me, leave me, I've got a baby' or 'I'm old'. Nothing helped; people were dragged down. Entire families vanished. Nothing and nobody was left. The next day you went up to the flat and it was empty.

Then, to make it still easier for themselves, the Nazis put up announcements on the wall: 'Anybody who will report to work voluntarily will be given three rations of bread and jam.' You can understand there was no shortage of volunteers because they had starving families at home. But when we saw that these people didn't come back . . . that's when we realised there was something wrong.

---

53 An extermination camp in Nazi-occupied Poland that operated from July 1942 to October 1943 and where 700 000–900 000 Jews were gassed.
54 The Jewish Police were auxiliary units organised by the local Jewish councils in the ghettos to enforce Nazi orders and sometimes to control the council. There were about 2 500 Jewish Police in the Warsaw Ghetto.

Chapter 4

Ghetto

Ella is always the one to open the door when I ring the bell at her Bordeaux flat. Her ever-present carer, Joan, hovers a few steps behind but Ella is determined to be the one to unlock the latch and throw wide the door to her world.

While Ella clearly depends on Joan for much and is accustomed to her company (including at shul services, which Ella attends every Shabbat), she prefers not to have her within earshot while we talk. She encourages Joan to take the opportunity to go for a walk on the beachfront or do her shopping, leaving the two of us to talk in private. I find this reticence intriguing because I doubt it is rooted in shyness or inhibition – Ella is renowned for her willingness to speak about her past. I consider whether it is perhaps a function of the professional relationship, that Ella does not want to expose too much of her private life to Joan who, though intimately involved in Ella's every day, is primarily her employee. That theory holds some water, but it's not airtight: after all, Joan is Ella's round-the-clock companion and is thoroughly familiar with Ella's personal life and effects.

By now, I have spent at least fifteen hours in interviews with Ella and there are many more to go. Our discussions are not chronological or linear; the shape of her memories is a corkscrew, a zigzag through time and place. Though I may only now be writing the beginning of her story, I have already heard the end, the middle, and many sidebars in between. Ella is worried about jumping around so much in her narrative and I have to keep reassuring her that it is my job to sort through it all and pull everything together afterwards. For me, the tributaries are as important as the river, perhaps even more so. It is those offshoots and junctions that make a story unique, that take us into its core, beyond the well-worn speeches, articles and photographs that the world sees. It has taken many hours to bring Ella to a point of comfort in recollection, to just allow her mind and heart to wander, without script or destination. She has done interviews before, plenty of them. But this is the first time she has sat down, one to one, and allowed her story to unfold without constraint. From beginning, to end, and back again.

I follow Ella's narrative from bud to bloom. Though it is a story about so much death, I watch it unfurl with life. Early interviews are like earthworms – touch them and they shrivel. As we spend more time together and our own relationship grows, interviews unearth memories that Ella hadn't realised she had buried, and the memoir blossoms.

This unfolding is sheer privilege to witness. With it comes the fullness of the story and a new depth of vulnerability, one that even 'unsentimental, direct and matter-of-fact' Ella Blumenthal is only just starting to reveal. And that, I realise, is why Ella does not want Joan – or anyone else – in our space.

ELLA:
I have given many speeches about my life. Usually, they give me half an hour, 45 minutes to speak, and I've got to try and get everything in. I'm going to give you one of these speeches to read so you can see what I mean. But with you . . . it's different. When I talk to you, I don't want it to sound rehearsed, like a speech. With you, it's more from the heart.

So far, I've told you everything in detail until we were herded into the ghetto. I never told you how overcrowded the ghetto was, fifteen to twenty people living in a room. And of course, the bodies put out every morning and the little children dressed in rags, begging for food. We couldn't survive on the food rations, it was impossible to live on the little bread and saccharin they gave us. The wealthier people bought food on the black market, but unfortunately others couldn't survive. How was it that there was a black market? There were people who had connections with the Nazis – they must have bribed the top officials. The guard at the gate of the ghetto was also bribed and he pretended not to see, he moved away when food was moved into the ghetto and then sold at exorbitant prices.

There were men who were employed in the German workshops outside the ghetto. So every morning they were marched out through the gate with Nazi guards on the side. Every so often they managed to buy some food from the Poles and smuggle it into the ghetto; sometimes they were searched at the gate and they had to get rid of it. Mostly they just had enough for their families, but if there was extra then it was sold. There were also young boys who took to smuggling. Seeing that their little bodies were so thin, they managed to squeeze through cracks in the ghetto wall and they found themselves on the other side, the Christian Aryan side, where the Poles lived. Maybe they sold the mother's wedding ring, maybe they simply begged for food. They were often caught when they returned: at best they were beaten up, but most of the time they were shot. *Ella's voice falls, as if off a precipice of horror, to a well of tears below.* You saw the little bodies on top of the wall, or on the ground in a pool of blood. They were just children! They tried to save us by bringing in a bit of food!

For a time, people found ways to make a little bit of money, like by making and selling the armbands we were forced to wear.

In the ghetto, we had to wear a white armband on the right arm. We did not wear the yellow star that you have heard about. The yellow stars were in Germany and certain parts of Poland, but in Warsaw and perhaps in different parts of Poland also, the Jews were wearing the white armband with a blue star on it. People made them out of different fabrics. The cheaper ones were on linen. The more expensive ones were on celluloid or silk that you could just wipe down. Everyone wore them, me included – you had to.

I told you about the round-ups in the streets and in the flats, how people were caught and sent away, as we believed, to forced labour in the east. As a result of these constant raids and deportations, the population was shrinking and so the Germans tried to concentrate us into a smaller and smaller space – the ghetto was shrinking too.

My family was no exception.

When the first member of my family disappeared, we were living at Gęsia 12. My brother Luzer had got married but I don't really remember his wedding; I think my father married them, gave them the *chuppah vekiddushin*[55]. A lot of people got married just to save themselves because the men, some of them young boys, were working in German workshops and they were told that they and their families wouldn't be deported if they worked for the Germans. So they'd say to the girls, 'Come, let's get married to save ourselves.' For Luzer, there was no big celebration. Two or three men brought a *tallit*[56], my father made the *brocha*[57], and they were married. Not long after, Luzer was there with us in the flat and we were eating, trying to get down some watery soup. And he says, 'I must go. My wife is waiting for me. I can't stay here without her, I can't eat without her.' And he left. We never saw him again because as he went out the door there was a round-up. We never heard of his wife again either.

Then it was the maid, the Jewish girl who had worked for Roma's parents before the ghetto. When we were all relocated to the ghetto, she didn't have anywhere to go so she came with us. One day she went out to buy bread and never returned. Caught in a round-up. They closed up streets and they caught anybody who was there. You couldn't run away because you were surrounded by SS men, Jewish policemen, Ukrainian guards, Latvian guards . . . So this maid

---

55 The Jewish engagement and marriage ceremony under the marriage canopy.
56 Jewish prayer shawl with knotted fringes, often held aloft to serve as a *chuppah* – the marriage canopy.
57 Hebrew for 'blessing'.

didn't return and my sister-in-law, Sala, went to look for her. Then *she* was caught. *Ella starts to cry.* I remember my little niece of six, Ruth, sitting at the table and knocking her head on it: 'Where's my mummy? Where is she?' A child of six. There was also Moishe, a little boy of three, but he didn't understand. Their mummy never came back.

Sala was married to my brother Froim – remember their wedding was near Lodz and I had to get a train ticket? That was her. And now she was gone.

My brother Heniek, the dancer, left the ghetto with his wife and little girl. Some friends told him it's better to be in the country, so they went to a place near Lublin called Janów – a tiny place, smaller than a village. A farm. He had left some goods with us, which we sold for him and then sent him money to live on. So Heniek was there and he was never sent to Treblinka. We only found out later what happened to him . . .

While we were there at Gęsia 12, at Froim's home, Roma's two younger sisters were out – they must have been on an errand or in the street – and as they were coming back home, there was a raid. A Jewish policeman caught them, and one of them said: 'Please let us off, we're small.' To which the Jewish policeman replied, 'I have got to bring ten people today. If I don't bring ten, then I'll have to present my own family,' and they were sent to *Umshlagplatz*.

When they didn't come back, my sister Golda was crying with worry. She couldn't sleep, she was tossing and turning and we were trying to comfort her by saying, 'Maybe they just got lost!' Even in the morning we didn't hear from them. Golda was out of her mind. They must have been about 9 and 11 years old – Roma was 13 by then.

The building we were in was very big, with a long courtyard which our windows faced. We always had somebody on duty watching out the window in case there was a raid. So late morning, whoever was standing by the window shouted, 'The children are here!' The two girls ran up the staircase, filthy dirty, and we couldn't believe they were alive. Behind them trailed a Jewish policeman.

They told us later that, when the train arrived, they pulled back and ran to the building adjoining the *Umshlagplatz*. They ran up the stairs right to the top and hid in the toilet. There was a bucket with dirty papers, and the bigger sister pushed the little one into the bucket and covered her with the dirty papers; she covered herself too and hid. When the train left and they could hear no more noise – it was the middle of the night – the older one told her sister she could relax.

They spent the night there in the toilet. Early in the morning, the older one looked out through a little window and saw the gate with the Jewish policemen, Ukrainian police and SS men at the entrance to the *Umshlagplatz*. She decided to take her little sister and they walked down. She spoke to one of the Jewish policemen. He said: 'Where were you? You came from the other world!' And she said, 'We want to get out of the *Umshlagplatz* . . . We are relations of Mietek Pressburger—' *Ella interrupts herself to explain, 'Mietek Pressburger was a Jewish policeman but he wasn't there that day. I'll tell you about him when I speak about my sister Pola.'* So the policeman replied: 'Are you telling the truth because if you are lying we're going to sort you out.'

Somehow they believed her.

There were some workers who were cleaning up, about to march out from the *Umshlagplatz* onto the street. So this Jewish policeman took the girls and joined the crowd of workers. He escorted them back to Gęsia 12. And this is how he came to be standing there with us now, while they told us the story.

The policeman started getting agitated. He said, 'I'm in a hurry. Fix this up now, I need to go.' He told us, 'I had to bribe the Ukrainian at the gate so now you've got to see to it . . .' Golda gave him some jewellery, some valuables, and he left.

So the girls were smuggled through and got back to us *[tender voice]*. They survived that battle, but they would not survive the war.

We had to find ways to keep ourselves going.

When we moved into the ghetto, we were ordered to bring all our valuables. Our furs were sent to the Russian front for the Germans – we found out afterwards. Everybody had fur coats, or coats with fur collars, especially the grownups, even men. It was the only way to keep warm in the Polish winters. When we had to hand over our furs, we knew it would be difficult to survive without their warmth, so people started manufacturing synthetic furs in the ghetto. They weren't as warm, but at least they were warmer than nothing.

We also tried to keep back some of the silver we were ordered to hand over so we could sell it for even a little bit of money. One of the few ways to sell was to the Poles who had permits to enter the ghetto. Some Poles had official reasons for coming in and they used the opportunity to buy up the Jews' silver. The Polish police were often smugglers but used the pretext of doing something official. Roma's mother sold men's suits. Other people brought their last belongings, their most precious items, anything – as long as they could get a little something to buy food on the black market. These Poles also used to smuggle in food and they took out the stuff they bought. Somehow they got through, maybe they bribed the person at the gate. But this was also a way of living in the ghetto.

The round-ups continued well into 1941. And the raids.

We devised a way of hiding in our flat. We pushed a big wardrobe against the door at the end of the flat, just before the last room. We cut out the back of the wardrobe, hung clothes in front of the opening, and crawled through to the room behind. We closed the door of the wardrobe, and the cut-out behind the clothes, in case the Germans came up searching for us.

Then it was already 1942, Tisha B'Av, and a new order was pasted on the walls. Every person – old, young, male, female – must leave their homes, bring valuables and food for three days, and present themselves in a big open space. Everybody. Even those who worked in the Jewish Council. From there, selections were made and those who were pulled out were sent to the *Umschlagplatz*. This went on every day for almost three weeks. Anybody who was found inside the flats would be shot.

Around this time, my sister Pola and I were working in a German workshop called *Werterfassung*[58]. Our job was to go into buildings that were empty and pick up valuable items that were left by the deported people, whether it was paintings, furs, silver, porcelain, beautiful pieces of furniture, carpets . . . We used to carry them down and load them onto trucks, which were sent to Germany. It was simply robbery of Jewish possessions.

We young people were starting to realise what was happening. Most people, like my parents, said the rumours were impossible – they can't kill people or gas them and burn them, like we heard. But I believed the rumours and I left the *Werterfassung* to go underground.

My family went into hiding in a building that was now outside the designated area. I didn't stay with them. I joined a group of young people who were hiding in cellars and bunkers. I never ever trusted the Nazis.

By now, my brother Itche had a baby, only two or three weeks old. There was some discussion as to whether they could hide with the baby and my brother wondered if they should rather present themselves. Apparently, he looked at everybody who wanted to stay in hiding, and he looked at his own baby, and he said, 'We can't take a chance, we'll go down. They say we're going to work in the east.' So he went down and was of course deported.

My brother Froim had a runny stomach and the only thing to help him was to get some rice. My family knew there was rice where I was. So Golda and my father took a chance and tried to get through to me. Golda had told Roma: 'Don't move from here, look after the children.' But Roma wanted to come too, so she in turn told her siblings, 'Please stay; don't move,' and followed her mother. When they had almost reached my place, Roma caught up with her mom and

---

58 Literal translation of the German is 'value acquisition'.

grandfather, but suddenly there was a round-up! They followed some people into a building and climbed a staircase right up into the roof, to an attic. They sat there through the night while the SS were downstairs searching, and Roma lay the whole night close to her mother just to hear her breathing. Only in the morning did somebody go out to check if it was safe. My father, Golda and Roma went back to where they had left the rest of the family and found only rucksacks. Their own. All the others had taken their belongings with them when they were discovered and deported. My mother, my brother Itche and his wife and new baby, my brother Froim and his little children Ruth and Moishele, and Roma's three siblings.

I met a woman later who said she saw this group of people marching to the *Umschlagplatz* that day; she said my mother was holding the infant in her arms as they were marching. I never heard of or saw any one of them again. It was done. But the rest was a miraculous chain of events – that they came to me for rice, that I was alive, that my father, eldest sister and Roma were alive. Only the four of us remained from the entire family.

This was 1942.

We called this particular time the *kesl* – Yiddish for the 'cauldron'. The whole ghetto, which was already small, was surrounded by guards – Lithuanians, Latvians, Ukrainians and Germans – not Jewish, no more Jewish guards. It was so tight that nobody could sneak out. We called it the 'cauldron' because it was so terribly hot – the hottest time of the year in Europe: July, August, September. And everybody who was presenting themselves to the Germans was wearing thick coats and padded fur because they didn't know where they would get warm clothes in wintertime. So many members of my family were lost in the *kesl*.

Ella rifles through the many notes she has stacked beside her today; hand-written pages, printed notes, pictures, books, leaflets, folders – to which she occasionally motions or glances. Now she picks out a page of scribbles serving as a placeholder in a brochure of sorts.

I have notes here that the resettlement of the Warsaw Ghetto's Jews started in July 1942. We didn't realise at the time that our people were being sent to death camps, not labour camps like the Germans said; we couldn't fathom that such things could happen. And the ones who helped send our people away were the Jewish Police. We hated them because they did the job that finished off hundreds of thousands of Jews; they collected them for the Germans.

Here I've made notes that Adam Czerniaków was a willing collaborator of the Nazis. Czerniaków was the chairman of the Jewish Council, the Judenrat, and he eventually committed suicide. I was reading this when you arrived – this is in Polish but here it is in English, just a short summary *[Ella reads]*:

> On Saturday July 18, Czerniaków officially informed the clerks that the German authorities categorically deny all rumours concerning displacement of the ghetto inhabitants . . .

This was when we had all heard it was confirmed that they were going to finish us off. So he called everybody – his orderlies and clerks – and he denied it.

> When however Czerniaków grasped the whole truth, seeing the erroneous reasoning, he committed suicide by taking poison. The news of Czerniaków's death spread like lightning and startled people because they immediately saw in this act of despair the omen of further tragic events. As it can be seen from the last of his notes, the Gestapo gave Czerniaków to understand that the displacement of Jews from the ghetto is tantamount to its liquidation. The suicide committed by Czerniaków augured the extermination of the Warsaw Jews. On his table was found a short letter to his wife in which he wrote as follows: 'They demand from me to kill the children of my nation with my own hands. There is nothing left for me but to die . . .'

You know the story of Janusz Korczak – the head of the orphanage who refused to leave the children when they were deported? Well Czerniaków had to give the order for them to go; the Germans told him that the whole place must be sent to Treblinka. So he had to organise it. That was the last straw for him.

> As it was later written, the death of Czerniaków was a shock and a warning. How this terrific tragedy grew to its climax tells the diary left by him which, besides the Ringelblum archive[59], is surely one of the most valuable documents of the Warsaw ghetto.

This piece that I read to you comes from a bulletin of the Jewish Historical Institute, based in Warsaw. Czerniaków wrote in his diary every day – between September 1939 and the 23rd of July 1942, when he committed suicide. And this is when the destruction started – it was the end of July when the ghetto was surrounded and we were doomed. *Ella points to some hand-written reproductions in the bulletin from which she is reading.* He wrote in Polish, daily. That's his handwriting. Of course, we heard immediately when he had committed suicide; the news came through and we realised something terrible was coming to us.

Ella dips in and out of the bulletin, opening pages randomly and reading extracts from Czerniaków's diary. She reads about the weather, his regular interactions with officials such as Józef Szeryński –

---

59 Dr Emanuel Ringelblum was a Polish Jew who led a secret group in the Warsaw Ghetto known as Oyneg Shabbos for which historians, rabbis, writers and social workers chronicled life in the ghetto. Between September 1939 and January 1943, they collected documents, diaries, decrees, drawings, essays, milk coupons, chocolate wrappers, and all sorts of material describing daily life in the ghetto and the community's struggles. This is the Ringelblum Archive. As it became clear that the ghetto's Jews were unlikely to survive the war, Ringelblum had the archives stored in three milk canisters and ten metal boxes, which were buried in the ghetto. Two canisters and ten boxes were unearthed after the war. One canister has never been found.

the head of the Jewish Police whom the Jewish Underground viewed as a traitor and attempted to assassinate – and the SS; she reads about budgets, electricity and gas. She still grapples with the role of the Judenrat and Jewish Police, of all the tainted Nazi proxies, shaking her head as she reads of Czerniaków's daily tightrope struggles. I point out that she earlier referred to Czerniaków as a 'collaborator', a word with such pulsating moral judgement.

We thought that he was! But I see from what I just read that actually he was trying. He meant well but his tactic was wrong. He thought that delaying will help to save us, trying to execute the Germans' orders slowly. But as time went on, they kept demanding more and more from him. The Judenrat was actually responsible for rationing the food in the ghetto. They organised the forced labour and the administration of the community services. There were 24 members, I think. Actually, it was difficult for them because they wanted to cooperate with the Germans to avoid major killings and prevent the deportations, but once decrees were out, they couldn't help. At the time, I don't think we realised, or maybe we didn't want to realise, that they themselves were placed in this extremely difficult situation.

Czerniaków was an intelligent man – an engineer – which was probably why he was chosen for the position. Dr Seidman too, also a fine man, also a member of the Judenrat; Hillel Seidman had worked with my brother-in-law, the journalist Samuel Rothstein (Shmuel, Roma's father). Dr Seidman was a religious writer and he kept a diary, which is famous now.[60] And he had *smichas*[61]. Shmuel also had *smichas*! Here in South Africa, when you have *smichas* you're called 'Rabbi'. But for us in Poland it was a normal thing; to me it was like matric – you learn a lot, you go through your studies, you pass. Anyway, just to show you that these were intelligent Jewish people that the Nazis chose to do their dirty work.

---

60 Hillel Seidman, who survived the Holocaust, authored many books, most famously *The Warsaw Ghetto Diaries*, written in Yiddish and focusing on religious life in the ghetto. He was an activist in Agudas Yisroel. Ella and her family would cross paths with Dr Seidman at numerous points in their life story.

61 Rabbinical ordination.

Ella hauls out Yehuda Bauer's A History of the Holocaust *again and flips feverishly through the pages, jabbing at the photographic evidence of her account. She hardly looks up from her pictorial trip down the dark alley of memory. If I comment or ask a question, she indulges me with half an answer and continues to barrel through the book at pace.*

See, look, there's a picture here of Czerniaków; and this is the Jewish Police. And here is a member of the Judenrat. Can you see this cap some of the men are wearing? That's how my father and my brothers were. You see the rabbis? And here you can see the armbands. Look, this is a picture of Czerniaków's office; can you see all the propaganda? The Germans organised footage to be taken of the Warsaw Ghetto and they took pictures in his office; you can see the new orders on the wall. All the proclamations were written in German, Polish and Yiddish, signed by 'Adam Czerniaków, engineer.' This is a picture of a proclamation from 13th of June 1941 – it says here we were going to get something new . . . a box of matches! There was no box of matches. And here on the 13th of February 1942, a proclamation that we were going to get two eggs for children – *zwei Eier*.

And another proclamation to do with bringing out furs – what is the date here? The 25th of December 1941, wintertime; we had to hand over any garment that was made out of fur. Some of us burned them instead of handing them over.

Look here is a photo of a gazette, a Jewish newspaper. And look! Here is the building of the Judenrat on the street Grzybowska 26; the first window from the right on the first floor was Czerniaków's office; that is where he committed suicide. Can you see how he is wearing the star here [*she points to the lower arm*] and not here [*upper arm*]? It is around his cuff. Even during his life before, it was known that he was a pedant; and during the war, he kept his notes and everything so pedantically and scrupulously. He noted all the happenings of the day, every problem in the ghetto, every order he received from 'The Occupant' as they called the Germans.

And look here! Hillel Seidman also! He was eventually in charge of Agudas Yisroel in Paris. He was French-speaking, a rabbi and a doctor, a good friend of my brother-in-law before the war because he was also a writer. Seidman was also on the Judenrat.

Oh and here he mentions a book about Hillel Seidman – I must get it for you. You've got so much to read! There is so much . . .

I don't think we should carry on with this—

Wait! The Warsaw Ghetto Uprising – here is a picture of Marek Edelman. He was one of the fighters in the uprising and the only leader to survive. He actually came to Cape Town. I went to his talk. He couldn't speak English, though. He spoke Yiddish, or Polish, and he had a translator with him.

Ella consults her leaflets and books before she continues. She reads out loud and apologises for repeating facts and figures, but I for one appreciate the reminder; sometimes, the facts and figures are so incomprehensibly large or shocking as to be unbelievable, so I need the repetition to help keep the story straight.

In the summer of 1942 the Nazis began liquidating the ghetto. From Tisha B'Av to Yom Kippur,[62] between 250 000 and 300 000 civilians, our people, were sent to 'work camps' . . . but the only way we went was to Treblinka. While we did not yet know the whole truth of what was happening – we couldn't believe we were being sent to death – we also doubted the idea of the labour camps. How come they're sending old people to work? How come children, disabled people? Surely these people cannot work in labour camps! We tried to talk ourselves into believing that it was labour camps when, in fact, it was a slaughter.

Now, after this *Grossaktion*[63], it was just the five of us left from my family. The ghetto was already so small, the population was shrinking.

---

62   These major fast days in the Jewish calendar are about eight weeks apart.
63   The *Grossaktion Warsaw* (Great Action) was the Nazi code name for the round-ups, deportation and mass murder of the Jews of the Warsaw Ghetto, starting in July 1942. This is the period Ella refers to as the *kesl*.

I was hiding with my young people; we were close to the members of the Underground, the ones who were thinking of revolting. Pola was living elsewhere, and the other three – Roma, my father and my sister Golda – paid good money to get into a German workshop called Többens. There was Többens and also Schultz – two prominent German industrialists who had the most Jews working under them; these two workshops were outside the ghetto.

There was a building next to the workshop where the three of them were given a room with two iron beds (Roma slept with her mom) and a gas stove. Every morning they used to report to work, and every evening they returned to that room to cook a bit of food and to sleep. So for this time, they were effectively living outside the ghetto. If they wanted to come in, they couldn't just show papers that they were working for the Germans; they had to join those columns of workers who came from inside the ghetto but worked outside, building roads and repairing things. These columns used to leave every morning and return every evening, so my family would have to sneak in and out as these workers came close to the gate.

Now remember I told you that my sister's husband Shmuel had left Warsaw even before we went into the ghetto, and had made his way to Palestine. What I haven't yet told you is what happened once he got there. He immediately went to the British consulate and said, 'I have a wife and four children in Warsaw under the Germans, can you give me a visa for them?' And he received it.

Soon after Shmuel left, he asked Golda to send him a photo. I went with her and the children to a photographer to take a picture and we sent it to him. I still have that picture. It was this picture that he produced at the embassy. We used to call it a certificate, but now I'm calling it a visa. It arrived when we had already been relocated into the ghetto and everything was a complete mess. Roma went to the place functioning as the post office. Her three siblings were already gone; only her mother was left. She gave one address and then another and they pulled out an envelope and somebody in the queue said, 'Look! You've got a paper! Entry to Palestine!' She didn't believe it.

When Roma brought the paper to her mother, my sister said, 'I don't want it; how can I think of going to Palestine? What will I say to my husband when he asks me what have you done with my three children?' Her other children were gone. She and her daughter, Roma and our father were working at the workshop outside and I was inside the ghetto hiding with my young people.

Everybody told my sister that she had something valuable. But what should she do with it? Should she take it to the headquarters of the Gestapo in Warsaw on Szucha Street? 'No,' people said, 'If you go there they will kill you.' They killed everybody there; they wouldn't want to listen! It was the worst possible place; when they caught a Jew on the Aryan side, they brought him to Szucha Street and tortured him. He would be sold out by Polish people who got everything out of this Jewish person, said they wouldn't report him to the Germans, but then handed him over to Szucha Street. We called them *schmaltzownicks* – *schmaltz* means 'fat': Polish youths who walked around on the Polish side of Warsaw, looking for a face that looked a little bit Semitic, or frightened eyes – you could see it's a Jew: 'Come on, give me all you have, all your valuables; I won't report you.' When they got what they wanted – cleared all the *schmaltz* off them – they handed them over.

So going to Szucha Street was not an option for Golda. Eventually, she decided to get advice from Dr Hillel Seidman – because of his position on the Jewish Council and because of him knowing her husband. But he was in the ghetto. So Golda had to get back inside the ghetto to go talk to him. She left the certificate with Roma (outside the ghetto) and smuggled herself into the ghetto between the commandos – that's what we called the groups of people who worked for the Germans. It was the 17th of January.

I don't know if Golda ever saw Hillel Seidman but when she presented at the gate with her card showing that she was working for the Germans outside, they closed the gates and nobody could leave – not even those who were employed by the Nazis. Everybody who was near there was sent to the *Umshlagplatz*, to Treblinka, and my sister was among them.

This was in January 1943, around the time of the first Jewish uprising[64] in the Warsaw Ghetto – it was a small uprising, the first time our Underground youth had resisted the Nazis with shooting. It was the first time that the Nazis locked all the gates and you couldn't get in or out. So even people who worked for the German workshops were stopped and deported, even the commandos. And of course, my sister.

The Nazis gathered people at the *Umshlagplatz* but did not send them away immediately. Sometimes they had to wait for the trains. So Golda was in a building that used to be a school or a hospital, adjoining the *Umshlagplatz*. She was kept, along with others, in the cellar there and she met a man, a religious man. She offered him jewellery – I'll tell you later that we all had jewellery sewn into our clothing. This man said he could get her out but he didn't have anything himself. She said: 'I've got, can you save me?' So he got out everything from her – gold coins and jewellery – and he saved himself. Not her.

How did we find out? Roma met a woman afterwards who said, 'So your mother managed to save herself?' Roma replied, 'No, she did not.' This woman was there. She was in that cellar with my sister and

---

64   This 'small uprising' as Ella calls it, was the first act of armed resistance in the Warsaw Ghetto and paved the way for the larger, better-known Warsaw Ghetto Uprising a few months later in April 1943. By January, only 60 000 of the 440 000 Jews confined in the Warsaw Ghetto remained. Jewish lives were lost to starvation, illness and deportation to Treblinka and other camps, particularly in the mass round-ups (*Grossaktion*) of summer 1942, which prompted the formation of underground Resistance movements in the ghetto. In January 1943, a small resistance effort to another round-up was partially successful and spurred on the Jewish and Polish Resistance groups to plan further action, also influencing the behaviour of ghetto inhabitants, who hid in their own homes instead of responding to Nazi calls to gather in the *Umshlagplatz*.

the religious man who took her valuables. She heard them talking. She herself managed to get out – I don't know how she managed it, you could bribe sometimes – but she knew Golda had handed over her jewellery and the man had got out, so she assumed my sister had too. Tragically, Golda had not.

My father subsequently met that man in the ghetto and confronted him:

'Do you know Samuel Rothstein?' my father asked.

'No I don't know him.'

'You know him very well and you know his wife and you know what you have done to her – you sold her; you got everything from her, all her valuables, and you saved yourself and let her perish.' My father was shouting. There were people all around them and my father was shouting. There was nothing, nothing he could do.

This man eventually also perished; he did not survive either.

So now there were only four of us left: my sister Pola, my father, my niece Roma, and me.

Chapter 5

Mila 19

The floodgates have opened.

Today, Ella starts talking before I have even sat down, and I barely have time to switch on my recorder. I saw her just yesterday for a halting, tearful account of disappearance and loss, but today she has the fire of the resistance fighter about her and there is no time to waste with biscuits or small talk.

Moments like these belie Ella's 96-some years. Her high energy and long memory often astound me but there is something different about her manner today. The buzz in the room extends to her cell phone, which is constantly ringing with calls that Ella can only answer through the speakerphone; so I get to hear both sides of numerous conversations, ranging from the electrician arranging a fridge repair, to the Director of the Cape Town Holocaust & Genocide Centre arranging a lift for Ella to and from an event they're hosting. In between, there are calls from her children and grandchildren all over the world – quick 'how are you's' and 'send love to's' and 'thanks for callings' as she tells them she is busy with an interview. Then it's back to business amid a torrential energy that I'm sure will keep me up late into the night.

ELLA:
There were rumours going around, people saying that the transports were not going to workshops in the east, that they were taking our people to die. We just did not believe it – how could it be? Surely it's just rumours?

But by 1943, the Underground confirmed what was happening. And the rumours became more precise. In her book, Roma writes about hearing from a young man who said:

> 'I've just returned from Treblinka. It's a small station north-west of Warsaw; it was a miracle that I managed to get away . . . Dante's Inferno is what I saw in Treblinka. The innocent little village station voraciously devours trainloads of people that keep coming relentlessly. We have been horribly deceived; they are not taking us to work camps but to a well masked death factory.'[65]

I look at Ella quizzically. Not wanting to offend the sanctity of memory by casting doubt, I say cautiously: 'It is hard to imagine how someone could escape and come back to the ghetto to tell you all.'

I believe there was a way of getting out – of course it must have been very few who managed.

There were people who worked at the arrival in Treblinka, sorting all the belongings that the victims left when they were told to undress: money, diamonds, jewellery hidden in clothing, food. After sorting, the clothing was packed into those same wagons they'd arrived in, and sent to Germany. Some individuals managed to hide themselves among the clothing on the wagons; then in the middle of the night they jumped out of the train, and headed back to Warsaw. I know there were cases, not many, maybe one or two like this. And when we heard this, we knew that we'll never, never see our loved ones.

We couldn't doubt it any more – we still wanted to believe that they were sent to work in fields for the Poles, not even labour camps. As I've said before, we ignored the question of how old people or babies might work in the fields. We deluded ourselves.

But when we eventually heard it from individuals and from the notes of the Underground, we understood. This is truly happening. And we must not be caught – the few of us that are still alive!

---

65   Roth, R. 2002. *Here There is No Why.* Rachel Chencinski Roth.

We realised that we have to hide, all of us. So my sister Pola and I decided to bring Roma and my father back inside the ghetto to find a bunker and hide. At that stage, they were still at the Többens workshop outside the ghetto and did not know about Golda being deported. We smuggled ourselves through to them and they were so surprised to see us. Roma immediately asked, 'Where is my mom?' – she didn't realise . . . We made up a story: told her that Golda had been trying to get back but was shot and was in hospital. 'We want you to come with us into the ghetto to visit her.'

They had heard that the factories were moving to places such as Poniatów and Trawniki, where conditions were supposed to be much better. 'We don't believe it,' Pola and I said. We told them it was another trick, that we would not let the Nazis lure them into a trap with beautiful words. We said we had stopped believing their lies about their idyllic work camps. We told them we would build a good bunker, get food and provisions somehow, and we would hide there until the end of the war.

So we brought my father and Roma into the ghetto.

Not long after, we had to tell Roma the truth about what happened to her mother. What I didn't mention before was that when Golda found the gate was locked, she rushed back to us with the terrible news that the ghetto was surrounded. At the time my friends and I still did not have a good hiding place so she decided to stay with Pola, who was married and living in an area that was thought to be safe from this round-up. On the corner of Mila and Zamenhof Street, a Ukrainian caught them both and pushed them into the column of people being marched to the *Umschlagplatz*. Pola's husband was concerned because she had not arrived at work; he guessed what must have happened. He bribed a German on a motorcycle to help him, to chase after the column. The German pulled Pola out by force. She didn't want to leave her sister but the German didn't want to risk his own life – he was scared to take two people out of the column. Pola's husband tried to get Golda out but it was impossible. So he took out Pola only and Golda, Roma's mother, was sent to the *Umschlag-*

platz – to that holding area where the con man took her jewellery – and then to her death.

I couldn't protect Roma from the truth for long, but I could try to protect her from harm. So once Pola and I got Roma and my father back to the ghetto, I had to organise our hiding place. I was with my young people – two boys and a girl. We were friends in Warsaw before the ghetto and we were together in the ghetto also. We found an abandoned flat in an abandoned building – 19 Mila Street; the people had already been deported – we found a pot of food on the stove so there must have been people still living there yesterday! But there was no time for tears.

Some people were still employed in the German workshops outside the ghetto. The rest of us, who did not work for the Germans, were considered 'wild'. I was one of them. As Roma explains, '"Wild" is the term to designate those who are unemployed and of no use to the Third Reich, living in the ghetto illegally.' Even here, in this hell where the Nazis forced us to live, we were illegal.

After those who worked on the Aryan side left for work in the morning, the ghetto was empty; there were no people in the streets and it was not safe to go out if you didn't work anywhere, if you were one of the 'wild' like me. You had to sit in hiding and only when it was dark, and the people arrived back from the German workshops, could you go outside. The streets filled up with people then and you could go out to buy some food and hear news.

It was my father, Roma, myself and my three friends, and we immediately started working on our hideout. We decided that we must brick up a whole room – not like they did back in Gęsia Street, with a hole in the back of the cupboard, but actually brick up the doorway leading to the last room of the flat. So we bricked it up and shifted over a heavy mahogany wardrobe to camouflage the place. That flat was on the second floor. Directly above us, on the third floor, the flat was set out exactly the same. And it was also abandoned; the people had been deported. So we found a spot on the floor that led to our room below. We cut out the flooring, broke through the ceiling and put down a stepladder through that opening onto a wardrobe inside our bricked-up room. The ladder wasn't long enough to get to the floor, it only reached the wardrobe and from the wardrobe we jumped down to the floor. We made a trap door to fit the hole exactly and the last person who went down pulled the trap door shut. We also pulled over a broken cot, just to camouflage it more, so at the same time as you pulled over the trap door, you also pulled the old cot.

We sat inside this room every day. We could hear the Nazis walking around the streets or marching in early in the morning, shouting, calling, 'Where are the Jews?' Shooting, we could hear shooting. One time we even heard them on our staircase. All day we sat and listened. I suppose we exchanged some words among us but we were mainly sitting and listening to know if they passed our building. Only at night we used to crawl out because at this stage the Germans did not come into the ghetto during the night – later on yes, but not at that time. So we used to climb out at night and cook a bit of food in the kitchen.

We knew that this bricked-up room was not the safest place to survive and we decided to build a bunker underground, under the cellar. We couldn't go out in the streets, but we found that in our building, Mila 19, there was a long corridor in the cellar. You remember I told you that every tenant had a little partition, to keep coal – like in my brother's building where we stored our things. This building had the same arrangement. When you walked through you saw locks hanging on the door to each partition. At the end of this corridor, we dug through the foundation of the building to make an opening to the last cellar. Everyone managed to get tools of a sort in the ghetto, and we worked at night to make the opening. We found a broken toilet in the passage and, after we had squeezed through to our bunker, the last person pulled the toilet over to cover the opening.

We put some wooden planks down, raised off the floor of the bunker, and put food provisions on them. Why on a plank? So the mice and rats shouldn't get to them. We stored some dried pieces of bread, water, candles and some horse fat there. It was very difficult to get fat at all; the only kind you could get was horse and it was very expensive. Once, my father realised we were cooking with horse fat because the taste is different – it's sweet – and he refused to touch the food! He would not touch the unkosher food. But we had to have it to sustain ourselves.

Every night we used to squeeze out of the bunker to straighten our limbs and to get a bit of fresh air. The bunker space was very small. We could only lie flat or sit, we couldn't stand up because the ceiling of the cellar was very low. So we climbed out every night when we thought it was safe; you would see other people emerging from their hiding places and bunkers. Like ghosts coming out at night.

What about practical things like using the toilet?

Well you had to hold it – there was no way to use a bathroom during the day. As soon as it got a bit dark at night, we used to crawl out, one by one, and relieve ourselves. Yes of course; you're quite right. I was never asked this question before!

There was somebody else with us who I've forgotten to mention. When we were hiding in the bricked-up room and in the cellar, there was a couple. The man's name was Moishe and before the war he had a bakery in this very building of Mila 19. So we called him 'Moishe Baker'. He had a wife and a young child. He saw us when we carried the bricks to brick up the doorway, and he said: 'You're going to have a bunker, a place to hide. I have a wife and a child and I haven't got anywhere to hide. You've got to take me in.' We were afraid – even afraid of other people, we couldn't trust anybody – but we took them in and they were with us all the time in this bricked-up room. Whenever we heard the heavy steps and the shouting of '*Wo sind die verfluchten Juden?*' – 'Where are the cursed Jews?' – the mother had to cover the child's face with a pillow in case he cried or made a noise. But this child knew he had to be quiet; he had seen us preparing.

This is how we lived for some time, though I couldn't tell you how long because we had no concept of time.

I must tell you, I do wonder about it – maybe because I'm an old person – I think: how did I manage to survive, to be so strong? I still can't believe it myself. But when you've got fear and the will to live, it gives you strength. We are stronger than we think, you know that?

We didn't believe that the rumours about death camps were true until our young people started trying to make a revolution against the Germans. The Underground movement printed leaflets that forced us to realise the truth.

The Underground organisation had a building on Mila Street 18 and we were hiding in Mila 19, exactly across the road.[66] I know the building, a low, small building opposite our large one, their gate was always closed. You wouldn't realise anybody was living inside any of these buildings anyway – they looked completely deserted, yet there were people hiding inside in cellars and bunkers.

All this time, Ella is rifling through her many papers and cuttings. She insists she has something to read to me and, even though we have been talking about difficult memories for a while now and she should be tiring, that earlier nervous energy still shoots out like sparks from a welding iron.

I also notice that Ella's account of these months of hiding, deprivation and loss is delivered with unvarnished stoicism, different from

---

66 18 Mila Street was the headquarters of the Jewish Fighting Organisation (Żydowska Organizacja Bojowa, ŻOB), which spearheaded the Warsaw Ghetto Uprising. Its leader, Mordechai Anielewicz, organised defensive Jewish groups in the ghetto after reports of mass murder filtered through in 1941. The Jewish Resistance made contact with the Polish Home Army and smuggled weapons and explosives into the ghetto. Their first clash with the Nazis in the 'small uprising' of January 1943 set the stage for the larger one in April 1943, for which Anielewicz employed guerrilla tactics, using a network of tunnels, bunkers and roofs prepared over the preceding three months. It is this time period that Ella is describing now.

her usual straightforward manner. Although strong, we've seen how genuinely and easily her voice can crack; her stories and expressions quickly elicit emotion – both hers and her listener's. But today feels different, more hurried – even the memory of Moishe Baker's wife putting a cushion over their child's face is recalled with restraint.

I wonder if what I'm seeing is a cooling off, a necessary distance from trauma induced by self-defence. Has she reached a point of desensitisation in her telling? But we're only near the start of the war memories – surely it's too soon?

It is. Way too soon. The worst is most certainly yet to come. It is not that Ella is blocking out or glossing over sadness and it's not that she is feeling the distance. If anything, the opposite is true: each time we talk, Ella reinhabits the girl she was then – like method acting, except she's not acting. And her one throwaway statement earlier today is the key to understanding this particular time period: 'There was no time for tears.' There wasn't time then, in the rush to find safe harbour, and there isn't time now, in the rush to tell me all about it. No time for tears.

I'm looking for that leaflet the Resistance printed. To me, this *[Ella finds what she is hunting for]* is so important. When we got this information we realised there was something wrong. It took time. We had always believed what the Nazis said, that the people who were sent away were going to work for the Germans. But our Underground youth printed leaflets and they were distributed among us. I'll read one of them . . . *Ella sits up straight and puts force and volume behind her words, like a call to arms:*

> Citizens! Jews! Awaken from your lethargy. Stand up and fight. Do not believe that they are sending us to labour camps. It is a vicious lie. Our brothers and sisters are being brutally murdered in the death camp Treblinka. Brothers, prepare to defend yourselves; those who are not fit for fighting should go underground and hide in cellars and bunkers. Turn every

building into a fortress as we have no right to occupy the surface of the earth because we are condemned to death.

When she's finished reading, Ella shows me a piece of paper with this message written out in a bold and looping script.

After the war I wrote it down. I always read it out to audiences these days when I give talks because this is what really made us understand and believe the awful truth. From these young people we had to believe it. They worked with the Polish Underground on the Aryan side – they used to communicate with them, so they knew exactly what was happening to our families. I don't know how they got in touch with each other; I suppose they got information on the radio. And they bought arms from them – although often the arms were useless, paid for by good money.

When we were living in that apartment in Mila 19, the Resistance people would come to us for money, for support. They knew where people were hiding. And they used to distribute flyers to tell people the truth:

> Brothers and sisters! Open your eyes to the bitter reality; don't let them deceive you. Don't believe stories about work camps for old people and children. Only 90 kilometres from Warsaw there is a death camp Treblinka where the Nazis are killing our mothers, sisters, children, fathers and brothers, in cold blood. Don't believe the unabashed lies that specialities will be released from deportations . . .

Specialities means people who have a trade or a skill. They told us while we were in the ghetto that those who work, who are employed in the German workshops, will be immune to the deportations; if you work for us you will stay in the ghetto.

> Death awaits us all in the camps of Treblinka. The voracious dragon is devouring tens of thousands of victims daily. The

silent witnesses are the empty wagons . . . After the unfortunate victims have been murdered, the wagons return to *Umschlagplatz* for more Jews . . . Look the terrible truth straight in the eyes . . . Don't let them deceive you . . . The ghetto in Lublin and those in other cities and towns have already been liquidated. The inhabitants of those ghettos were shot in the nearby forest or deported to Treblinka. We must prepare to fight. We will defend our honour with our lives and the lives of our dear ones. Death to the Nazi bandits.

Long live the Jewish Fighting Organisation.

I must interrupt the narrative flow here to point out that this very flow is in fact a literary device – it is imposed, by me, in an attempt to fashion a largely chronological account from what would otherwise be a pastiche of memory.

Ella's recollections are not linear, and the more time we spend together, the more she loosens up and allows memories to rise, sometimes unbidden, from the mental vault in which she stores her past. At first, she apologises every time one comes barging in; she considers them unwelcome visitors, disrespectful of the appropriate time and place for the telling. It takes me a long while to convince her to let them in, to speak them as she remembers them, and allow me to untangle the collection later. There is no telling what might trigger a flashback: a word, a smell, a facial expression, a request to spell a name . . . and I encourage Ella not to self-censure.

Now, at the time of writing, I must keep a handle on the threads and keep them at once distinct and interwoven. I feel like an octopus with a maypole. For the sake of narrative flow and integrity, I must keep a tight hold on each of the many strands, let them billow and settle, braid and untwist. I must remain independent but connected, much like the strands themselves.

While this book is driven by a verbatim account of Ella's testimony, it is of course not a direct transcript of our interviews. So readers may not appreciate just how many times Ella starts and stops a particular thought. And the place she first references a memory is not necessarily the place that I insert it – either because it is out of sync, or incomplete or, as is the case with what we are about to explore, because she is not sure that she wants it written in the book at all.

We're talking about her sister Pola, closest in age to Ella of the siblings and, up to now, hardly mentioned. By this stage, Ella has told me what became of all members of her family – except Pola. She darts in and out of that subject with occasional allusions ('I must tell you about my sister Pola') which go nowhere . . . until she can quash it no more.

Ironically, it is not the tragedy of Pola's fate that underlies Ella's reluctance to share her sister's story. It is that age-old Jewish Achilles heel . . . Shame.

My sister, I want to tell you about my sister . . . but I don't know if you want to put it in the book.
Why not?
I'll tell you.
Okay.
I'll tell you.
Okay.
When we were hiding – I don't think anybody knows about it, Roma's the only one who knows about it because she was with us . . . When the Germans – no, I can't say 'Germans', I must say 'Nazis' because it's hurtful to Germans. Like the consul general here in Cape Town. I was invited to him just before Christmas two years ago. His family came from Germany and he liked me, we had a very nice association with him. Roma was here on holiday as it happens and she went with me to his house for tea with some others. They wanted to know my story and while I was talking, I couldn't say 'the Germans'. So I had to watch myself to only say 'the Nazis'. Are you with me?
Oh yes.
Now, I was going to tell you something.

You were going to tell me about your sister...

But there was something else, in the beginning of the war, when we were still in—. It will come back to me just now. I had it in mind but I've forgotten. Sometimes I can't remember the ... the ... is it 'consequence'?

You mean chronology?

Yes, chronology. And I'm jumping around with my stories because certain things I never speak about. So I was going to tell you about the bread—

You wanted to tell me about Pola, something that you said you're not sure if we must write about because you don't know if anybody knows.

But this wasn't what I was going to tell you before Pola. It will come back.

Okay.

It's something to do with the beginning, when they occupied Warsaw. But I don't want to waste time. I want to tell you about Pola, I want to get it off my chest. When we were— Ah! I think this is what I was going to tell you.

When Warsaw was invaded, we left our homes in Praga. Roma's family and our family went to my brother in Gęsia 12. Remember we had to run down into the cellars when there was the bombardment? And in this block of flats, do you remember I told you there was a synagogue at the bottom? *Ella sketches the building's layout with her fingers on the tabletop.* Every flat had an iron balcony. We were on the second floor and on the third floor, across the courtyard from us, always sat a woman with grey hair. The reason she was remarkable is because you could see her own grey hair – very seldom did you come across a woman who didn't wear a *sheitel*. And she would sometimes sit on the balcony. I didn't know who it was, my brother and sister-in-law had nothing to do with a woman like this.

When we went down to the cellar, there was a young man, a son of this woman, who used to come hide on our side. He could have gone down his staircase but instead he would come and join us, waiting until the bombardments were over. He had an eye on her, on my sister Pola, though he was much older than her. He spoke French because he had brothers in Paris and he himself had already been in Paris. He was smartly dressed with a smart hat, a modern Jewish person. I don't know how to explain it to you – we just did not have contact with people like this.

When the Germans occupied Warsaw, we went back to Praga and he started coming round frequently, following Pola, taking her out. When I told you that I had typhoid and I said somebody got us a doctor who came dressed as a tradesman . . . It was he who got the doctor from Warsaw. We were quiet, old-fashioned people; we couldn't have arranged that. He was a man of the world.

Eventually, in the ghetto, he became a policeman. He was a good-looking man, a toughie. And as a policeman, he was better off in the ghetto. At some point, my parents gave the blessing that he and Pola should get married but I don't remember who married them or when it happened. Then he was a relation.

I don't know if you should write that in the book; I don't want to speak badly, I'm just telling you this because it's part of my story . . .

Now you remember when the two girls, Roma's sisters, were caught and they said to the policeman at the *Umschlagplatz* that their relation is Mietek Pressburger? That's him. That's Pola's husband.

I don't know if you should put that in the book, though. It's a blame on our family – with Mietek Pressburger . . .

I must look puzzled because Ella glances at my face and tries to clue me in. What she is getting at is just how controversial the figure of the Jewish policeman, or the member of the Judenrat, was during the Holocaust. To many, they were Nazi collaborators, an impression led largely by the role they were ultimately forced to play in rounding up fellow Jews for deportation; but to historians, and arguably the policemen themselves, their position was a means of survival as they could – only initially – avoid deportation themselves and save their own family. The war-time behaviour of the Jewish Police, and other Jewish pawns of the Nazi state, is complex, fraught with nuance and judgement. But Ella's overriding sense is that the mere association of such a person with her family is shameful.

Pola was blinded by him; he was so strong in his ways and his movements and his whole being. What is the word for how you get by a witch?

Enchanted? Bewitched?

Yes, she was bewitched. He was so much stronger, she had no say over her life. I didn't know when they got married, I just knew afterwards that they were husband and wife. And she would have gone to live with him – the policemen had their own quarters.

But in the end, it did not save her.

There was talk in the ghetto that there will be an exchange of citizens – whoever has got a foreign passport will be exchanged for a German citizen overseas. So they started to print foreign passports – South American, British – some real, some not kosher. I don't think there were consuls in the Warsaw Ghetto. Some consuls, like Japan, gave permits for Jews to leave the country, but many were not legitimate.

Pola's husband, Pressburger, got South American passports; he must have paid for them but for sure they were not kosher. We don't know exactly but Roma and I heard that they had passports for a country that the Germans did not approve of. And they were all sent by train to Treblinka. They disappeared.

So this is what happened to Pola. And her husband . . . a policeman. Even to policemen.

In the end it did not matter who you were. If you were Jewish, that was enough.

During the time of the *kesl*, with the mass deportations, almost 300 000 people were lost. People who were working for German workshops were also sent away. Jewish policemen were deported. Even the head of the Jewish Police, the convert Józef Szeryński, was arrested; he was released back to the ghetto and then there was an attempt by our Underground to assassinate him.[67] No one was safe. Even some who worked for the Judenrat went. The only ones who remained alive after this 'cauldron' were people like me who were in hiding, and people who were chosen and pulled out of the selections. The German owners of the workshop, the big bosses, could stand there during a selection and pull out their workers – like a Schindler story.[68]

After this, life carried on with a much smaller number of citizens in a much smaller ghetto. And as the ghetto was shrinking, so too was the size of my family.

* * *

It was Pesach, April 1943.

I remember my father sharing a piece of *matzah*[69] that he had saved from the previous year. He gave small little bits to everybody. And then he recited the blessings over the *matzah*. After the blessings he prayed to *HaShem*, asking that he should save us like he saved the Jews from bondage in Egypt. Save us.

The next morning, the Nazis marched in. Every morning they used to march into the ghetto, looking, searching, calling to find Jews to deport them. And we sat in that room with the curtains closed. You couldn't see from outside which window is which because all the windows looked exactly the same. And the buildings were grey, so from the street they wouldn't know that there were people in a bricked-up room.

Usually, they marched in happy, with a song. But this time they

---

67 Ella mentions Józef Szeryński a couple of times in interviews, emphasising the fact that he converted from Judaism to Christianity (which did not save him) and was viewed as a collaborator by the Jewish Underground in the ghetto. Ella believes he was eventually killed by the Underground, though internet sources say he committed suicide after the deportations in January 1943.

68 A reference to German industrialist Oskar Schindler, Nazi party member, who saved the lives of 1 200 Jews by employing them in his factories and bribing SS officials to prevent their execution.

69 Hebrew: unleavened bread; integral to the Jewish holiday of Passover.

were met by Molotov cocktails, homemade bombs. There was shooting coming down from rooftops. The SS men were taken by surprise and they withdrew, leaving their dead and injured. Believe it! There was German blood flowing in the streets of the Warsaw Ghetto! But the next morning they came back with a new commander, reinforcements and tanks in retaliation, and still the Nazis found that our young men and women would not give up – they were falling, but they fought on.

We didn't know about the uprising before it happened. We knew there was an underground Resistance but we did not know their plans. They asked me sometimes to get involved. I never went to their headquarters – nobody could get into the place where they were hiding – but I did sometimes deliver notes and things for them. My family was scared about the Underground though, because we knew that if they revolt, the Germans are going to kill us all, they're going to retaliate – which they did. In fact, that was the same attitude that the Polish people, and the Polish Underground, had to the Jewish Underground – they feared that the Poles would be next after the Jews; they did not want to provoke the Nazis.

Our people in the ghetto did not agree with the underground organisation, at least not at first. We were also afraid to provoke. We helped them when they came to ask for money to buy arms. But we were afraid.

Still, when we heard the shooting, we said, 'It's our boys, our boys!'

The fighting went on for a couple of weeks. But unfortunately, our people couldn't stand up to this mighty, well-equipped German army and the uprising was crushed. The SS found the Resistance headquarters at Mila 18 and they threw gas down. Very few of the Resistance fighters survived. Some of them managed to get underground through sewers from the ghetto to the Polish side. But most died.

With the uprising, the Nazis decided to liquidate the ghetto. It was the only way to get rid of us. Anyone who was left was hiding in bunkers and cellars, and whoever was alive was not to be caught! They couldn't find anybody in the streets, or in the homes. The only way was to smoke us out. So they set the ghetto on fire . . . building by building.

We had to get out of our bricked-up room. We could smell the smoke and see the flames. It was the middle of the night when we went up the stepladder and out the burning staircase; the main gate of the courtyard was already in flames but we went through. It was night and the whole ghetto was burning. We wanted to get to our bunker, where we kept some provisions. We managed to make our way to it and squash in.

It became unbearably hot. We couldn't breathe.

We realised that the façade of Mila 19 was now also on fire. The fires had caught up to this place and we knew we would suffocate if we did not get out.

So one by one we climbed out.

There were people from other bunkers who found themselves in the same situation. We were all in that last courtyard and it was burning. We saw people jumping out from their hiding places, bodies caught on balcony rails – we could see them hanging from high up. People were running around with their clothes burning, their hair singed, their skin scorched.

There were informers among us – Yiddishe people. Sometimes a Jew was caught and told by the Nazis: 'You won't be deported; you will stay alive if you show us where the Jews are hiding.' Some nights, when we climbed up from our bunker, we might see a person whose clothes were not even creased – someone who was bought by the Nazis with the promise to live. Now, one of those said: 'You don't want to be burnt alive. There are SS men in the street behind the gate but you won't be shot. You will be resettled to the east where you'll work in the German workshops, with your family.' Some people chose to follow them. As they got out beyond the gate they were rounded up and sent to the *Umschlagplatz* and of course the next stop, Treblinka. But we, our little group that kept together – my father, myself, Roma and my friends – we stayed together all the time and, even in this dark hour when we were trapped, we still refused to submit.

Now we were outside and Moishe Baker pointed out a narrow space in the courtyard where he used to keep bags of flour for his bakery – it was dirty and concealed by things lying around and over it. We lowered ourselves into that narrow space – I think there were about thirteen of us – and we stood so tightly pressed together there that we couldn't move our limbs.

That's how we stayed.

I want to just say again that, even in this dark hour when we were trapped with nowhere to turn, we still resisted and refused to submit. *Ella repeats this sentence a few times – now, and often over the coming days as her memory casts back to the dying days of the Warsaw Ghetto.*

In the morning we heard heavy footsteps and shouting: '*Raus! Raus Juden!*' – 'Get out! Get out Jews! If you don't come out, we will send gas.'

We had been betrayed.

One of the informers must have seen us crawling into our narrow hiding space. There was no escape from here, nowhere else to hide. We had no option but to come out.

It was May 1943, almost three years since we had first entered the Warsaw Ghetto.

* * *

We blinked in the brightness. We were outside, blinded by the daylight we hadn't seen for such a long time.

We were ordered to stand with our hands up, facing the courtyard wall. We waited to be shot. I prayed to God that I should be shot first before my father. Roma was standing on the other side saying the same prayer. I didn't want to see my father being shot. But we were not shot; we were only searched for weapons because they knew that we Jews were armed. We were ordered to place all our valuables into a sack and then we were chased out into the street. We could see some of the buildings still smouldering. Warsaw Ghetto was in ruins. It was already three weeks after the start of the heroic uprising and I'm convinced that we were among the last survivors holding out under the burnt-out ghetto. I don't know if there were any Jews caught afterwards – there could have been some still trapped.

We were marched to the *Umschlagplatz*. There was no train yet, so they put us in an adjoining building, I think it could have been a hospital or a school before. It's still there. And we had to sit – not only us but hundreds of people had to sit on the floor of an empty hall. There must have been other halls because there were a lot of people.

At night, the Latvian guards in their black uniforms – not the green army uniforms of the Nazis – marched into our hall and pulled out young girls. We were sitting against a wall; my father covered Roma and me with his coat.

In the morning we were ordered down the stairs to the train platform, but at the end of the staircase we were sent back because the train was already full – so we spent another night on the floor in that hall. The following morning again we were ordered down. There was an old man going down the staircase in front of my father. I think he was a rabbi. I saw my father giving him a piece of loaf sugar – you know that crystallised sugar, like a square? *A sugar cube?* Yes! A cube of sugar. Not a loaf! Well, my father had saved a cube of sugar in his pocket and he gave it to the old man. As we got to the platform, the old man was motioned out of the line. And he was shot. Right there. Almost at our feet . . . He was too old to make even the last journey.

* * *

That was my own experience of the Warsaw Ghetto Uprising and the dying days of Jewish life in Poland. But I want to read to you what was written by Jürgen Stroop, the new SS commander who set the ghetto on fire and got most of us out who were still hiding.

I was caught in May – the 7th or the 8th of May – and the report was sent soon after that. Stroop wrote this in his report about the destruction of the Warsaw Ghetto:

> The former Jewish quarter of Warsaw is no longer in existence. The large-scale action was terminated at 20:15 hours by blowing up the Warsaw Synagogue . . .
> Total number of Jews dealt with 56 065, including both Jews caught and Jews whose extermination can be proved . . . With the exception of eight buildings (police barracks, hospital and accommodations for working parties) the former Ghetto has been completely destroyed. Only the dividing walls are left standing where no explosions were carried out.'[70]

Actually, he was preparing this report for Hitler's birthday, which was in April. Stroop wanted to advise Hitler that there were no more Jews left in Poland.[71]

Quite a birthday gift.

---

70 The SS and Police Fuehrer in the District of Warsaw. *Progress of large-scale operation on 16 May 1943, start 10 000 hours. The Warsaw Ghetto: the Stroop Report – 'The Warsaw Ghetto is no more'*. Jewish Virtual Library. https://www.jewishvirtuallibrary.org/the-stroop-report-may-1943. Last accessed 20/12/2022.

71 Yad Vashem, Israel's official memorial to the victims of the Holocaust, is the preeminent resource in Holocaust history. The museum, on the slopes of Mount Herzl in Jerusalem, charges no admission fee, and the website (www.yadvashem.org) offers unrestricted access to its trove of material. Of particular interest at this point in Ella's story is the online exhibition of The Stroop Collection, showcasing some of the many photographs taken during the final liquidation of the Warsaw Ghetto. These unique images document the very moments Ella herself endured and remembers here.

Chapter 6

Majdanek

Gone is Ella's stoic, distanced tone of earlier. Now, remembering this close-up of Nazi venom, putting herself back on that platform for the start of what she believed to be her own last journey, the timeworn trauma leaks from her eyes, lacing her voice with a frightened vibrato.

ELLA:
We were pushed along. I said to my father: 'Stand up straight and walk straight, not bent.' The guards were shouting, '*Schnell, schnell, schnell!*'[72] knocking and hitting us. They pushed us into the wagon, that cattle truck, until we stood so tightly pressed together that they had difficulty shutting the heavy doors before bolting them. We waited, pressed together, in the unbearable heat, and when the train eventually moved, there was still no air coming through. There was one tiny window and a few friends managed to stand there and get a bit of air, but inside it was so hot you couldn't breathe. Some people were fainting, others were dying even in the upright position. There were no facilities, no water. I heard later that some people jumped from those trains. That friend of mine, Marysia, she jumped out of a train. I don't know how – it couldn't be by the windows because those were barred; some people said you cut out the floor, but then you'd still be under the train. I have read about

---

72 German for 'quick'.

Majdanek

people having survived this way – maybe some of the windows were not barred? But not on my train.

Somebody said we're heading for Treblinka but in fact, thanks to God's will, the train stopped just outside Majdanek, a camp not far from Lublin. The station was called Lipova 7 – *siedem* in Polish – and that is where we stopped.

When we got off the train, we couldn't manage to lift up my father; he couldn't remember where he was, he was just lying there, so we had to go out, leave him. We found some water dripping from a broken tap somewhere; people were pushing, everybody tried to get a few drops. And then – listen to this! – I looked around and I saw a familiar figure walking towards us in long white underwear, in Yiddish it's called *gatkes*[73]. It was my father! Walking towards us! Only after the war did I find out how it happened.

Two of my friends that I had been hiding with, two boys, were ordered by the Nazis to clean out the cattle truck. They recognised my father and as they took him out, he revived in the fresh air. But while we were travelling, he must have undressed himself because it was so terribly hot. Now he remained in the white underwear. He kept asking: 'Where is my *kileh gartel*[74]?' You see my father had a rupture and he used to wear a special orthopaedic belt to hold in his tummy. He put it on every morning. It was beige leather and it had kidney shapes on the ends. It was this belt that he was asking for.

Why was he so worried about this belt? Well, back in the ghetto, my parents had divided their valuables among all of us. Even before the ghetto, when the war started, we used to buy gold pieces – like here in South Africa we have a Kruger Rand. We knew we needed something we could use to bribe people if we were sent away – we thought we were going to work in fields on Polish farms, and we could bribe our way and help ourselves with gold. Money was worthless, so there was a market for buying and selling foreign gold pieces.

---

73 Like long johns.
74 Yiddish for 'hernia belt'.

There were Russian gold pieces we called *chazzerlach* – a *chazzer* is a pig so I don't know why they were called *chazzerlach*. There were English pieces also. But I remember mainly the *chazzerlach* because of the name.

The gold pieces were easy to hide so each member of our family sewed them into their clothes, into panties, undergarments, though not into coats because you could lose a coat. My father had his in that belt, the rupture belt. So when we found him, he was dazed and kept on asking me, 'Where is my belt, where is my belt?' He must have taken it off when he got undressed.

We were formed into rows, five abreast, and marched to the actual camp, Majdanek. I must have been the last one in my row, not in the middle, and we were surrounded on each side by Nazis with dogs on leashes. I still don't know even today what exactly happened, but I tripped and fell, crawling, trying to keep up with the others while a dog was biting into my back and I was waiting to be shot. Not until the Nazis had enough fun and stopped laughing was the dog called off. I got up and tried to walk; I was in pain.

We arrived at the camp, which was surrounded with barbed wire, and there were sentries all around pointing guns at us. Women with babies, children, older women, were immediately taken away from us and ordered straight to the gas chambers. Then it was the turn of the men . . .

My father was among the group walking in front of me. He turned back to have a look at Roma and me and he was hit over the head. He bent under the blow and that was the last I saw of him. I've never . . . *[sobs]* . . . never seen my father again. My father's ashes are there . . . *[openly crying now]* . . . My mother's, brothers', sisters' ashes, I don't know where they are . . . But the ashes flying there at Majdanek that day, those were my father's.

As if on cue, a strong gust of wind blows through the windows thrown open to the sea view, and a door slams shut with a loud bang. Ella startles at the noise and is jolted from this most painful of memories.

Majdanek

We were standing and waiting. They were sending away the older women and the very young children. We saw famous Rabbi Ziemba's daughter-in-law, his son Luzer's wife. She and her children were taken away to the gas chambers in that very first selection.

Roma, one of my young friends and I were standing together and, while these things were going on around us, I asked: 'What am I to do with my valuables?' So the others stood tight around me and I dug a hole in the ground with the heel of my boot – I was wearing beautiful boots. I tried to get as much ground out as I could and then I took some of my gold pieces that were sewn into my clothes, and buried them. The girls stood close, holding hands around me, so nobody could see, and I put ground over the pieces, tapped it down with my foot, and said I would come back to find the place. Apparently, I wasn't the only one because they found a lot after the war.[75]

Now we girls had to go through a selection, young girls. With one wave of the whip you were sent, *rechts, links, rechts, rechts, rechts, links, rechts* – right to life, left to death. I was afraid that I wouldn't pass the selection because of my bleeding back, and my knees which were scraped from crawling on the gravel. Roma assured me: 'If they send you to the left, I'll follow you.' So when it was my turn to go past the selection, I used all the strength that was left in me – I lifted my shoulders and held my head high – and I was sent to the right. So was Roma. Right to life.

We were sent to the showers to be disinfected and there was an area with hooks to put up clothes. There was an old-fashioned iron-cast stove; it had a chimney going out, a place to put coal, and ash

---

75 In a later interview, Ella will read to me from one of the many books and papers she has collected on the Holocaust. This extract, from the *Staten Island Advance* newspaper, November 2005, describes the excavations at Majdanek and the discovery of the personal treasures buried in its grounds by victims: 'A child's ring, twisted reading glasses, a few gold coins, scraps of personal dignity, hurriedly buried in the last act of defiance to keep them from falling into Nazi hands . . .' As she shows me, Ella remarks: 'I just want to tell you that it's true, what I did there; other people did the same.'

underneath. I found that type of stove again when I came to this country in the house that we rented – of course we did away with it; the previous owners had used it to heat the house. Anyway, the rest of my possessions, I left in the ash in that stove.

We were given showers and lice-infested clothes and ordered into an empty blockhouse – there wasn't even a piece of straw; we slept on the bare floor. Roma was still getting her period in those early days. Later, we never got our menstruation; I think they put something in the food to prevent us from menstruating, so we never got it. But it happened in the beginning and we had no paper, no sanitary towels, nothing. So I tore off pieces from the shirt underneath my dress for her – until it was almost gone.

We were sent to work in different labour groups – *Kommandos*, the Nazis called them – building, in the fields, cutting grass. There was a group that was really one of the best, called *Scheiße Kommando* – you know what *Scheiße* is in German? It's faeces. We girls were ordered to push a wooden cart filled with human excrement. Two girls were harnessed to the cart in the front, like horses. The rest of us were pushing from the sides and the back. When it rained, the wheels would get stuck in the mud and we struggled to move the cart, we'd be hit and whipped so hard that *[talks through tears]* eventually we'd get it out. When we got to the field, we had to open the cork to let it all out and we got covered with faeces. And that was a good job! Why? Because men came to work in the field so we could sometimes pass a word – this one's still alive and this one's gone. There were no toilets in Majdanek. There were buckets close to the wire partition between the women's and men's camp. *[Ella giggles]* we could show our— *[points to her backside]*. I can laugh now but back then...

There were transports all the time, people were sent away to different camps and of course to the gas chambers. Some of the girls, our friends, couldn't take it – the tempo, the life; the food was a piece of black bread, gooey like clay, and the soup was watery, with rotten leaves floating in it. Some girls became swollen, especially the feet and the faces, they said it was because we were living underground in the darkness for such a long time in the ghetto – a reaction.[76] Maybe. Others got TB, others typhus. When we were not working, we used to sit and clean up our clothes, especially in the seams, because we knew the lice in the clothing was causing typhus.

One day, when we came back from work, we were ordered to assemble in a big open place. *Ella's voice drops to a sensitive tone.* One of our friends, one of the girls, was led to a – to a place where you hang, from the neck. *Like the gallows?* Yes, gallows. She was led to the gallows and the SS woman kicked a box from under her feet and she was hanged. We had to stand and watch. The *Kommandant* of the camp stood there; he proudly announced, with his white gloves knocking his little whip against his shiny boots, 'This is what's going to happen to any one of you if you try to escape. So that you shouldn't forget it, you're going to stay here the whole night until dawn when you will go back to work.'

So we stayed. The whole night. We remained and watched how the little body of our friend was moving in the wind. It was a terrible sight.

She had probably tried to escape. But there was no way to escape. And we had to stay the whole night. So we stood close to each other to keep warm. Roma had a brainwave. She said: 'I'm going to tell you about the Friday nights in my house where we lived before the war . . .' and she described how her little sisters were all dressed up with plaits and ribbons, everyone in shiny, beautiful Shabbat clothing. The little boy went with his father to the synagogue, and the smell of the food coming from the kitchen was wonderful. And when the father came back, how he sang *Shalom Aleichem*[77] and the table

---

76 The swelling was often due to starvation. Epidemics raged in the camps, exacerbated by the lack of sanitation and nutrition: typhus (which claimed the greatest number of lives), typhoid, dysentery, tuberculosis, meningitis and scabies were rife.
77 Hebrew: peace to you; traditional song sung on Shabbat (Friday) evening after returning from synagogue, welcoming the Sabbath.

had all the shiny silver and how the food came from the kitchen after he made the *brocha* for *kiddush*[78]. *Gefilte* fish, how the sauce was jellied and how it looked, and tasted so beautiful. And then the chicken soup with the *lokshen* floating in it, it was delicious. And of course the roast, the meats were outstanding, the roast meats and boiled chicken. Everybody was just swallowing saliva and tasting the food, thinking of those beautiful Shabbat Friday nights at home before the war.

We stood like this until dawn when we were sent to be counted again and off to work. It was then that a woman walked up to Roma – she wrote about this incident in the preface of her book because it was so important to her – and this woman said to her, 'You know, I am not Jewish. My grandmother converted to Christianity, but I was sent here as a Jewess. I don't know your rituals, but the way you described it, it's so beautiful and I was with you all the time.'

It was not unusual for a Christian person to be sent to the camps. Back in the ghetto, we had two churches – they happened to be in the area designated as the ghetto. And there were quite a lot of people whose parents or grandparents were Jewish who were also sent away, even though they identified themselves as Christian. Like this lady, who now said: 'Look at my feet – I'm swollen, I won't survive. But you've got to. I want you to remember that you must carry on, you must try to survive to tell the world what has happened.' Roma says she kept her promise to this woman, although in her book she apologises 'to you, unknown' that it took her so many years to write her story.

We always tried to avoid being caught and sent away. Even though they might say you were being sent to another camp, it was often to the gas chamber.

But one day – it was summer, July, I think – we couldn't avoid it.

We were caught.

We were put in a row and at the head was someone sitting and

---

[78] Jewish blessings recited just before the meals on holy days.

writing down numbers. We were not tattooed, but we had numbers stitched on our clothes. Roma and I were in that row and we kept on moving back, back, back, trying to disappear. An SS woman was behind us, watching . . . and she closed the count exactly behind us!

We were transferred to the men's camp and placed into an empty blockhouse.

When the men heard that women were in their camp, they came into the blockhouse and asked: 'Have you perhaps seen my wife Sala? She was wearing a floral dress . . .' or 'Have you seen my little girl Yehudit? She has big blue eyes . . .' – and so on. The men were soon chased out by the guards but not before a Polish man had sat next to Roma and me. He was not Jewish but he heard that we came from the ghetto and he wanted to know the latest news from Warsaw. He gave us a leg of chicken – he must have worked in the kitchen – and he . . . he tried to be fresh with me. I was so scared! I whispered to Roma, 'Hold me, hold me.' Anyway, when they ordered the men out, we were left holding that piece of chicken. Roma and I shared it, savouring every morsel.

In the middle of the night, they chased us out from this blockhouse.

It was so very quiet and still. Except for the dogs, the barking dogs on leashes. The Jewish men who came to us earlier told us this blockhouse was right next to the gas chamber. So we knew, as we were chased, frightened and trembling, by the SS men and their barking dogs . . . we knew where we were headed.

I clung to Roma's hand.

We were pushed into a bathhouse, the ladies' one. The next building was the men's.

The heavy doors shut behind us. We stood, crushed together, crying, praying, terrified, looking up at the ceiling – expecting the gas, the poisonous gas, to come down any second.

The last moments of our lives.

We screamed for help, scraping the walls with our nails. When death is staring you in the face, it is simply instinct to try to escape. There was no way out.

I don't even remember what it looked like in there. There was only fear; you could almost smell it.

And then we were praying to *HaShem*, calling: *[talks through tears]* '*Shema Yisrael*,[79] listen to us *Ribono shel Olam* – we are young girls who want to live!'

I took Roma's hand and I was whispering, holding tight. I said: 'Don't be afraid; I don't think it will hurt, it won't even take long and we will soon join our loved ones.'

As I finished, the heavy doors opened and an SS man came in and shouted: '*Ruhe!*[80] You are not going to be gassed!' I was too afraid to even look at him.

We could not believe it! We thought it's another German trick that they are playing on us. But some of the girls fell to his feet and kissed his boots. He didn't even notice.

The ceiling was high and up top there was a tiny window, which was shut. One of the girls asked the SS man if he would allow us to open it. He granted permission but no one could reach it – it was so terribly high. So one girl got onto the other's shoulders, climbed up, and opened it. It was dark and terribly claustrophobic in there, so the window helped a little. And the fact that the SS allowed us to open it was proof that this was no trick – they were not going to gas us.

Still, we were too afraid to fall asleep, and there was no room to lie down. We sat huddled together. No one spoke. I just held Roma to feel that we were still together and alive.

At dawn, we were let out.

We couldn't believe it! Roma and I still clung tightly to each other. All I could think was: I am here! I am alive!

'Happy' does not describe it well enough – there must be another, much stronger word to describe the feeling that we had survived a gas chamber to see the light of another day.

Outside, in the faint morning light we saw women getting off the

---

79 'Hear, O Israel' – these are the first words of Judaism's central prayer.
80 German for 'Quiet!'

train onto the platform. They shuffled past us and were directed straight into the gas chamber we had just left. There was no way to speak to them, warn them; we didn't know what was going on. There were some Jewish men prisoners working on the ramp – they told us the SS received an order to gas 500 Jewish women and not 700. We were 700.

They were so efficient, so orderly. It was due to German orderliness that we evaded the angel of death; 500 unfortunate women took our place in the gas chamber, and we took theirs on the train. We were shoved straight onto the very cattle cars that had brought them to Majdanek – the same train now bound for Auschwitz.

Chapter 7

Auschwitz

Of the many Holocaust stories I've read and heard, I have never heard one quite like this . . . Ella literally walked free of a gas chamber. She lived to exit through the same door through which she entered, coming face to face – first with her would-be executioners and then with the unfortunate substitutes who would meet their deaths in her stead. The sheer improbability of this, if not the impossibility, makes it nothing short of miraculous – so miraculous, in fact, that I feel her story should end there.

Surely, after having suffered through ghetto life, deportations and the war's most famous act of resistance; having endured the cattle-truck transport, dog bites, forced labour and starvation; having held her niece's hand as they walked free of an actual gas chamber . . . surely her redemption comes now?

But no. It is 1943 and the war is far from over.

So is Ella's story.

ELLA:
Do you know that when the museum opened in Majdanek, they were trying to find any of the women who were in this transport? They found two in Israel, Roma in New York, and Roma told them about me in South Africa. Just four that were traced. I sent them a whole lot of things . . . they wanted my history in pictures. My whole life story is in the museum in Majdanek.

Auschwitz

We travelled a few days, nights – I think it was two, I can't remember how many – to Auschwitz.

Some years ago, when I was in Poland, I visited the Jewish Historical Institute in Warsaw. After providing my number and my transport, they gave me a lot of documentation. They'd found that my transport to Auschwitz was going to be sent back to Majdanek because we were not suitable to work in Auschwitz: a lot of us were very sick, some were injured, some were even dead. They were going to send our transport back, but the order was overruled and we remained. I have a copy of the order, even the name of the SS man who ordered the return of our transport, and the one who overruled it. I didn't know about it back then; I only learned about it when I visited Warsaw.

If we had been sent back, I wouldn't be here today. If I'm not mistaken we were almost the last transport to be sent out of Majdanek. The rest of the camp was destroyed, all the prisoners were gassed. No one survived Majdanek.[81] So can you see the miracles, one by one?

As we arrived in Auschwitz, there was an orchestra playing – a prisoner orchestra – as if to 'welcome' us. And in front of them were all the *Kommandants* of Auschwitz. Among them was Josef Mengele who was afterwards described as the 'Angel of Death'. I came face to face with him! Afterwards I saw him at different selections.

First, our arms were tattooed. Roma and I were ordered into different queues; they divided us according to surname, from A to M, let's say, and the other half of the alphabet was in the next queue. My number was written bigger than Roma's because the woman who tattooed mine had a heavy hand. Roma's tattooist was a prisoner.

My number was 48632 and there was a triangle below the number. Different nationalities were arriving, and this is how they iden-

---

81 Towards the end of Majdanek's function as a camp, the SS dug large ditches outside the camp fence and conducted mass shootings in those pits. They played music through loudspeakers to drown out the noise. This massacre of approximately 42 000 Jews was known as 'Operation Harvest Festival'.

tified us – the triangle was the sign of a Jew. This type of tattoo was used only in the beginning, the first two years of the existence of Auschwitz. Later, when the transports were arriving more and more frequently, they would tattoo people on the inside of the arm, not on the outside, and no triangle. There were very few survivors with numbers, and even fewer with numbers on the outside of the arm or with a triangle, like mine.

From then on, we were no more known by our names but by our numbers. When I had to report at certain times, I used to say *Häftling 48632* in German – *Häftling* means 'prisoner'. Nobody knew our names.

Next, all the hair was shaved off our heads, and from the whole body. Then we were disinfected. They used a rag at the end of a big stick, like a mop, with a terribly strong liquid to sponge us down. They gave us other clothes; we had to leave ours – if you can call them 'clothes' *[Ella's voice drips irony]* – more like rags. But we were given other, lice-infested clothes, terrible. I looked around for Roma because I couldn't see her anywhere *[crying]*.

I called out, 'Roma, where are you?'

'I'm right here,' she said. 'I'm right here next to you.'

I couldn't even recognise her *[soft sobs]*. I couldn't—. She-sh-she had a lot of beautiful long hair. In Majdanek we had kept our hair and she had a very small, narrow face, tiny build . . . I couldn't believe it was her! 'Here I am,' she said, 'Right next to you.'

So we were given these terrible clothes and chased into a blockhouse where we had to sleep ten girls to a bunk. We were lying head to toe, five each way, three levels of bunks. There were more than a thousand in a blockhouse, and no space to move. There was only one blanket for the ten of us; it wasn't even a blanket, it was like a rag, but it was something to cover ourselves – all of us with one horrible piece of rag. When it got dark, the rats came out from between the bricks, crawling over us. We got so used to it because we knew they were only looking for food; we would sometimes keep a little piece of bread over for the morning and they knew to look for it. You slept with a piece of bread under your head and a rusty bowl – everyone had to have their own bowl. Sometimes the bread was stolen by other prisoners, right from under our heads.

And then of course we used to stand at roll calls every morning whether it was rain, snow, hail or burning sunshine. There was a *Nachtwache*, the night watchwoman, and she used to knock with a stick early in the morning, '*Aufstehen, aufstehen!*' – 'Get up!' I think we might have got a bit of watery coffee just to sip.

I remember the mornings – some frosty, some mild, some boiling – standing in mud, five abreast for roll call. The head of the block, the *Blockalteste* – we called them *blokowa* in Polish – would count us; this was the woman who was in charge of the block, usually Slovakian or Czechoslovakian girls who came to Auschwitz earlier – the Germans invaded Czechoslovakia a year before us. You remember it was Austria, then they marched into Czechoslovakia. Only then they invaded Poland. That's why people travel now to Prague because it's intact; in the Warsaw Ghetto there's nothing.

So these *blokowa* were Jewish girls, and they were quite cruel actually. Their attitude was: 'We lost all our families, we came here long ago, we suffered, there are so few of us.' They didn't realise that we came from the ghetto, that we also lost our families. Who knew about Treblinka? They didn't know. They used to call us sometimes 'you Polish pigs', like the Germans. A lot of them spoke German, especially the ones that were in charge. They had numbers, much earlier numbers than we had.

So we had to stand while they counted us, again and again. They kept on forever counting. Whoever was sick was pulled out. You could see some people collapse. We wore wooden clogs on our feet and stood for hours. The *blokowa* would wait for the SS women to arrive to take the count, and she would report: so many sick in the blockhouse, so many standing out, so many dead, and so many are ready for work. Then they released us and we started walking, five abreast, always with SS men on each side of us, heading towards the gate.

At the gate, they counted us again – how many of us are leaving? We worked outside the gates of Auschwitz, not inside. Nobody was allowed to remain in the blockhouse in the camp, only the people who were in charge of this blockhouse. The sick ones were sent to a blockhouse called number 25 – I think it was 25 – which was a death block. They kept them there until a transport arrived from one of the European countries for the gas chambers. When the gas chambers were working, these people were taken to the gas chamber at the same time. We used to see them at Block 25. The small, narrow window was closed with grates, and they were looking up; we could see they were lying, they couldn't even sit, *[tearful]* looking up at us – without food – they must have been dying there also.

I worked in different *Kommandos*. The main one was building roads, carrying heavy bags of cement, of sand, on my shoulders, pushing heavy trolleys with stones. When I think of it now, I don't know how I managed to do this heavy work. But the will of survival kept me going: I knew I wanted to live. I was trying with all my might to carry on.

For a little while I did work sorting shoes. Heaps of them. Men's shoes, women's shoes, flat shoes, high heels, elegant shoes *[tearful]*, children's shoes and little babies' shoes. The shoes were so fresh, the actual whiff of the people who had worn them was still there. It was a terrible job . . . the shoes lying in heaps and their owners lying in piles.

I worked at an outdoor *Kommando*, in the fields, picking some green leaves with thorns on them – prickly green leaves, we didn't know what for. Probably they just wanted to keep us working, even if they didn't really have proper work for us. Those prickly leaves burned our fingers, but we were outdoors, hoping something would fall from the trees that we could chew.

When we got back to the camp, we were counted again at the gate, checking if nobody had run off. And then there was soup. We would stand and wait for a bit of warm soup that was dished out into our

Auschwitz

rusty bowls. It was just watery soup with some green leaves floating in it. It was difficult to swallow, just like that bread we were given in the morning, gooey like clay. We had to stand with this rusty bowl waiting to get to the *kesl* – a big pot, like a cauldron. I always tried to move back in the queue because the later you got there, the thicker the soup would be, and at least there was something floating in it, maybe a piece of turnip or a little piece of potato, or a rotten leaf.

The *Blockalteste* would dish up and every blockhouse got its pot. We sat on the ground outside to eat. Sometimes you spilled, sometimes somebody knocked it out by moving. You did not mix with people in the other blockhouses – you couldn't, there were over a thousand of us. Everything you did was with your blockhouse. To this blockhouse you were knocked, chased, woken up early in the morning . . . everything.

So we got the bread once a day, the soup once a day, and that coffee which wasn't coffee. During the day, nothing to eat.

They put something in the food to stop our menstruation. We never had any periods until after the liberation. For me, it took a long time to come back; Roma's came back right away. I don't know what it is that they used. They couldn't have used medication to stop our menstruation, of course not – that would have been too expensive. It was some preparations that they made, some poison to affect the workings of menstruation.

I do not want to disrespect Ella and her memories, absolutely not, but I do wonder about her assertion that the Nazis laced the food with a menstrual suppressant. Initially, I found no ready reference to such a practice in my internet deep dive, however a recent article on a website dedicated to neuroscience research news points to new support for the theory that synthetic steroids were indeed administered by the Nazis into the food supply of female concentration camp inmates.[82]

---

[82] Neuroscience News.com. 21 September 2022. *New research provides theory on why women stopped menstruating upon arrival at Nazi death camps.* https://neurosciencenews.com/female-menstruation-holocaust-21463/. Last accessed 20/12/2022.

Perhaps this then, in addition to malnutrition, shock and stress, induced amenorrhea. The issue of fertility was a difficult one in the camps, both its presence (there are stories of women falling pregnant during their incarceration, requiring abortions, being subject to medical experiments and even successfully giving birth) and its absence (women's fears of becoming infertile and not being able to bear children should they survive the camps). Moreover, struggles with menstruation have been noted as a point of cohesion and defiance for women, during and after the war . . . sisterhoods bonding over this unique aspect of their suffering.

The question of how women handled the physical and social challenges of menstruation during the Holocaust has long fascinated me. How did women manage their bleeding if they barely had clothing, let alone underwear or toilet paper? Sanitary pads were surely not accessible, and neither was the more common homemade menstrual rag; as for washing or cleaning, inmates were barely given water to drink, let alone bathe with.

It is one of those supremely female experiences about which I have never heard or read much in mainstream accounts of Holocaust survival. So I was grateful when Ella raised the issue spontaneously, but somewhat stumped when she shut it down just as quickly as she brought it up. Whether or not her captors poisoned her food with a suppressant, Ella was clearly one of those (lucky?) women who, from fairly early in her concentration camp experience, did not have to endure the vagaries of the female reproductive system.

Apart from the associated physical discomforts, there was the very public nature of an otherwise private process. 1943 was not the body-positivity, open-communication era of today (I write this as my teenage son comes in to ask if I have any 'female products' for his friend who has just got her period and wasn't expecting it; no blushing, no eye-rolling, no shame – these are the simple facts of life). In the camps of World War II, menstrual blood would stain already sullied bodies and clothes, outing a personal condition which was, in any case, treated with distaste and concealment even by women them-

selves. I can barely imagine the discomfort and humiliation. Trying to imagine convinces me that Ella was indeed lucky, at least in this instance, not to have to suffer even further degradation.

I wonder if Ella's theory about the 'poison' is due to a lack of her own clear memory around the issue, a coping mechanism to help or block it out, or perhaps a fallback onto the myth of the military's use of saltpetre or Blue Stone to reduce carnal urges in soldiers. When I comment: 'You were probably so malnourished anyway, it's no surprise you lost your period,' Ella shrugs off the possibility – 'I don't know if that alone would stop it, in any case . . .' and moves swiftly along.

It was dangerous to get sick in the camps, yet sickness was unavoidable.

Roma had typhus. She was sent to hospital but she was lucky because the Jewish lady doctor, also a prisoner, told her to get out. 'But I still can't stand on my feet,' Roma complained. But that lady said that Mengele was coming that day, as he did frequently. When he comes, he orders the whole hospital to be cleared; all the sick people are sent to the gas chamber. So she said, 'My child, get out. You must!' Roma crawled out of there with two other girls.

When I got typhus later, I realised if I'm sent to hospital I might not be as lucky as she was, maybe there won't be anybody to warn me when Mengele comes. I had been lucky so far; when there were selections, Mengele was often there. We really never knew when there would be selections, we'd just hear suddenly, and we'd quickly pinch our cheeks to get a bit of colour. Mengele would stand with a whip and we would have to present ourselves, standing five abreast, undressed, while he swung his whip – *links, rechts* – indicating to death or to life. I always used to stand straight, with my head up, looking strong. But with typhus, there was no way I could do that. So I decided to stay in the camp. We were not allowed to stay behind – only the *Blockalteste* remained when we went to work. But I took a chance, there was no other way.

With typhus you get pimples all over your body, and a very high temperature. So when we had to stand at the roll calls, I tried to stand at the back, between people, so that I would not be recognised. When my *Kommando* was ordered to walk, and after we were counted, I disappeared somehow and I hid myself in toilets and then behind blocks during the day. I waited for the labour groups to come back and, when they counted us again, I was there. Eventually my fever dropped and the crisis was over – it was just luck that I felt I was getting better – and I rejoined the *Kommando* even though I could hardly walk.

Then I had enteritis. The toilets were very far and if you dirtied on the way you were punished severely. You know our toilets consisted of stone slabs with holes on each side; you just had to sit there with everybody, back-to-back and facing, and do your business. Washing was limited. During the winter, the water froze in the taps, and I used to wash myself with snow.

One evening, the girls were talking and I heard one say she is from Janów. I remembered my brother Heniek and his family went to a farm near Janów, outside Lublin. We used to send support for him from his business to this farmer, Jan Parish. We had always thought that Henry was mostly with the farmer, not in the ghetto there in Janów.

So I asked this girl: 'Have you ever come across Heniek Frank?'
She said, 'Of course, I knew him. He used to sing and dance.'
'What happened to him?'
'Same as to my own family. All the Jews were moved into the Janów ghetto. From there, they were all sent into the forest and shot.'
She escaped somehow, probably as a Christian girl . . . *Ella is crying and takes a minute before she continues.* This girl was working as a *Schreiber*[83], she had a higher position in the camp. She asked me, 'What can I do for you?'

---

83 German for 'clerk'.

'Help me by giving Roma a job not under the skies but under a roof.' In the open field it was raining, snowing, cold or hot; we used to come back wet, frozen, or burnt by the sun. 'Please help me keep Roma dry.'

It took some time, but eventually they called out Roma's number and sent her to work in a department called the *Bekleidungskammer*, where the girls sorted out clothing from those who had been sent to the gas chambers. As Jews were rounded up around Europe and the *nebbishes*[84] sent to Auschwitz, they were told to bring all their essential belongings with them. When they arrived, those belongings were confiscated and stored in large warehouses next to the gas chambers. And of course they all had to undress first, so the clothing, panties, socks, children's clothing – it was all collected. This department, where the victims' belongings were stored and sent out, we called *Kanada* – because Canada was thought of as a very rich country. So the belongings went directly to *Kanada* and from there to departments like the one where Roma was sorting and folding.

Roma's job was wonderful because they worked under a roof and they could shower every day; they didn't stand to roll calls. Only selected girls worked in this department because it was very difficult to get in there. But Roma was now in and I was happy.

That was one way to have a higher chance of surviving Auschwitz: if you worked in the *Bekleidungskammer* and *Kanada*.

Girls who worked in *Kanada* were so well-off as they had things to exchange. Sometimes they even found bread or food that people had brought with them stuffed in their pockets. But mainly they found jewellery in the clothing, like I had sewn in our gold coins. *Kanada* was the top department in Auschwitz.

Although I never worked in those departments, it helped me that Roma was there. I told you I had enteritis – a runny tummy – and I needed panties, I had no underwear. Roma used to take from work, put on an extra panty, and I begged her not to do it: 'They'll catch

---

84 Yiddish for a person who is regarded as pitiful, unfortunate.

you, she'll catch you,' – I was talking about the supervisor there, a German woman, also a prisoner and very strict. But Roma kept on bringing for me. I would again mess myself and need another one, and Roma brought.

I also had a problem with my leg. My left calf swelled up, becoming red and so painful. I couldn't walk, I couldn't go to work. I found someone to ask and they said we'd have to amputate the leg because it became like a balloon. At the *Bekleidungskammer*, Roma managed to get a scarf which she gave to a woman doctor prisoner as 'payment'. This woman got something for me, a medication, and the leg slowly came down. If they had had to amputate it, I wouldn't have survived. That woman doctor saved me, she must have had access to medications through the Nazis; you know the Nazis used some of the prisoners who were highly qualified – doctors, lawyers, engineers – in the camps. Remember there was that Jewish doctor in the hospital who warned Roma? Anyway, I don't know what sort of medication it was – it couldn't have been antibiotics, like penicillin, because there were no antibiotics in those days. But whatever it was, it helped. And do you know where that painful leg came from? It was from climbing up the bunks to where we slept. Remember there were three levels, and I always slept at the top – here, let me show you . . . *And Ella proceeds to demonstrate, right there in her dining room, miming the action of clambering up one level and then another, stopping just short of climbing onto a chair for height! 'Oh! I've got a cramp!' she exclaims, and sits back down with a cheeky chuckle at herself.* I got this injury from scraping against the edge of the wooden pallet, I must have cut myself and then the cut got infected.

So there was trading in the camps, in different ways, and Roma's position in the *Bekleidungskammer* was a help, both to her and to me. Roma and I were always together, in some or other way. This helped us to survive I think. What also helped was *protectsia*[85], through the men – Jewish men – especially those working in the *Sonderkommando*[86].

The girls who worked in the *Bekleidungskammer* had, like, 'boyfriends' working at the *Sonderkommando*. These boys had all the valuables left inside the victims' clothing; they passed some on and also used them to bribe the Nazis who were in charge of the different departments. Every girl who worked in the *Bekleidungskammer* had a man who 'recommended' her to that German woman supervisor – a man who paid for her. That strict woman knew that Roma was not one of them, that Roma got in there some other way. So she watched her like a hawk and Roma was going crazy, she was so afraid. Every day she came from work and she'd say, 'I'm still here, I'm still here.' But she was terrified that she'd be kicked out.

Eventually she *was* kicked out! But at least she was working for some time there and it was a bit more protected.

As for me, I was still working outside. And Roma came back to join me.

Roma heard they were looking for some girls for a wonderful job. People had to go and put their numbers down and they were waiting until the quota was full. When she heard this, Roma came looking for me but I was nowhere to be seen. When she eventually found me, she said: 'Come, come, there is a good job for us, maybe we can still manage to get it.' But we were too late. When we got there, the quota was full.

We found out afterwards what it was for – it's called *der Puff*: where the Germans used women as prostitutes. These girls were going to serve the Nazi soldiers. It was pure luck that we were too late to make that quota!

One day we decided to go *nach vorne* – that means 'to the front', referring to where the SS had their offices. We decided to work up

---

85 Hebrew word for 'using connections to your advantage'.
86 Death camp prisoners, usually Jews, who were forced to dispose of the corpses from the gas chambers.

the courage to speak to one of the Nazi officers. We didn't go right up but close enough so that somebody could see us from the office block. An SS man walked up and stood in front of us and I said, 'Häftling nummer 48632.' Roma reported her number too. And then we said what we had learned how to say in German: 'Can you please help us by giving us a job under a roof?' So he looked again at our numbers – we showed him like this *[holds her arm out]* – and he said with surprise, in German, 'Are you still here?' . . . because not many people with our numbers were alive.

We left thinking nothing would happen. But sometime later they called out our numbers and we were sent to another blockhouse to work in *Weiberei* – where you knit or make material – a weaving mill. Our job was to plait strips of plastics which were used for the army. Roma was lucky, she got a job sitting – I think it was to cut the material; I had to stand and plait. But at least we were under a roof.

I think our good fortune was thanks to this one Belgian girl in the offices at *nach vorne*. Right now I can't remember her name but she was so good to us. She was a Jewish prisoner herself – they had prisoners working at *nach vorne* too, those who could speak fluent German were sometimes chosen for this – and she was very kind. One day we heard sirens blaring, the warning sign that somebody had run away. Then we heard that this girl had run off – Mala! That was her name! Mala! We heard she ran off with a man who probably also worked in the offices. We could see that she wasn't standing where she always stood, next to one of the *Kommandants*. So we said, '*glückliche Reise*' – it's what you wish someone when they go on a journey, 'Happy travels!'

For two days, we heard nothing and we were so happy. Three days, four, five. She was free! It was almost a week when we came back from work and all the blockhouses were assembled, the whole camp in one place. And there they brought Mala . . . into the middle *[Ella talks through tears]*. She was bleeding, so beaten up – like a sausage – we couldn't even recognise her.

They brought her into the middle and she spat at one of the guards and said something very strong, with no fear, about how they would be punished for what they were doing to our people: 'You will get your end, you'll get what is coming to you.'

The *Kommandant* said, 'You deceived us,' – because she had been working with them – 'We're going to finish you off.' The SS woman standing there said, 'She deserves to be smashed, killed right away.'

And then Mala. Sweet, beautiful, kind Mala . . . cut her wrists. Herself. Standing there. And collapsed.

What we heard afterwards is that she managed to get SS women's clothing and the man who ran off with her got the men's uniform. They got hold of a car and must have driven quite far because it took a few days. But in the end, they found them.

I never thought about trying to escape because I knew there's no way. Although . . . I'm remembering now . . . every time I talk, I remember something else . . . *Ella stops for a few moments, grows contemplative and quiet. When she looks up at me again, she shakes her head and squeezes her eyes, as if to rid them of cobwebs and tears.* Roma approached me once while in Auschwitz and said, 'Come, let's end this struggle. We won't survive – what is the use? Come, join me on the electrified wires.' In any case the only way to get out of Auschwitz was through the chimneys, 'So come, let's finish it and join our loved ones, they're waiting for us.' The memory is not clear, but it took me a long time – days and days – trying to persuade her. I can't remember this part but she writes in her book that she did go one night, tried to get to the fences. We were in different blockhouses at that time because I was working in a different place. A shot came through from the towers! She crawled back to safety and she realised – apparently I said, 'Thank God that you're here, I thought you were going to do something silly.' I don't remember exactly; it's impossible to remember everything.

Our world was Auschwitz. We seldom heard news from outside.

In the ghetto, yes, we would hear news from our Underground who were in touch with the Polish Underground. I remember we heard that the Germans had a disaster on the Russian front – that they had to withdraw and lost so many of their army. Some thought that maybe they would leave us alone after that. Others said, 'No way; it's going to get worse.'

In the camps, we hardly ever heard news – although one time we got news we wished we hadn't.

Sometimes two or three Jewish men from the men's camp were sent into the women's camp for repair work – to fix the roof, the plumbing, the floors or the wall or locks. Once, they told us Yom Kippur was coming up. We had no real sense of time in the camps. We tried to keep what we called the *luach* – Hebrew for 'calendar'. In the days of the ghetto, the serious new orders almost always came out before a big Jewish holiday, like the *Grossaktion*, which lasted from Tisha B'Av in July to Yom Kippur in September. This was one way to mark time.

So this year in Auschwitz, when we heard about Yom Kippur approaching, a few of us girls decided to fast – we'd keep that day's piece of bread hidden for the following night. I went to work but I didn't eat.

The news came through a few days later that they had made a mistake – they got the wrong date for Yom Kippur! There were no calendars, so it's hardly surprising. They worked it out again and gave us another date. We fasted again – although most days were a fast day anyway and we got used to the lack of food.

So as far as I recall, that was the one time we had news from outside. We couldn't even rely on new arrivals to tell us what was going on.

When the transports came into Auschwitz, different nationalities arrived but we didn't always know from which countries because of the many languages. Some of them could speak a bit of German or some French.

Already long after we arrived in Auschwitz, a certain transport came and the women were sent to our blockhouse. We just couldn't figure out if they were Jewish – by that time the markings of the tattoos, even the placements of the tattoos, had changed. We tried to talk to them; we tried Polish, Yiddish, French, German – no reaction, nothing. What else could we do? So we thought we'll ask them about food, and we said the word *cholent*. They looked at us blankly. What else? Shabbat? And they burst out, with wide eyes, 'Shabbat, Shabbat, Shabbat!' *Ella becomes excitedly charged here, her voice pitches upwards and she looks ready to jump around the room.* Shabbat! They knew Shabbat!

They were Jews from Greece, as it turns out. Thessaloniki. In Polish it's Greczynka which means 'Greek girl' but we called it 'Saloniki'. I heard afterwards that the Jews from Thessaloniki were religious. And of course Shabbat is something all Jews have in common. Every time I think of it, I am overwhelmed. Can you believe it?

But they were falling like flies because they came from a warm climate; they couldn't get used to the harshness of Auschwitz. They got so thin and sick – typhus. They couldn't take the conditions and most of them were gone. I don't know how many of them survived.

Not only Jews were the victims of the Nazis.

In Auschwitz, when we marched to work, we passed a camp – a place surrounded by barbed wire. We could see through and there was a blockhouse with children playing on the ground and there were men and women – Gypsies. We used to see them every day, entire families were living together in the middle of Auschwitz in the camp, separated by barbed wire *[Ella talks through tears]*. And we used to cry: 'Look at the children playing in the sand! Where are our children?' Our children were already gone. We were so jealous.

On the way back from work we used to see them – I can't remember if it was weeks or months, possibly days – we passed the same scene: men, women, children playing in the sand.

One morning we went to work, and we passed the same place, expecting to see the same scene. But it was completely empty.

They had taken them all out during the night to the gas chambers. All gone. Every single one.

That was the end of the Gypsy camp.

Ella gives a visible shudder and shakes her head as if to clear it, but that seems a task as impossible as digging a hole on the beach at the edge of the waves: as quickly as the sand is shovelled out the water refills it; an endless supply of fresh memories just waiting to take the place of their predecessors. All a survivor can do is wait for the tide to recede, however momentarily, to catch a breath.

As time went on, we became smart and learned what one has to do to survive in Auschwitz – how to deal with sickness, how to keep clean, manage the lice.

An early incident I remember clearly.

They woke us up in the middle of the night, shouting '*Aufstehen, Aufstehen,*' hitting at us with sticks. Where could they be taking us in the middle of the night? There was only one place . . . to the gas chambers. Remember what happened in Majdanek? They also took us in the middle of the night to the gas chamber.

Instead, they chased us into a *sauna* – a room where showers were coming down – and the German woman in charge shouted '*Entlausung!*' – delousing. They couldn't do it during the daytime because we had to go to work, so they chased us into the sauna at night. We had to stand, lift our arms, and they washed us down with a rag dipped in disinfectant. They took away our clothes and dipped them in disinfectant; they were wet when we got them back.

But the relief! No gas chamber! We were so thankful to *HaShem* that we weren't going to be put to death!

We were so very happy that we were talking, laughing, chatting loudly to each other. The German officer reprimanded us to keep quiet. But we were so relieved that I guess there was still a noise coming from us. So she said: 'You're going to be punished,' and pulled five girls out of the bunch. The punishment was to have their hair shaved off – by that time our hair was already a little bit grown back; our faces were so terribly thin but hair made us look a little more human, more feminine. So to have your hair shaved off, to look like a skeleton, meant certain death – it was much more likely you would be a candidate for the gas chambers looking like that.

I was among the five pulled out.

They did shave the other four girls' hair to the skin, nothing was left. As for me . . . There was a tall nurse at the table where they were cutting hair, writing down the numbers of each of the girls who was picked. She had a red triangle and the letter 'P' on her chest indicating a Polish (non-Jewish) political prisoner. When it was my turn to come up to the table, I looked straight at her and spoke with my eyes: 'I know you,' I said silently . . . 'I know who you are. Let me off.' And she did. She didn't write down my number. She pushed me back into the line and she saved my life.

How did I know this woman?

I was at Chavatzelet school with a girl named Guta Bankier who was also sent to Auschwitz. She had two sisters – one two years older, the same age as my sister Pola; and a third who was older still. The eldest one did not look Jewish – she had blonde hair, Aryan features, and she spoke Polish well. She had been deported to Auschwitz-Birkenau as part of a mixed transport of Jews and Poles from a prison in Bialystok; she must have run away from the ghetto. Now when anyone arrived in Auschwitz, they took down your name, your birthday, your number, and then you were tattooed. But when the *Schreiber* – that's the scribe who wrote everything down – was registering the new arrivals in Auschwitz and saw this girl's prominent Aryan features and blonde hair, she registered her as an Aryan, as a Pole. Non-Jewish prisoners were not subject to selection the way that we Jews were, and the camps were a bit easier for them. There was a number on her arm but she didn't have the triangle indicating that she was a Jew.

She gave another name, and she was in Auschwitz as a *goy*, as a *shiksa*.[87] Her real name was Lena Bankier.

I knew it, Roma knew it and her sister Guta knew: two sisters in Auschwitz together – Lena as a Pole, Guta as a Jewess. They only met at night for fear of being found out; if you had seen them together

---

87   Yiddish: both terms refer to a gentile (non-Jew); *shiksa*, specifically to a girl or woman.

you would notice the family resemblance, especially the smile. Yet Lena wore the emblem on her chest that she's a Pole and her sister wore the striped uniform.

The first time I ran into Lena, I instinctively wanted to embrace her. But the red triangle with the letter 'P' on her chest kept me from doing so – I couldn't let on that I knew her so I passed her by. I kept my knowledge to myself, afraid that if anyone found out about her, she might be denounced, God forbid.

Lena worked as a nurse in Auschwitz. And she was the one who was supposed to shave our hair that day, the one who saved my life.

After the liberation, Roma and I landed up in Paris and we scraped together a few pennies to buy tickets to the opera. We sat up on the fifth floor; we could see the ceiling and the walls of this beautiful big opera house on Place de l'Opéra. We loved watching *Faust*.

At the interval, we came downstairs and there was Lena Bankier. It must have been in October or November 1945, soon after we arrived in Paris. There she stood: she was tall like you, very presentable, dressed beautifully, on the arm of a Polish officer! He was a tall, elegant man, dressed smartly with all the insignia.

She remembered me and I remembered her. We talked.

Lena's youngest sister Guta, the one who was my age, also survived Auschwitz and settled in Israel – then still Palestine. Their middle sister left school the year before the war to go to Palestine. So the two were there and Lena, who survived Auschwitz as a 'non-Jew', was in London. You remember, the Polish army were all in London; when they ran off from Poland, they formed a government in England and he was one of them.

Roma was in touch with Guta and she heard that Lena married the Polish officer and had children in London. She converted to become Catholic (because most Polish people were Catholic) but her children were actually Jewish. Once when I was in Israel, we were with Guta's sister who had left before the war. She was showing pictures from school, including ones of my sister Pola, who was in the same class. I still have some of those pictures. One photo is the whole class on the day we played truant. We did it on the 1st of April – we called it *Prima Aprilis* in Latin – and I have this picture from that day in 1938.

Some years later, my husband and I were going to London and we arranged to meet Lena and her two sons for dinner; she said her husband couldn't come. Well, the night before we were due to meet, I got terribly sick – I was so sick that my husband phoned reception and asked them to send a doctor. I couldn't stop vomiting! A doctor came and, believe it or not, it was a Polish doctor *[chuckles]* and we spoke Polish! Anyway, I was too sick to go for dinner with Lena Bankier. My husband couldn't disappoint them so he went by himself; I did not get to see her, nor did I see her ever again after that.

In 2013, I got an email from a gentleman in London, asking about Lena. In April of that year, the British government organised a ceremony in honour of British heroes of the Holocaust. Here you can see the invitation. Very fancy. There is also a letter addressed to Mrs Maton – Lena's daughter – saying: 'Dear Mrs Maton. As you may be aware, your mother Mrs Helene Maria 'Lena' Lakomy née Bankier has been nominated for a Holocaust Heroes Award for saving the life of Hela Frank. It is with a sense of great pride that I can now confirm that the British Government has agreed to bestow this award on your late mother. Her selfless actions saved the life of Hela Frank who was destined for the gas chambers of Auschwitz, and clearly demonstrate an extraordinary act of courage . . .' Signed by The Rt Hon Eric Pickles MD, Secretary of State for Communities and Local Government. It is quite amazing.

By the way, Guta Bankier also worked in *Kanada* while we were in Auschwitz – her sister must have arranged it. And I must tell you that they nearly turned Lena in! Somebody found out about her false identity and denounced her – is that the right word? She had to stand at the *politische Teilung* – the political division – and they ask you your mother's name, your father's name, do you know the prayers? Lena denied her Jewishness. If the Germans had discovered the truth, Lena would have been condemned for special punishment. There was a punishment barracks, separate from the rest of the camp. The inmates of this colony were not permitted any contact with other prisoners; they belonged to the *Strafkommando* – the punishment commando – an internal unit that had to perform hard labour at an extremely rapid pace for fourteen hours a day.

It wasn't easy for her to convince the Germans that she was Polish; they demanded absolute proof from her. The hardest question is 'Does anybody know you?' She managed to get a Christian Polish woman to vouch for her; she swore under oath that she knew her from home. She must have been prepared in case something like this happened. Another life-saver.

That was the beginning of Lena's journey to becoming a Catholic. And it is how she survived the war.

In 1944, the transports were coming from Hungary. Instead of French and Dutch, we could hear another foreign language being spoken.

Usually, the transports arrived at night when we were locked up in our blockhouses. They also made a *Lager ruhig* – it means like 'quiet in the camp' – because they didn't want the people they brought to see how we looked. If it happened that new transports arrived in the day, there was *Blocksperre*[88] – you remained in your block and couldn't go out, or to work. We were not even allowed to go to the toilet; there were buckets in the blockhouse to relieve ourselves.

At night, when transports came, we could hear them, people talking. And the next morning, you couldn't hear a thing. But the chimneys were bellowing smoke and fire and the smell was all over of human flesh and hair and fat. We knew exactly what was happening, but what could we do?

I think the transports from Hungary were almost the last transports that came to Auschwitz. I was already an old prisoner. And you know me . . . I was around, I made myself known.

---

88 German for lockdown, literally 'block lock'.

Auschwitz

I was offered to become a *Blockalteste* of one of the new blockhouses which had opened for the new arrivals who were selected to be sent to work – the others were sent to the gas chamber.

I want to tell you what it meant to become a *Blockalteste*.

At the entrance to the blockhouse, there was another door to a small alcove where there was a little window with a piece of curtain, a narrow bed and a little stool and table. It was tiny but it was a bed and a sheet and a blanket and a pillow. Remember the rest of us slept on crowded, rat-infested bunks sharing one blanket. But this alcove was for the *Blockalteste*.

The *Blockalteste* did not go to work of course. She was in charge of the block and she had to be cruel: she had to hit those who were too slow to walk fast or who couldn't stand properly. And at roll call, she stood in front and pulled out the girls who looked sick or who were collapsing, then stood aside and waited for the SS woman to come and get the report of the roll call. Also, when bread came, she would receive it and, instead of cutting it into say ten portions, she used to cut it into thirteen or fourteen portions and keep the extras – therefore the slices were becoming smaller, narrower, thinner for us. And what did she do with the bread? She would exchange it. There was a little market in the camp in the late afternoon – I'll tell you about it. But I want to finish off why I refused that wonderful job. You didn't have to stand to roll calls, you were not beaten, you had plenty of food, you had a bed . . . But I said no. I said I won't take the job because I've got Roma. So they said, 'You can take Roma with you.' You see, each one of these girls had a . . . uh . . . a . . . I don't know what it's called – like a lover; they're allowed to have somebody with them. So I can have Roma. I said, 'No,' I still refused. I'm not going to pull out my sisters, my Jewish children, and hand them over to the Germans. I'm not going to hit them. I can't do it. I won't be a traitor to my own people. Even if it meant I would be well-off – how could I do it? *Ella is very emotional.* I'm not going to steal even a piece of bread from my own people, put them aside to be sent to Block 25, to the death block. No. Absolutely not.

And I never thought of it any further.

Many years later, when I arrived here in Cape Town, I met a few survivors. We formed a meeting group and we would sometimes get together at people's houses. One day, a Sephardi lady said: 'You Polish girls, you were so cruel. A Polish girl was in charge of our blockhouse.' Funnily enough, I don't remember any Polish girls as *Blockaltestes* – they were all Czechoslovakian girls, as I told you. But there must have been one who was offered the position, like I was. Also, many Sephardi people arrived late – this lady was from Rhodes Island, and they came late to Auschwitz.

'This Polish *Blockalteste* was so cruel, she used to hit us,' the lady told us. And I thought to myself: thank God I never took that position. I survived with a clear conscience.

So now: the market.

Everybody who worked in different departments used to – in plain language – 'steal' something. But we didn't call it 'stealing', we called it 'organising': 'What did you organise today?' Like Roma 'organised' panties for me from the *Bekleidungskammer*, or the girls who worked in the *Kartoffel*[89] department, where Roma also worked for a little while, they used to put half pieces of potato in their clothes. Sometimes they would get caught; mostly, if they heard from others walking past that the SS were conducting searches, they would throw the stuff out and you could find it on the road.

Remember there were not only Jewish prisoners in Auschwitz. There were Christian Polish and German women – political prisoners, prostitutes, homosexuals – who got parcels from home. They were allowed certain things like onions or garlic. They didn't get cigarettes though – and you know before the war, even after the war, every second person was smoking; I myself used to like smoking, later when I lived in France, but not much, and not for long. The women got their parcels of garlic or onion and the cigarettes were smuggled in by men. How the men got cigarettes I don't know; most probably from the belongings of people who were sent to the gas chambers.

---

89 German for 'potato'.

Auschwitz

So the people who needed cigarettes used to exchange, let's say, garlic or a piece of bread or a scarf like Roma took, for two cigarettes. There was an exchange market – no money changed hands but there was business going on. Sometimes, with jewellery or valuables, they could pay off an SS man, an ordinary soldier – they were also human beings, they also wanted to do business.

And so, we survived.

You had to be smart. You had to know how to mingle, to work your way in the camp. You couldn't just sit and wait for a piece of bread and a bit of soup; you would never survive that way. You had to know all the intricacies, *ganove*[90], you know . . . the crook business; you had to know all the tricks.

During the first eight, nine months in Auschwitz, when our hair was still so very short and we were starving, we looked like skeletons. But we learned a way to live, to survive the camp, and we even began to look smarter because we could get an extra bit of clothing, a jersey or something. Some girls were lucky, they got shoes – maybe they organised them at the markets. I was wearing wooden clogs; when the snow accumulated during wintertime under the clogs, I walked as if on stilts.

I met a man I knew from the ghetto – I think he was in the same Mila 19 hiding spot as me – at the fence at Auschwitz. He saw me and shouted, 'Wait! I'm going to give you something!' And he threw me a jersey – a thick, beautiful jersey! I was so happy! But *[Ella suddenly becomes tearful]* I had to get rid of it, can you believe it? It was full of lice! And my body was crawling with them.

When Roma and I had been in Auschwitz for quite some time already, we were walking to work, five abreast, and we marched across the road at the same time as a men's *Kommando* we had met before. One of the men called: '*Warszawa! Warszawa!*' – and we raised a hand to greet. The next time we saw the same *Kommando*, some-

---

90 Yiddish for 'thieves' referring to tricks or illegal activity.

body threw a piece of paper to us, for Roma and Hela. It was Moishe Baker! Remember from the hiding place in the ghetto? Years later, Roma found him or he found Roma, in Israel. He survived the war. But his wife and child did not.

Anyway, the third time we passed his group, Moishe Baker threw us a cigarette; for a cigarette we could get two or three pieces of bread! The following time we got a packet of cigarettes from him. From then on, we were rich! Roma got into the *Kartoffel* block and I already had a mind for business; I suppose I put it to good work then too – at the little market in the late afternoon in Auschwitz.

Auschwitz

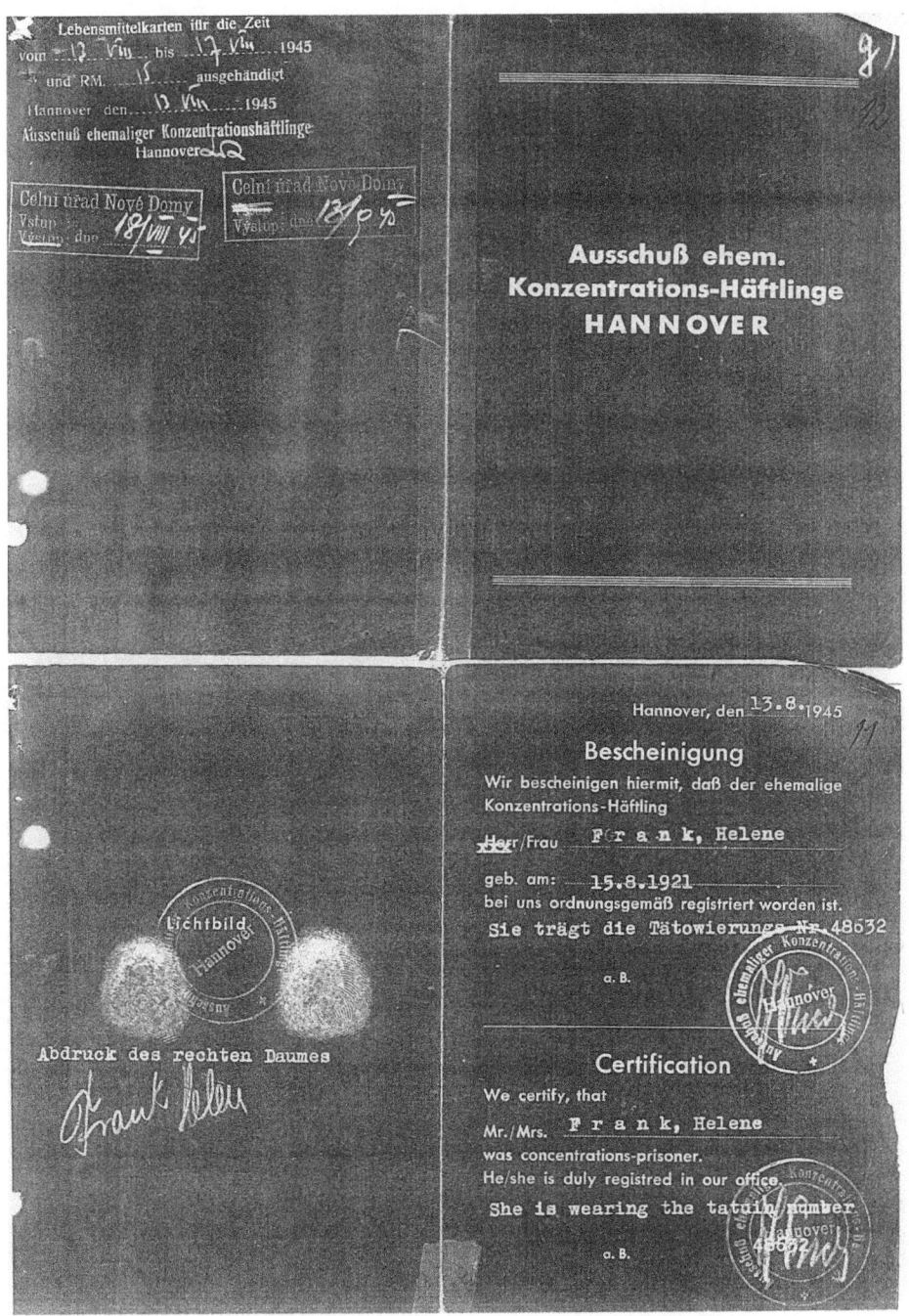

Ella's prisoner certification document.

Chapter 8

Bergen-Belsen

Many of my sessions with Ella start with her saying: 'I think I told you already . . .' and then proceeding to repeat some element of her story. Every repetition differs slightly – whether in perspective (like when she reads from a formal account of an experience she herself lived through), or detail (like when she finds a photograph to illustrate her verbal narrative or remembers a specific name or feature). But her stories' sentiments and bare bones are unwavering. Despite her advancing age and distance from the time of the war and its immediate aftermath, Ella's memories remain intact – perhaps some yellowing around the edges here, a bit of fading in the colour saturation there, but intact.

ELLA:
Towards the end of 1944, our numbers were called, and Roma and I were sent out of Auschwitz.

We were moved onto trains and again into cattle trucks. We didn't know where the trains were going. It must have been about two nights and three days that we were closed in these cattle trucks. They must have been transporting cement before because we became covered in a kind of white dust, and when the train stopped, we couldn't shake it off!

We arrived at Bergen-Belsen concentration camp. I know we travelled a long time because the trip was from Auschwitz in Poland deep into Germany. Bergen-Belsen was still new – it wasn't properly organised yet and there was no water to wash ourselves of the cement. There was hardly any food and they didn't send us to work; it was nothing like Auschwitz. They didn't know what to do with us. There were not even blockhouses. There were tents and when it rained, the storms tore them away and we were under the sky, wet – no, more than wet, just lying there in the water. Terrible conditions. But the transports kept arriving.

I found out that there was a new kitchen opening and decided I had to get in there to work. There was an enormous queue of girls standing all day, trying the same thing. I used to come back at night and tell Roma I wasn't successful, I never got close to the end of the queue. The girls were even fighting in the queue, trying to get to the front. When I came back on the fourth day, I had cuts and bruises on my face because people were hitting, trying to get closer to the front. I told Roma I'm not going back and she said, 'But you must! You must carry on!'

On the fifth day, I got in – but not to the kitchen. Next to the kitchen we were sitting on low stools, peeling turnips. Turnips for days and days and weeks. It was out in the open, cold and miserable, windy – and I was sitting and peeling turnips into water.

Eventually, luckily, they put me into the kitchen where I was mixing with heavy wooden utensils, difficult work for which you had to stand up and work with a huge basin. I became quite well-off. I would smuggle out a little piece of turnip or potato to Roma. There were two Hungarian sisters we were very close to – one was Ettie Weiss, I can't remember the other's name; I used to sometimes hide a bit of food for them too. 'We will never forget you,' they said.

Once I tucked a piece of turnip under my clothes and the SS man, the *Obersturmführer*, noticed it. Next to me was standing a Russian man, a Christian Russian, who worked with me in the kitchen; he was pushing a wheelbarrow with ash and he quickly said to me: 'Helenka, drop it in.' The *Obersturmführer* – he used to call me the '*kleiner dicker*[91]' – I had put on weight already! – called me to his

---

91   German for 'little fat one'.

office, which was at the end with a glass window. He searched me but couldn't find anything. Had he found it, I would have been shot. So this Russian boy saved my life.

He said to me afterwards, 'If we survive the war, you are coming with me to Russia. I saved your life.'

I said, 'Alright.'

And when we were eventually liberated, we were still working in the kitchen, and he said, 'Now I am going home, back to Russia. You're coming with me.'

'I can't, I've got Roma, my niece who has been with me all the time. I can't leave her.'

'Bring her with!'

'You go,' I told him. 'You go and I'll follow you.'

Of course I never did.

Some months later, all the *Kommandants* from Auschwitz arrived, and once again we were standing at roll calls. It became almost like Auschwitz, the same rigour, the same discipline. Most of that time I worked in the kitchen, which was lucky because I didn't have to attend roll calls.

It was while I was working in the kitchen that I helped a friend from school who was in a different section, separated from our camp but still inside Bergen-Belsen; it was called the *Internierungslager*[92]. It was an international camp where men, women and children were together. They were Jews, but with their families, separated from us by a wire fence. They had passports from different countries – I think they weren't European, so rather Palestine, America, South America – or maybe with different papers, like the *Aliyah*[93] certificate my sister and her husband had from Palestine. These people were told they were waiting to be exchanged for German citizens in foreign countries. In Warsaw, there was a rumour on the Polish

---

92 German for 'internment camp'.
93 Hebrew: to go up; the immigration of Jews from the diaspora to Israel.

Bergen-Belsen

side that there was going to be an exchange of Jews (with passports or papers) for German citizens, taking place at the Hotel Polski. People flocked there. The German authorities called out names and people went forward, thinking they would be sent to the country for which they had papers. Instead they were sent to Bergen-Belsen. My friend – Bronka Kahan from Chavatzelet school – was in that camp. She had a pass from the British, to go to Palestine.

Now, in the kitchen, we had a big *kesl* where we cooked the food. And you had to stand on a stool to mix it with a wooden stirrer. When the men came to collect the big, heavy *kesls* of food for this *Internierungslager*, I used to put in some extra – a little more turnip, make it a bit thicker, sometimes a piece of meat . . . for Bronka. And she knew it.

These prisoners were liberated at the same time as us, Bronka too – she survived. After the war, I met her in Israel. She's done very well.

There was not much work in Bergen-Belsen until all the *Kommandants* from Auschwitz arrived with Josef Kramer, the *Kommandant* from Auschwitz-Birkenau, who now took over.

You know they made the prisoners walk from Auschwitz to Bergen-Belsen – the death marches. Auschwitz was liberated by the Russians in January 1945 and these death marches took place in the months before, when they were trying to get the prisoners out of Auschwitz as the liberators advanced. It must have been early in January or end of December and they came exhausted. They had been marching for weeks.

There were all nationalities in Bergen-Belsen, but mainly Polish and Hungarian girls from Auschwitz; not many Greek girls had survived. But I do remember one who gave me a piece from a *mezuzah*[94]. I think I've still got it somewhere – a little piece of the parchment. Maybe it wasn't *mezuzah* or parchment exactly, but it

---

94 Hebrew: small box placed on the right-hand doorpost of Jewish homes and containing parchment inscribed with Torah verses.

was a paper with some Hebrew writing, perhaps from a *siddur*[95]. We even had two little precious stones, like small diamonds, but I don't remember how we got them in Bergen-Belsen. One looked good and the other didn't look very genuine; the good one I gave to Roma and the other one I kept. I was liberated with it and looked after it for years but I think I misplaced it when I lived in Johannesburg. But that Hebrew piece I've still got somewhere: it was wonderful to have some Hebrew writing, we hadn't seen that for years, since the ghetto.

In the camps, it was each man for himself. Especially in Auschwitz. Everybody was trying to survive; there was no pity. Of course I'm speaking in general. There were some wonderful people, but normally everybody was fighting for themselves. In Bergen-Belsen, I was the well-off one, I could be the helper. But not in Auschwitz.

I was in Auschwitz from July 1943 to October 1944, nearly one-and-a-half years. And then in Bergen-Belsen for six months. But each day felt like ten years.

Survival is very basic. Eventually, you become desensitised; you have to, if you are to survive.

For a religious Jew to be stripped naked in public, no modesty, no privacy – it's unthinkable. Yet this was not on your mind. You marched – *links, rechts, links, rechts* – and you were chased – *schnell, schnell, schnell* – and your only concern was not to drag your feet. At first you might try to help the next person to carry on and it was terrible to see how people were falling, it was shocking. But eventually, bodies lying where they fell no longer made any impression on you.

I wasn't ready to die yet. You remember what I said to Roma? I wanted to carry on; I wanted to live as long as I could, manage to stand up in the morning to the roll call and march out to work. I hoped for a better tomorrow. The will of survival was a burning will.

---

95   Jewish prayer book.

Why did I have that will more than others? More than Roma even? I don't know; I simply can't answer that. I just know that I wanted to live.

I know I am strong, I can manage, I'm not falling yet and I'm not going to give in. There's nobody left – I've got to carry on.

Only a miracle would save us. We could see that the Germans could not be defeated. We knew what had happened in Russia; even when the Germans surrendered there, they didn't leave us alone. We thought that they would release us, but they didn't. It became worse.

Only a miracle. We read the history of the Jewish people and we see the miracles. Take the story of Passover and the exodus from Egypt – we were slaves during the Holocaust as we were slaves in Egypt. The Egyptians didn't even kill us en masse then like the Nazis did here. This was unbelievable! Unheard of! You cannot even imagine really what happened to us, what happened to me. It's—

Ella stops. Mid-sentence. Just stops talking. Her eyes grow wide and fill with tears. She remains silent for a few long moments and, when she speaks again, it is softly and with a tone of utter disbelief.

When I think of it now, I - I - I can't believe it! I can't believe that I have lived through it and survived. Why? How come?

To this day, I don't know where I found the strength, for any of it.

My most difficult job was on the roads – building, digging, carrying bags of cement and sand, crushing stones, pushing heavy wheelbarrows. Where did I get the strength and the willpower? Roma was struggling. I just did it.

Even the job of pulling out weeds. Even when there was nothing really to pull out, we had to pretend – bend, dig, pull.

We were punished. All the time and for no reason. We were hit with heavy sticks until we couldn't walk any further. It was unbearably, unbearably hard. That's why so many fell; they just couldn't carry on, couldn't even swallow the food.

Another day, another winter. You stood there frozen. People falling down next to you and you just wait to be counted, wait until she comes to count you.

Now that I'm going over it— how did I manage to get through this hell? And yet . . . there was always a sparkle of hope in me: as long as I'm not put to death, as long as I'm not sent to the gas chamber; if I can still walk on my feet then I must carry on. I always had hope.

We sometimes sang together. When new transports were arriving, they locked us in and we sat on the coir sleep-mats and sang. Polish songs, Jewish songs. We were dreaming . . .

Only the young and strong survived. That's why the people who came at the end, in 1944, the Greek girls – even the Hungarian girls – not many survived. By then, we were 'old' prisoners; we had been through so much, starting in 1939: the ghetto, losing our families, then Majdanek and then Auschwitz and now Bergen-Belsen. We had already survived, so we carried on.

Now I'm sitting here talking to you, letting you know what happened to me, how I got to this stage. And yet immediately afterwards, I didn't want to talk about it. I couldn't. People didn't understand the enormity. People didn't know what happened. Only in Israel there were so many of us who came from the camps, but there was no time to cry, to talk about it; you wanted to get on with life. When I came to South Africa nobody knew that I was in the camps – not my neighbours, co-workers, even relations of my husband. They didn't know what it was. Nobody realised yet. And I didn't know how to begin to describe it.

And there was more! Things I only discovered after the war. Like the fact that they used to gas people in mobile vans, not only in the gas chambers. I didn't know! I also learned that Jewish people had the terrible task of removing the lifeless bodies of our brethren; they had to pull them out of the gas chambers and burn them. This was the *Sonderkommando*. And then, when a new transport came, the Nazis chose a few strong ones to do this job; they sent the *Sonderkommando* themselves to the gas chambers and replaced them with new ones from the transports. It's unbelievable – even to me, who was there!

Ella rifles among her many clippings and articles and pulls out one to read aloud. She intersperses each sentence with her own assent, confirming that this is, indeed, what happened to her. She segues in and out from press clipping to personal memory for a while, seeming to verify her own account and validate her memories with the facts as presented in this particular piece. If it is in print, it must surely have happened, and just as she recalls it. And then:

Ah, here it is. This is the sentence I was looking for: 'The camps were really factories of death . . .' As simple as that.

Factories of death.

Ella stops again and shakes her head. You know, after talking to you for the last few days, I come to think of it now myself – is it me who went through it? I can't believe it. No wonder people ask me to give them a *brocha*. It must be only holy people who could survive such a battle and yet I became normal and I wanted to carry on like all the other people around me. I wanted to have a family, I wanted to get married and have children.

I was in Bergen-Belsen for six months: from the end of October 1944 to the 15th of April 1945, when I was liberated by the British.

Chapter 9

Liberation

The more we talk, the more Ella wants to talk.

Each time I arrive for an interview, she has unearthed more memorabilia, dusted off more books and paged through more newspaper cuttings. On one occasion, I walk in to find her seated at her dining table virtually surrounded by stacks and she tells me she was up most of the night 'preparing' for her time with me.

At first I fear that the apparent reliability of these third-party sources are a risk to the integrity of her own memory; I am concerned that she may use the testimony and reporting of others to fill in the blanks in her own memory that time has necessarily forged. But Ella seems wary of this pitfall of memoir too. Instead, she combs through the material like a locksmith searching for just the right key; not all fit but those that do are catalysts rather than replacements – mechanisms that open the door to her own recollections, rather than usurping them.

I also find that, the more she reads from the voice of others, the more she finds her own. Whether it is the affirmation that she gets from these sources – 'yes, this is how it was, this happened to me too' – or the unlocking of a long-sealed deadbolt, Ella's head of steam is only building.

Today, as she looks up at me from her perch among her papers, eyes bright and red nails flashing, she remarks:

'You know I never realised that I'll be able to talk to you with such openness. When I talk to you, I tell you exactly what happened; I *don't use highfalutin language like in these documents I've got here.'*

I ask: 'When you tell me all the stuff you were thinking about last night or read in your papers, do you feel like you're getting it off your chest?'

'Yes. And also, I worry that otherwise I might forget it or miss it. I was digging through it all and wanted to make sure to show you.'

ELLA:

We could hear planes flying above us, circling.

We could hear explosions and we worried that bombs would come down and hit us.

We could hear shooting. And sirens.

We knew help was coming. Even if we were to fall in the crossfire, we knew help was finally on its way. We weren't afraid that we would die that way because it's better to die from our own saviours than from our murderers.

The shooting intensified. The Germans were fighting back.

Outside, most of the watchtowers stood empty; in others, the Nazi soldier wore a white armband, but we didn't know if that meant surrender.

We did not go to work or stand for roll call; there was no one in the kitchen, no food, no normal life in the camp.

I noticed once that the SS men were pushing heavy trolleys with documents in the main road of the camp – lots and lots of documents. I now know that they were clearing their archives, but of course not everything was burned because my name was there – that I was in Bergen-Belsen.

It must have been a few days of this, at least.

After some time, we came out to look around. The British army was already approaching, trying to get into the camp. All of a sudden we heard and saw a British tank and sitting on top of it was Josef Kramer, the *Kommandant* from Auschwitz/Bergen-Belsen, wearing a white cape. He didn't look at us, just stared down . . . pathetic . . . not the same person with the white gloves and shiny boots who used to strike such fear into us. Next to him was a British officer and this time Kramer was the prisoner.

We couldn't believe it! Everybody ran towards that wonderful tank. I had scraped my feet on the wooden clogs and my legs were too sore to run; Roma helped me. Some of the girls were kissing the ground where the heavy vehicles were coming past. Somebody shouted, 'Long live England!' in Polish or Jewish or German. Maybe somebody in English. There were announcements through loudspeakers: 'You are now liberated by the British army. Food and medication is on its way.' We were all so jubilant and happy; we just couldn't believe we were free! There are no words that can describe the joy after so many years of suffering – there are not sufficient words now and even back then. The only words I could come up with were those of the Hebrew prayer that we say on very special occasions: '. . . *shehecheyanu, v'kiyimanu, v'higiyanu la'zman ha'zeh*[96].'

It was one of the most beautiful moments of my life, when we were liberated. It's hard to express it. Never, never will I forget it.

Around us, it was the British who were crying; they couldn't believe what they were seeing: skeletons coming to hug the trucks, piles of bodies lying all around. And of course there were many they did not see because people were too sick to even come out of the barracks. By that stage, we had no food or even water left.

Afterwards they painted letters of the alphabet on the sick people: one for TB, another for typhus . . . Some of the sick were even flown to Sweden; I have friends who landed up there; Sweden took in a lot of survivors, sick, sick people.

---

96   The full prayer translates as: 'Blessed are You, Lord our God, King of the Universe, who has granted us life and sustained us, and allowed us to arrive at this time.' *Shehecheyanu* is a prayer of gratitude for new and unusual experiences or possessions from which one derives pleasure or benefit.

Liberation

They told us to go back to our barracks while they sorted everything out. Someone found powdered milk in the storerooms; it had been useless before because we had no more water. The British must have brought water with them and we mixed the powdered milk to give to the sick.

They also found storage containing loaves of bread, but someone – must have been one of the SS men who knew what was good for him – warned the British that the bread was poisoned. The Nazis poisoned the bread before they left, can you believe it? So the British destroyed it.

The British shared their food rations and of course they didn't realise that they shouldn't have done it – normal food was too rich. I warned Roma, 'Don't eat it! Our stomachs cannot digest the meat in the tins and the beans and the tomato juice.' But some couldn't resist – we were so hungry and the smell of it! – and they paid with their lives.

Then the liberators reorganised everything. First of all, we were moved to the camp where the SS men had stayed. We took over their barracks and we had rooms. *Ella speaking through tears*: You won't believe what we had there! We had a bed, a proper bed – it was an iron bed but it was a bed – with a bit of a mattress and a white sheet with a decent blanket over it. And behind the door was a wash basin with running water, something else we couldn't believe. We took over the kitchen which the SS army had been using and I worked in this kitchen, with the same team.

I don't know where they moved the SS to. They still wore their uniforms – the men and the women – but without caps and without belts. The SS men were made to dig a big, wide hole in the field and the SS women had to carry the bodies that were lying all over the camp and put them nicely into this open space. These holes were enormous – the size of a swimming pool or bigger even, filled up with bodies. Can you just imagine?

We watched this, trying to get near, wanting to spit at them, but we couldn't – the British soldiers held us back, they wouldn't let us get near the women who had tortured us.

As time passed, we began to look more like human beings: the Red Cross sent food parcels and medication. We put on weight, our hair grew back, we had water, we were clean and received clothing from the Joint Distribution[97]. We looked like *menschen*[98].

I had not been as badly off as the others in Bergen-Belsen because I worked in the kitchen and I could feed myself sometimes. In Majdanek and Auschwitz I suffered terribly, but in Bergen-Belsen I was one of the 'elite'. That's why it did not take me so long to start recovering.

We made acquaintance with British soldiers. They even arranged dances and invited us. It was quite far so we had to ride in military trucks to the place and there was music and we danced. But eventually we decided not to attend these dances because we were annoyed and hurt that the British were not allowing Jews into Palestine. There were so many who wanted to go to *Eretz Yisrael*[99]. We Polish girls had nothing to go back to, no families left, our homes were burnt, and the only place to go was to *Eretz Yisrael*. But the British were still holding on. So in small protest, we stopped joining them on the dance floor. But we did make some friends with Jewish soldiers.

One of them was named David Levin. We didn't know at the time that Levin is a Jewish name. We knew he was English – he was from Manchester – but we weren't sure that he was Jewish. He couldn't speak Yiddish. So how did we find out? We invited him on a Friday night; we put a sheet on the table in our room. The chaplains had given us *siddurim* and candles, so I lit the candles for Shabbat. This soldier Levin then made the *kiddush* – and so we knew he was Jewish!

While we were eating, one of the Hungarian girls who was with

---

97 This refers to the American Jewish Joint Distribution Committee and Refugee Aid (JDC or Joint), established in 1914 to organise relief efforts for Jews in Europe and the Middle East during World War I and beyond.
98 Plural of *mensch:* German/Yiddish for 'human'; a person of integrity.
99 The Land of Israel.

Liberation

us – you remember I told you we were very close to those Hungarian sisters? Ettie and . . . and . . . Clara! That's it! Ettie and Clara Weiss – well they were sharing this room with us. One of them was cooking and David Levin didn't eat the food! Most probably it wasn't tasty enough. So we urged him: *'Ess! Ess!'* Yiddish for 'Eat! Eat!'

And he says, 'I'm no SS!' *[Ella laughs]*. It still sticks in my mind! I'm no SS!

There was another British soldier who brought a bicycle into the camp and we used to ride out, past the houses of the Germans living nearby. The camp was right near a place called Celle. In fact, when we arrived from Auschwitz, the trained stopped at a station called Celle; we saw the sign. And then they marched us through woods and through fields to Bergen-Belsen. So after the liberation, when we went riding beyond the gates of the camp, we passed this country place and saw the homes where the Germans lived – small houses with gardens in front. But all the curtains were shut. These neighbours said they never knew what was going on at the camp. They were so close, how did they not know? Is it because there was no gas chamber and crematorium there? There was no need for one because people were falling like flies in any case, from TB and typhus, and of course hunger. When I arrived there, I saw a pile of bodies and skeletons and told myself I must not land up on top of it! But these people were right next door, and they deny knowing anything about it.

I share Ella's incredulity.

On approaching the camps I visited while touring Poland in 2015, I remember marvelling at the distinctly pastoral nature of their surroundings – and not simply as a matter of geography, but in tone and ambience too. Some were quite picturesque: rolling hills, whisps of wood-fired chimney smoke, sheep and cows grazing in open fields . . . apparently oblivious to the factories of death that lay just behind, or next to, or beyond. I scribbled my surprise in my notebook – that ordinary Germans living through a war might not have known what hell was unleashed in the compounds bordering their homes, or worse, may have ignored or condoned it. But beyond the war, still today: why would anyone want to live in a town named Auschwitz or Oświęcim (in Polish)? There is no shaking off the terrible association conjured by that very name and, even if you could see past the name itself, why settle with the towers of the crematoria in sight? This history is just too recent. Who could enjoy a tea-time pierogi while surveying the not-unnoticeable memorial stones of Majdanek? Not to mention the busloads of visitors who may come to pay their respects at these memorial sites and can't help but ogle the incongruous mundanity of the neighbours.

The days passed. I continued to work in the kitchens – the chaplains even worried about our *kashrut*[100]! And we grew stronger still.

I've got pictures from this time. Looking at us, you wouldn't believe that Roma and I were survivors. In one, I'm wearing a British uniform, sitting on a British tank or truck. I look well. It's one of the few original photos I have and I don't have many from before the war. The picture of my brother Itche's wedding in the ghetto was sent to Yad Vashem – it survived the war because it was sent to Roma's father in Palestine. The date is on the bottom and even the signature of the bride with a few words like 'This is our wedding. I'm your new sister-in-law.' The whole family is shown in that photograph – everyone except me. I was cut off. If you look closely on the far left, you will see my hand holding the arm of my brother Heniek.

Speaking of weddings, immediately after the liberation, some young people wanted to get married to have families. You know we were so happy just to be alive, and we didn't have anywhere to go yet. So in the meantime, these young people got married right there in Bergen-Belsen. There were chaplains in the British army; they put out *tallit* and married off the couple with a *mazeltov!* The couple even followed the tradition of breaking a glass under their feet, and they were given a room somewhere. This happened often.

---

100 Dietary regulations of Judaism.

There was a committee set up in the camp to run things; it was made up of Jews but under the British. Josef Rosensaft was in charge and he kept everything in order so we weren't living like wild people. They kept records of everything, the marriages, the births . . . There were many weddings and many babies! And some survivors remained in Bergen-Belsen for months after liberation, even years. In fact, Bergen-Belsen eventually became so crowded because refugees from other, smaller camps in Germany all came to Bergen-Belsen, which was big and well organised and where you could feel like a Jew again.

In the meantime, though, Roma and I registered in the camp as stateless. Other countries claimed their own citizens – French, Czechoslovakian, Russian, Hungarian; they all went back to their homes because they had not been destroyed. And if they didn't have families, at least their homes were there, their cities were there. But we Polish had nothing to go back to. Poland was in ruins. So we registered as stateless.

Even though we feared that there was no one and nothing left for us in Poland, we hoped that Roma's father – Samuel Rothstein – was alive in Palestine. So, soon after the British Army rode in, we decided to send him a note.

We wrote on a few different pieces of paper that Roma Rothstein and Hela Frank – his daughter and sister-in-law – were alive, liberated in Bergen-Belsen in Germany by the British army. We asked various British soldiers to post the notes to Palestine – you couldn't just send a letter from Bergen-Belsen as there was only field post, not normal post; so the soldiers had to go home to England and post from there. Roma remembered his address – Samuel/Shmuel Rothstein, Neve Shalom 9, Tel Aviv, Palestine – and we just hoped that one of these notes would reach him.

It would be many months before we heard anything more.

Bergen-Belsen was liberated in April of 1945 and in August, still with no word from the outside world, I decided to go back to Poland.

Although we knew what happened to our family, I thought maybe somebody had jumped from a train, maybe a miracle, let me go and just see. Roma wanted to go with me but I didn't allow her. Firstly, it was very dangerous to travel. The trains were packed! There were refugees, survivors, soldiers. You had to cross different zones, so to travel from Bergen-Belsen, which was in a British zone, you had to cross the border to the American zone and then to Warsaw, in the Russian zone. The roads and trains were not safe. Secondly, the most important thing: she might hear from her father. I told her, 'Don't move! If he receives our letters and looks for us but doesn't find us, we are lost.' So I left Roma at Bergen-Belsen and set off.

I went to Heidelberg and got a travel document which was half in English, half in German. And I gave myself a name – Helene. You know, Hela is a Polish name but Helene is more typical, so I said 'Helene Frank'. Apart from this, I had no papers, no documents, no money. But from this official document you could see that I'm a survivor with a prisoner number and I need help going to Warsaw to look for my family. When the train stopped at the different stations, I showed them my affidavit and got a piece of sausage or a piece of bread – they helped me.

I travelled with a woman who was much older than me who also came from Praga. She was about 40 and had survived with her daughter – it was very unusual that someone of her age survived. She also wanted to look for family. I met her in Bergen-Belsen and she had been in Auschwitz also – Mrs Pricowa, we used to call her 'Mrs Price' – and she became like my mother on this journey.

When I arrived in Warsaw with Mrs Price, I walked around and I couldn't believe it. *There's astonishment in Ella's voice.* I was walking on the ruins of the ghetto. It sounds like an expression – 'walking on the ruins'– but proper, *mamash*[101], that's what it was. Just bricks and sand. Nowadays it's all cleared up and rebuilt with beautiful buildings, but in August of 1945, the devastation was still fresh.

There was a central office for survivors to put down their names. The Jewish committee had a room on the second floor of a building,

---

101 Hebrew/Yiddish word meaning 'truly' or 'really'.

Top: Ella's brother Itche's wedding in the Warsaw Ghetto, December 1940. This is the only photograph Ella has of the family she lost. Ella herself is not pictured, though her hand is just visible holding the arm of her brother Heniek, far left.

Bottom: Ella's sister Golda (centre) with her children:
Roma (top left), who survived with Ella; Regina/Rywka (top right), who was killed in Treblinka and whose name Ella took for her entry permit to Palestine and retains to this day; Justyna (bottom left); Dawid (bottom right). Praga, mid-1940, before being moved to the Warsaw Ghetto. These photographs were sent to Samuel Rothstein, Ella's brother-in-law (Roma's father) who had left Warsaw and made his way to Palestine.

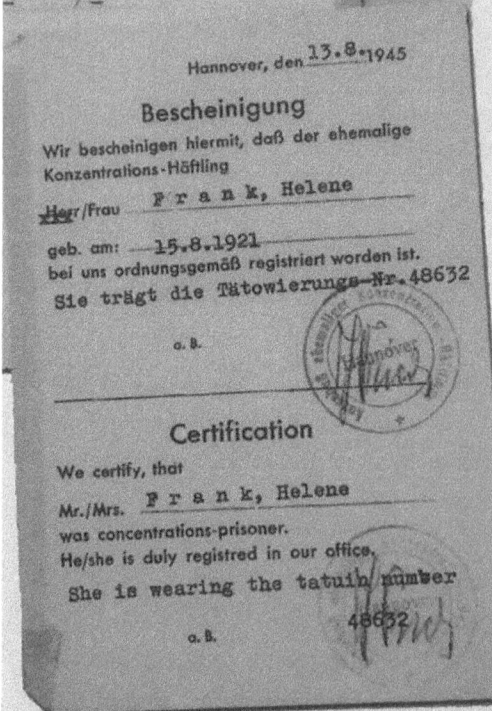

Top: Ella in the bathing suit given to her by her favourite brother Heniek: Ciechocinek, 1938.

Bottom left: Ella's prisoner certification document in the name of Helene Frank: Hanover, 1945.

Bottom right: One of the Weiss sisters (left), Ella (centre) and Roma (right) standing in front of a British truck in Bergen-Belsen after the liberation in 1945.

Above: I am Ella, Paris, 1946.

Left: Roma (left) and Ella (right), photographed in Hanover, Germany, a few months after their liberation in April 1945.

Bottom left: Roma (left), Simcha Sneh (centre), Ella (right): Eiffel Tower, Paris, 1946.

Bottom right: Roma (left) and Ella (right): Paris, 1946.

Top: Roma (left) and Ella (right) dressed in their tailor-made woollen suits at the Arc de Triomphe: Paris, early 1946.

Bottom: Ella and Simcha Sneh: Paris, 1946.

Top: Ella outside Monte Carlo Palace, 1947.

Bottom: Ella on a road trip in the Côte d'Azur, photographed at Menton on the border between France and Italy, 1947.

הגדה של פסח 440

בְּפֶסַח. ואמרתם זבח פסח: יָהּ רֹאשׁ כָּל אוֹן מָחַצְתָּ בְּלֵיל ש[ִׁמּוּרֵי]
פֶּסַח. כַּבִּיר עַל בֵּן בְּכוֹר פָּסַחְתָּ בְּדַם פֶּסַח. לְבִלְתִּי [תֵּת]
מַשְׁחִית לָבֹא בִּפְתָחַי בַּפֶּסַח: ואמרתם זבח פסח: מְסֻגֶּרֶת סֻגְּרָ[ה]
בְּעִתּוֹתֵי פֶסַח. נִשְׁמְדָה מִדְיָן בִּצְלִיל שְׂעוֹרֵי עֹמֶר פֶּסַח.
שׂוֹרְפוּ מִשְׁמַנֵּי פּוּל וְלוּד בִּיקַד יְקוֹד פֶּסַח. ואמרתם זבח פסח עוֹד
הַיּוֹם בְּנוֹב לַעֲמוֹד עַד גָּעָה עוֹנַת ח. פַּס יָד כָּתְבָה לְקַעֲקֵעַ
צוּל בַּפֶּסַח: צָפֹה הַצָּפִית עֲרוֹךְ הַשֻּׁלְחָן בַּפֶּסַח. ואמרתם זבח
פסח: קָהָל כִּנְּסָה הֲדַסָּה צוֹם לְשַׁלֵּשׁ בַּפֶּסַח. רֹאשׁ מִבֵּית רָשָׁע
מָחַצְתָּ בְּעֵץ חֲמִשִּׁים בַּפֶּסַח. שְׁתֵּי אֵלֶּה רֶגַע תָּבִיא לְעוּצִית
בַּפֶּסַח. תָּעֹז יָדְךָ וְתָרוּם יְמִינְךָ כְּלֵיל הִתְקַדֶּשׁ חַג פֶּסַח:

כִּי לוֹ נָאֶה. כִּי לוֹ יָאֶה.

אַדִּיר בִּמְלוּכָה. בָּחוּר כַּהֲלָכָה. גְּדוּדָיו יֹאמְרוּ לוֹ לְךָ וּלְךָ לָהּ
לְךָ. לְךָ אַף לְךָ. לְךָ יהוה הַמַּמְלָכָה כִּי
לוֹ יָאֶה. דָּגוּל בִּמְלוּכָה הָדוּר כַּהֲלָכָה וָתִיקָיו [יֹאמְרוּ לוֹ]
ולך וכו': זַכַּאי בִּמְלוּכָה. חָסִין כַּהֲלָכָה. טַפְסְרָיו יֹאמְרוּ לוֹ. לך וכו':
יָחִיד בִּמְלוּכָה. כַּבִּיר כַּהֲלָכָה לִמּוּדָיו יֹאמְרוּ לוֹ. לד וכו': מֶלֶךְ
בִּמְלוּכָה. נוֹרָא כַּהֲלָכָה. סְבִיבָיו יֹאמְרוּ לוֹ. לך וכו': עֲנָיו
בִּמְלוּכָה. פּוֹדֶה כַּהֲלָכָה. צַדִּיקָיו יֹאמְרוּ לוֹ. לך וכו': קָדוֹשׁ
בִּמְלוּכָה. רַחוּם כַּהֲלָכָה. שִׁנְאַנָּיו יֹאמְרוּ לוֹ. לך וכו': תַּקִּיף
בִּמְלוּכָה. תּוֹמֵךְ כַּהֲלָכָה: תְּמִימָיו יֹאמְרוּ לוֹ. לְךָ וּלְךָ לְךָ כִּי
לְךָ לְךָ אַף לְךָ לְךָ יהוה הַמַּמְלָכָה כִּי לוֹ נָאֶה כִּי לוֹ יָאֶה:

הנני מוכן ומזומן לקיים מצות כוס רביעי של ארבע כוסות לשם יחוד
קודשא בריך הוא ושכינתיה על ידי ההוא טמיר ונעלם בשם כל ישראל:

בָּרוּךְ אַתָּה יהוה אֱלֹהֵינוּ מֶלֶךְ הָעוֹלָם בּוֹרֵא פְּרִי הַגָּפֶן:
בריך

The page of the Haggadah that Ella found/was given in the camps and kept hidden.

Right: Ella's tattoo from Auschwitz – number 48632. This photograph was taken by Dr Jack Penn prior to performing plastic surgery to remove the tattoo in Johannesburg, 1948. Ella still has the blouse pictured here; she kept it as proof of this picture's veracity.

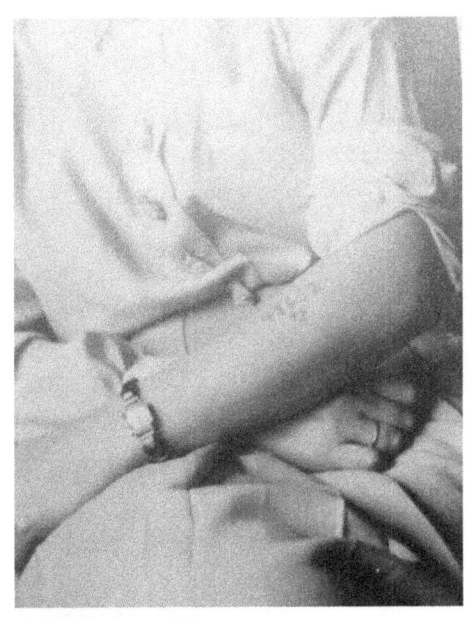

Left: The wedding of Ella to Isaac Blumenthal: 13 January 1948 in Tel Aviv. Ella wore one of her own dresses as she did not have the means to buy a wedding dress; she covered her number tattoo with a plaster 'to keep Auschwitz hidden' on her wedding day.

Top: Isaac and Ella with their first-born, Norman: Johannesburg, 1950.

Bottom: The Blumenthal family: Isaac and Ella with Norman (top left), Alvin (top right), Henry (centre) and Evelyn on Ella's lap: Brakpan, 1964.

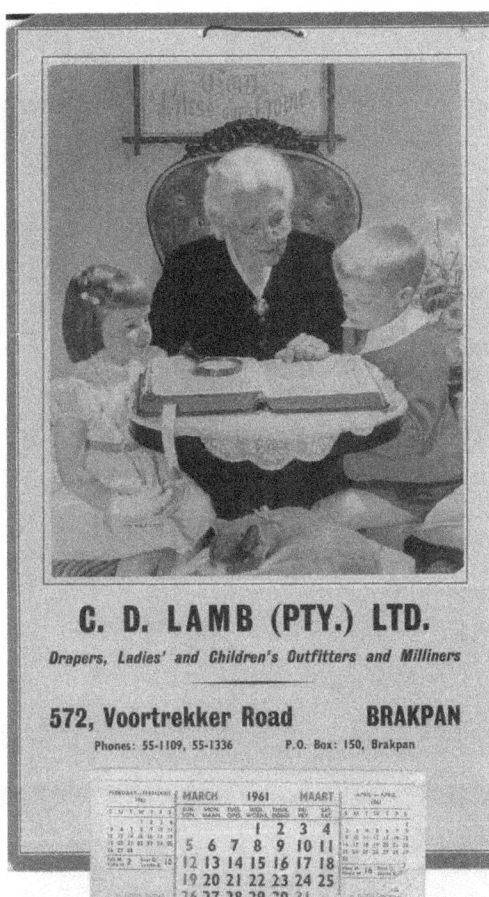

Top: A 1961 calendar from C.D. Lamb (later Lamb's), the business that Isaac and Ella bought in Brakpan.

Bottom: Store window of Lamb's, the family business in Brakpan.

One job for 45 years

Above: Ella in action in the 1970s at Roma's business in Borough Park, USA.

Opposite top: Alvin and Isaac at the front desk of Lamb's with driver and devoted family employee, Johannes Sibiya: Brakpan, 1980s.

Opposite bottom: Article in the *Brakpan Herald*, 1986, marking Maud Norman's 45 years of service with Lamb's.

Right: A classic Ella pose in the Brakpan house, 1980s.

Bottom: Ella and Isaac at their daughter Evelyn's wedding to Paul Kaplan: Johannesburg, 1989.

Opposite top: Ella in her element: Camps Bay, Cape Town, January 2021.

Opposite bottom left: Ella and Roma during one of Roma's last visits to Cape Town.

Opposite bottom right: A poster advertising a talk by Ella at the Marais Road Synagogue in Cape Town, 2017.

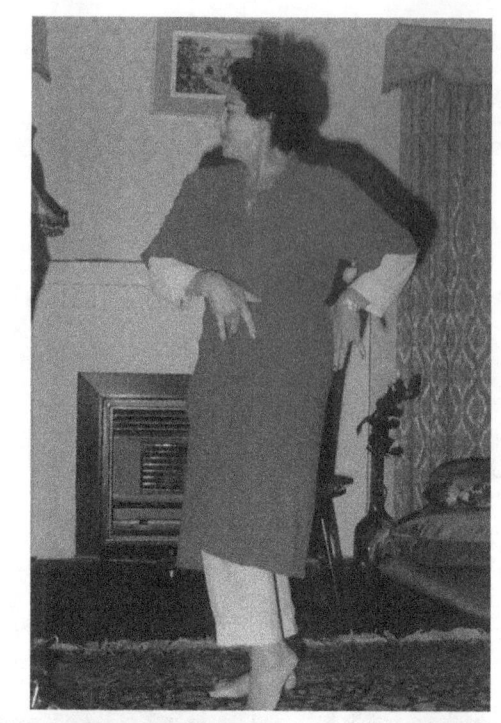

FEARLESS HERO
the triumph of faith

THURSDAY 18th SEPT
8.30pm - 9.30pm
AT MARAIS RD SHUL
Donation R20

session 1 - 7.30PM
Rosh Hashanah Learning
session 2 - 8.30PM

Ella Blumenthal

"I wasn't able to ta
about my sufferin
and fight for surviv
because the ope
wounds were st
bleedin

Now after mar
years, the tears hav
dried up and th
scars have heale
and I am now able t
share it with you

Motion to SA Parliament focuses on the Holocaust

On Friday morning 26 May the SA National Assembly set aside time specifically to debate a motion introduced by ANC MP Andrew Feinstein. The motion put before the Assembly read:

Noting:

That earlier this year the Prime Minister of Sweden hosted a 'Forum on the Holocaust' in Stockholm attended by the delegations of 46 countries, including 21 Heads of State. South Africa was represented at this important event which concluded with a Declaration which, inter alia, stated that:

• the unprecedented character of the Holocaust, and the terrible suffering of the countless millions of Nazi victims will always hold universal meaning;

• the international community shares a common responsibility to fight the evils of genocide, ethnic cleansing, racism, anti-semitism and xenophobia which still scar humanity;

• we will continue to encourage the study of and education about the Holocaust and to honour those who stood against it;

• we declare our commitment to plant the seeds of a better future amidst the soil of a bitter past, and

• we reaffirm humanity's common aspiration for mutual understanding and justice.

Noting further:

The excellent work undertaken by the Cape Town Holocaust Centre in educating South Africans about the Holocaust and the universal importance of tolerance, mutual understanding, justice and unity in diversity.

And acknowledging that:

Those who cannot remember the past are condemned to repeat it.

Resolves:

To support the work of those seeking to keep alive the memory of the victims and heroes of the Holocaust, believing that such education will:

• communicate an important message about the need to remember our own tragic past in order to build a just and tolerant future;

• strengthen the fight against continuing racism, ethnocentrism, anti-semitism, xenophobia and intolerance from whatever quarter in our young democracy; and

• reaffirm our commitment to plant the seeds of a better future amidst the soil of a bitter past in our country, our continent of Africa and the world.

In presenting the motion to the Assembly, Andrew Feinstein delivered what may well have been one of the most moving addresses the honourable members have ever been privileged to hear in that chamber. Not a member could be seen 'napping.' Indeed, while he spoke, one could not hear a proverbial 'pin' drop.

It may have been a source of surprise, even to the specially invited representatives of the local Jewish community, seated in the upstairs visitors gallery - which included two Survivors - to learn that Andrew Feinstein's own family were victims of the Holocaust.

His mother, Erika, also present that morning, spent those critical years in hiding with her family in Vienna.

At Parliament, l/r: Holocaust survivor, Hella Blumenthal, Erika Feinstein, her son, Andrew Feinstein MP and survivor, Irene Gloff.

In delivering his very fine address, Mr Feinstein's depth of sincerity and feeling, and the universality of his message was so strongly transmitted to the members of the Chamber that, at its conclusion, they rose spontaneously to give him a standing ovation.

Thereafter, one after another, representatives of each party (bar one), pledged their support for the motion, from their own particular perspectives.

For all present, parliamentarians and observers alike, this was a unique and memorable session.

Cape Jewish Chronicle article, July 2000.

Top: Ella at her 101st birthday celebration with three of her children: Alvin (left), Evelyn (centre), Norman (right): Cape Town, 2022.

Middle: Ella with the Kaplan family at her 101st birthday celebration, L–R: Evelyn, Brandon, Dani, Shane, Jade, Nate, Lisa: Cape Town, 2022.

Bottom: A Blumenthal family portrait taken at Ella's 95th birthday celebration: Cape Town, 2016.

Top: Ella being carried aloft on a chair at her granddaughter Dani's wedding to Brandon: Cape Town, 2017.

Middle: Four generations of Blumenthal women speaking at the Yom Hashoah commemoration event in Cape Town, 2018, L–R: Ella, daughter Evelyn, granddaughter Jade, great-granddaughter Deena.

Bottom: A 99 year age difference! Ella with her youngest great-grandchild, Nate: Cape Town, 2023.

and anybody who survived and heard about this committee went there. I looked through the names already written down to see if there was anyone from my family, anyone I knew. I couldn't find one. But I put our names: Hela Frank and Roma Rothstein, home address Bergen-Belsen.

Soon after we arrived in Warsaw, Mrs Price found her brother-in-law (her sister's husband) who had survived in hiding, with his children – I can't recall how many. Unfortunately, his wife was not alive. I remember him well because he had the same business as my sister Golda, Roma's mother: ready-made clothing. He invited us to stay there with him in this narrow room. There were two small iron beds separated by a narrow gap. I slept with Mrs Price in the one bed and he was lying on the other. At night he was trying to get fresh with her *[chuckles]* – maybe you shouldn't even mention it, but a man is a man and this was his late wife's sister, a survivor.

Since I had not found anyone I knew who survived, I looked for property. About two years before the war, my parents had bought a building as an investment in a suburb just outside Warsaw called Grochów. I went to have a look at this building; I remembered it was on a street called Kordeckiego, number 55. There was still a plaque outside: 'This building belongs to Naftali and Chava Frank.' The superintendent was also still there; he was a *goy* named Paul and he asked about my parents. I told him that I've lost them *[soft, tearful voice]*.

After I had located the building and saw it was still intact, I went to a lawyer and said, 'My parents bought this building and I'm the only survivor. Can you get it into my name? I can't pay you now but when we sell the building, you'll take half.' He took down the details of the building and then asked, 'Where do you live?'

'Bergen-Belsen,' I told him *[Ella is very emotional now]*. I couldn't give any other address!

Well, I never heard from him; how could he correspond to Bergen-Belsen? In any case the Polish authorities did not give any properties back – at least not in Warsaw.

When I went back to that building about eight or ten years ago with my daughter Evy, her husband Paul, and one of my grandsons from Australia, the plaque was gone. There was no superintendent and I asked two women standing outside, 'Who lives here? To whom do you pay rent?' They told me, 'To the government, to the municipality.' It wasn't a big building – just two storeys, about sixteen tenants. When the war broke out, it was the Germans who collected the rent, I suppose. Then it was the Russians. Now the Poles. But I have the title deeds and everything! It's an interesting story how I got them: Roma went to Poland about 20 years ago with her husband and son. I was supposed to go with them but my husband was ill and I needed to look after him. Remember Mrs Price? Well Roma met up with her niece – the daughter of her brother-in-law who we had shared the narrow room with. Roma told her we were very friendly with her aunt during the camps and they became connected; Roma used to send her parcels and she wrote letters back, always sending her regards to me. Roma told her about the building in Grochów and that I had tried to get it back. This woman went to so much trouble for us: she got hold of the title deeds and sent all sorts of documentation to Roma, who passed it on to me. It's because of her that I got the papers.

So when I was in Warsaw with Evy, I went to her place and rang the buzzer for her flat but there was no reply. I went there twice a day but there was no answer. On Shabbos we went to Nożyk Synagogue – the only one in the whole of Warsaw that survived. Although there were not many Jews still living in Warsaw, I asked about her. 'We buried her just a few days ago,' they said.

I paid my respects at the cemetery.

In August 1945, on my trip to Warsaw, I didn't entirely give up on finding family. Even though I did not find any of their names on the lists at the Jewish office, and in spite of what the girl from Janów – the one I met in Auschwitz – had told me, I still dreamed that my dancing brother Heniek, his wife and little girl, had survived. When

Liberation

we used to correspond, his replies always came from the farm area called Biała Lubelskie, with the name of the farmer, Jan Parish. I think they became quite friendly. I always remembered the address and this name. And I dreamed that this friendship with the farmer had saved my brother's family, or at least his little girl who had no Jewish features – she was fair, like his wife.

So I boarded the train in Warsaw to travel there. I would have to go as far as Lublin and find my way to Biała Lubelskie. But before I even got to Lublin, I was warned: do not travel any further on the trains because the Poles are killing Jews; they're pulling Jews off the trains, robbing and beating them, even killing them. Turn back!

I never reached Lublin. If I had, I would probably have managed to find that old farmer, Jan Parish. Years later, when Roma went there, she found that the farmer and his wife were already gone, only the children or grandchildren were there and they remembered something about Jewish people who had been around. Roma was wise enough to ask them to call the eldest people in the village and they brought two Polish women in their 80s. Roma asked them about my brother. They remembered him – also that he was singing and dancing and that the little girl couldn't speak Jewish like her parents, only Polish. They did not say much more, just that he used to make everybody happy – which is what that girl we met in Auschwitz said about him.

They also confirmed that yes, they were all shot. My brother, his family, the Jews of that area. Shot.

I was in Warsaw for about two weeks, probably less because I didn't have any money. There was nothing to find and nothing to keep me there. Nothing. I'd lost everybody and everything. I had to go back to Bergen-Belsen with no news for Roma.

But Roma had news. She had heard from her father!

One of the soldiers who took our notes had gone back to England on leave and, when his mother was cleaning out the pockets of his uniform, she found a note. She opened it and immediately sent it off, with her own letter attached saying she is glad to see that the recipient of the letter, Samuel Rothstein, has found his daughter and his sister-in-law (because Roma wrote: 'Your daughter and your sister-in-law are in Bergen-Belsen.') In her own letter, she apologised that it was so late, 'I only just found this note in the pocket of my son's uniform.'

Shmuel lived with his brother, who actually received the letter. It was Shabbat and he put it in his pocket to open only after Shabbat was over[102], but he forgot about it! A few days later was the festival of Shavuot; he found the letter and gave it to Shmuel, but he was not going to open it on a Jewish holiday either and, anyway, they were going off to shul. When they got home, he saw that the letter came from England, yet he didn't know anybody in England. He opened it, and went white – apparently he looked so shocked that his brother said, 'I hope you didn't receive bad news.'

This is why it took so long for us to hear back from Roma's father.

Anyway, he soon started to work on getting Roma out, and his first point of contact was his old friend Hillel Seidman.

Seidman had survived the war and was working with the Agudas Yisroel organisation in Paris – they were almost like the Zionist Federation here today – representing religious Jews. My brother-in-law must have asked Seidman for advice on how to get us out from Bergen-Belsen – just like my sister had wanted to ask his advice about the papers for Palestine that her husband had sent. Shmuel and Seidman corresponded and, being a good friend, Seidman started the ball rolling.

In his letter to us, Roma's father said we would be travelling to Paris and must contact Mr Hillel Seidman from the Agudas Yisroel at 9 Rue d'Antin, not far from Place de l'Opéra; and he gave the telephone number.

It took some more months before we could eventually leave the camp for good – we were liberated in April but we only left Bergen-Belsen towards the end of the year. I imagine that Seidman must

---

[102] In keeping with the Orthodox Jewish prohibition against *muktzeh* (items which may not be touched during the Sabbath or holidays) and tearing (forbidden on the Sabbath).

have advised the English authorities in Bergen-Belsen that he wanted us to come to Paris. Surely, if people had somewhere to go, the British were pleased to release them.

So they released us. And not only us. There were a few other people in the truck we boarded to leave Bergen-Belsen behind us.

We travelled in a British military truck under the auspices of the United Nations Relief Rehabilitation Administration (UNRRA). The truck had two benches on each side and a cover over it. I can still see that big hood around us, it was almost dark inside and it had flaps at the entrance.

I know we stopped in Holland and then we travelled to Belgium and slept over in Brussels. We got, I think, a franc each because we slept over in a hotel outside the city. And in the morning we visited Brussels. Have you been there? Have you seen the Manneken Pis? *[Ella giggles.]* What we saw was normal life. The shops were packed with goods, people were walking in the street, pushing prams with children. Life! We couldn't believe it. Where are our children, where are our parents, our brothers and sisters? The world was pulsating with life.

But not Jewish life.

As we walked past the shoe stores we thought of all the piles of shoes we had sorted through. As we walked past the clothing stores, we thought of all the discarded clothing left at the camps. It all came back to us.

The next morning, late October or early November 1945, we arrived in Paris. From our vehicle, we saw people walking with long, thin things under their arms. We were laughing because we didn't know what they were, and it seemed so strange. It turns out they were baguettes! A long, thin loaf of bread!

The truck we were in stopped at a café where we got off. Our truck had a name or some sort of marking – I suppose it had 'UNRRA' on the side – so people knew we were survivors, and they came rushing over, Jewish people, to ask us: 'Have you perhaps met my wife?

My daughter? My mother?' Somebody brought a picture of their child, others brought names, surnames – 'Have you came across this person in the camps?' Lots of people came. And what could we say? We never said to give up hope, even though we knew there was none. 'Wait,' we said, 'Some people are sick and still recovering. Maybe you will still find them.'

One of these men, we asked to do us a favour: we asked him to phone the number that my brother-in-law had sent us, ask for Mr Seidman, and tell him the name of the place that we would meet him. This man went out to phone and, when he came back, he said: 'Mr Seidman says you must wait for him outside, he is coming to fetch you.' So we stood outside and waited and waited. 'Maybe it's this man walking with the newspaper?' Roma said. 'Or maybe it's that man walking with a hat.' Maybe it's this one, maybe it's that one. Mr Seidman used to come to our home when my sister and brother-in-law were living with us in Praga for seven years. But I was a child at the time and I couldn't really remember what he looked like . . . until he started walking towards us on that street in Paris and I said to Roma, 'There. I think that's him.'

The main thing is they looked after us.

They placed us in a hotel. On Friday nights we ate at Mr Majerowicz, a very religious man who had lost his wife; he survived with two sons who were in the Maquis – the French Resistance – and a daughter, although I'm not sure how he and she survived. Mr Majerowicz was manufacturing woollen caps in his flat on a side street – Rue Amelot or Passage Saint Amelot, or something like that – not far from Place de la République. He knew my brother-in-law from Poland days; he used to read Samuel's newspaper articles before he settled in France.

'Welcome!' said Mr Majerowicz on that first Friday night Shabbat. 'Welcome the daughter of the writer Samuel Rothstein and his sister-in-law, welcome.' He and his daughter had cooked on a little gas plate and set a table just like at home, with a white tablecloth. It was a very small place and in the little room next door, the machines were clattering and the two sons were working. As soon as it drew near to Shabbos of course they stopped and introduced themselves. They all wore berets like real Frenchmen, Mr Majerowicz too.

We spent a beautiful Shabbat there. Just wonderful. And that is where we went most Fridays.

About 35 years ago, I went to Paris with my husband and my son Alvin, and I led them to this Rue Amelot, Passage Amelot . . . I wanted to show my family where I was so welcome and how people fed us, Roma and me, after the camps. Can you believe that the two boys were still there? Mr Majerowicz was lying on a bed in a room, maybe it was even a partition of the room. He didn't recognise us and he was clearly not well. The boys told us that the daughter had left for Israel but they remained with their father. He couldn't have survived much longer than that visit but I was still glad to see the boys and talk to them. They had been such an important part of my return to life.

I AM ELLA

Name	Vorname	geboren		befreit		gestorben	
Frank	Aron	10.10.19	Zwolle	-	-	14.03.45	Bergen-Belsen
Frank	Bernhard	26.05.99	Beszterce	-	-	-	-
Frank	Erik	15.11.43	Westerbork	23.04.45	Tröbitz	-	-
Frank	Eva	- . - .21	Budapest	-	-	-	-
Frank	Eva	13.04.44	Budapest	-	-	-	-
Frank	Fredericus	28.01.11	Borgerhout	-	-	01.04.45	Bergen-Belsen
Frank	Frederik	26.06.42	Amsterdam	23.04.45	Tröbitz	-	-
Frank	Gabor	15.10.46	Budapest	-	-	-	-
Frank	Gabriel	12.07.38	Budapest	-	-	-	-
Frank	Gizella	10.10.19	Pecs	15.04.45	Bergen-Belsen	-	-
Frank	Helen	- . - .22	Szaszregen	15.04.45	Bergen-Belsen	-	-
Frank	Ilona	20.03.87	Kunszentmarton	-	-	17.12.44	Bergen-Belsen
Frank	Iwan	16.04.98	Herzogenbusch	23.04.45	Tröbitz	-	-
Frank	Jacob	13.08.99	Herzogenbusch	-	-	29.01.45	Bergen-Belsen
Frank	Jolan	-	-	15.04.45	Bergen-Belsen	12.05.45	Bergen-Belsen
Frank	Josef	20.10.90	Beszterce	-	-	-	-
Frank	Jozefa	08.09.26	-	15.04.45	Bergen-Belsen	-	-
Frank	Judit	08.09.33	Budapest	-	-	-	-
Frank	Jules	26.06.15	Amsterdam	-	-	-	-
Frank	Lili	10.11.25	Tamasi	15.04.45	Bergen-Belsen	-	-
Frank	Lily	10.11.25	Tolna	15.04.45	Bergen-Belsen	-	-
Frank	Margot B.	16.02.26	Frankfurt	-	-	30.03.45	Bergen-Belsen
Frank	Marianne	27.12.09	Amsterdam	-	-	-	-
Frank	Marthe	22.08.35	Budapest	-	-	-	-
Frank	Moses	01.12.24	Fulda	13.04.45	Farsleben	-	-
Frank	Moses	14.12.21	Budapest	-	-	-	-
Frank	Nachama	15.08.21	Warschau	15.04.45	Bergen-Belsen	-	-
Frank	Nikolaus	17.10.39	Budapest	-	-	-	-
Frank	Piroska	- . - .91	Szeged	13.04.45	Farsleben	-	-
Frank	Richard Georg	16.05.87	Mainz	-	-	-	-
Frank	Robert	07.07.39	Overveen	-	-	-	-
Frank	Rudolf	24.11.34	Amsterdam	23.04.45	Tröbitz	-	-
Frank	Simon	05.12.94	Zwolle	-	-	16.03.45	Bergen-Belsen
Frank	Suse	17.06.07	Amsterdam	-	-	-	-
Frank	Violetta	29.08.18	-	-	-	-	-
Frank Abrams	Marika	- . - .25	-	- .04.45	Magdeburg	-	-
Frank-Broekman	Elisabeth	28.03.05	Appeldorn	23.04.45	Tröbitz	-	-
Frank-Coster	Rosa Selma	30.01.12	Hilversum	23.04.45	Tröbitz	-	-
Frank-Dien	Anna	03.11.11	Amsterdam	-	-	01.03.45	Bergen-Belsen
Frank-Kaufmann	Amalie		Vasarvar	-	-	-	-

Official records of prisoners of Bergen-Belsen indicating names and dates of birth (*geboren*), liberation (*befreit*) and death (*gestorben*).

Chapter 10

Separation

I'm growing used to Ella's tricks for jogging her own memory.

One is to check her personal archive of books, photographs and press clippings; another is to tap into the store she has created in her children and the few to whom she has confided the deepest details of her life story; yet another, and one which is also a source of comfort, is Roma's own memoir, Here There is No Why.

Ella gives me a copy but I prefer not to read it until all our interviews are complete. This is generally my strategy with research: I am wary of third-party material diluting or detracting from my own protagonist's story, so I tend to do all my background and supplementary reading only after my primary source has offered their own unfiltered account. But this situation, with Ella and Roma, is different, and it stands to reason. Bonds forged by shared trauma are unbreakable; family ties that outlast a forced severing are ironclad; when Ella and Roma emerged as their family's only Holocaust survivors, their already-close connection was fused so tightly that their two disparate selves merged in many ways, and their stories became synonymous with one another's. But herein lies a danger, for storytelling and particularly memoir: to assume that Ella's experience was Roma's and vice versa is to deny the uniqueness of the individual and counteract the very mission of biography, which is to preserve original memory. No two fingerprints are the same.

ELLA:
To start off with in Paris, we lived on goodwill.

We got packages from the Joint Distribution and collected food and clothing at the Agudas Yisroel office. American people sent clothing; there was a whole roomful, piled high, and we chose what we wanted. There was a beautiful fur coat that Roma wanted to take and I said, 'What do you need a fur coat for?' So Roma left it and a friend of ours took it. Roma has never forgotten that I did not allow her to take this fur coat *[laughing]*; it was a nice fur coat!

For many Shabbat meals, we went to Mr Majerowicz, as I told you, and even sometimes during Shabbat day, on a Saturday.

One Shabbat day, somebody brought a gentleman in a British uniform to see us. He was not actually a British soldier but in fact part of the Jewish Brigade[103]. He had gone to Warsaw to the Jewish committee to see if he could find somebody. He had lived there before the war and was engaged to my sister Pola's friend before he left to join the Brigade. Sadly, he couldn't find her name or any of her family in the register of survivors. But he found my name, Hela Frank, and that I was in Bergen-Belsen. So he travelled to Bergen-Belsen and there he got the address for me in Paris. Agudas Yisroel sent him to Mr Majerowicz where we used to eat on Friday nights.

There was a knock on the door and there stood this man – Simcha Sneh. As he walked in, he said, 'I'm looking for my fiancée, Nucia. Do you know anything about her?' Well, we didn't want to tell him that she had actually married somebody else after he left but we did tell him that the same happened to her as happened to all our families, to all the Jews. She was caught and sent away. She never survived.

Although this was more sad news, Simcha Sneh was so happy to have found us, people he knew. He even said, 'You are my family.' And he was wonderful to us. He was one of those socialists,

---

103 The Jewish Brigade Group of the British Army consisted of Jewish volunteers from Palestine who fought against the Germans during the last year of the war. They then helped create displaced persons camps for Jewish survivors of the Holocaust and helped Jewish refugees gain illegal entry into Palestine.

farbrente[104] . . . actually more of a communist I think. He travelled to England or Belgium, and he got us some beautiful material, grey with a little white stripe, pure wool. He asked a Jewish Frenchman, Mr Barrere, who had survived as a member of the Maquis and was now working at Agudas Yisroel, to make the material into suits for Roma and me. A skirt and a jacket each. You can see the picture – I was in front of the Arc de Triomphe in Paris. That suit was a French masterpiece. We wanted to pay this Mr Barrere but he said: 'I am not going to take money from two survivors. I am also Jewish.'

Those were the first new outfits we possessed. The best, the nicest, smelling so clean. I went on to get a few more beautiful pieces of Parisian fashion which I kept for years, but the first was thanks to this Simcha Sneh.

He even fancied me! Not only him – there were plenty *[there is that naughty chuckle again, even a wink]* – but Sneh wanted to marry me in Paris! I'll tell you more about that later.

In addition to Mr Majerowicz's place, we also used to eat at the home of the Warman family – remember 'w' is a 'v' sound in Polish.

They were very religious. She was a proper *sabra*[105], Mrs Warman, and he was a *shochet*[106]. She came from the very *frum* section of Jerusalem – Mea Shearim. They shared their flat in Rue Poissonnière with another family, I think their surname was David. They were the owners of the apartment – the Warmans must have hired a portion of it from them – and in the front half they manufactured clothing using hand-operated sewing machines.

In the back half of the apartment, the Warmans had two rooms and a tiny kitchen, if I can even say it was a kitchen – more like a partition. Yet Mrs Warman cooked like the best cook in the world! Mr

---

104 Yiddish for 'zealous' or 'devout'.
105 Refers to a native-born Israeli. A *sabra* is a fruit-bearing cactus adopted by Israelis as a national icon because the characteristics of this prickly pear fruit are supposed to mirror those of native Israelis – tough and prickly on the outside, soft and sweet on the inside.
106 Kosher butcher.

Warman used to bring kosher meat, which he got with difficulty because there was still very little kosher stuff. In their home we met many important Jewish people who came to them through Agudas Yisroel, all doing good work. Hillel Seidman used to come eat there Friday nights too. It was a *heimishe*[107], beautiful atmosphere. I remember one Yom Kippur we all ate together after the fast, all the dignitaries and the rabbis, squeezed tightly together at a makeshift table in this little flat.

The Warmans had two sons who were in a *yeshiva* in Aix-les-Bains, a resort town in the south of France. Now the sons live in New York, near where Roma had her business, in Borough Park. One of the sons is a rabbi there, with a lot of children; the other one is also very *frum*. When they were younger, they used to wear berets. I've got a picture with them, and one of them inscribed the words: '*A jullik*[108] Hela . . . David' *[giggles]*.

Oh, and that reminds me of one more thing. Quite a few months down the line, the last chief rabbi of Palestine, Rabbi Herzog, was in a conference in Paris. He was staying at the Hôtel du Louvre in Place de Louvre, with his entourage. I used to take food from the Warmans to the chief rabbi and his people in the hotel. And you know how I used to carry it? There were round dishes, white enamel outside, steel inside, with a lid. Three, four or maybe five of them stacked one on top of the other; they fitted nicely in a frame – it was a known thing for carrying food. And I didn't travel by taxi, I took the underground until the station de Louvre and then took the food up myself. You can imagine how kosher Mrs Warman was that the chief rabbi of Palestine was eating her food!

Mr and Mrs Warman eventually landed up in Venezuela. I think they were in America and maybe they couldn't get citizenship. They were very kind, and they loved me so much.

---

107 Yiddish for 'homely, cosy, familiar'.
108 Yiddish word referring, good-naturedly, to a boisterous, wild person.

Separation

When Roma and I first arrived, we stayed at a hotel in Paris where the Agudas Yisroel put us up. But we soon moved into a place belonging to a relation of Mr Majerowiz. The French authorities declared all homes had to be occupied – you couldn't have an empty property, you had to have tenants. The place this relation had was for her daughter and son-in-law, but they were waiting for him to come back from the war before moving in. So she said Roma and I could stay there until he returned.

He never came back. He had been caught on the street in Paris and never returned.

And that is where we stayed. It was in the Pletzl – the Jewish quarter in the 4th arrondissement. It had a beautiful bed, soft, with a duvet, and we had a little stove to cook some food. We were like *menschen*! We still used to get free meals, or we only had to pay very little for food, and this became a meeting place for some survivors in Paris.

The Joint Distribution offered for us to study something. So we decided to learn to become dental assistants. We went a few times and then dropped it! I don't know why; we just didn't have a feeling for it I suppose.

We also got visits from a lady named Jeanette. When Roma's father found out we were alive, he wrote to his cousin, Mr Krankimel, who lived just outside Geneva. Mr Krankimel had left Warsaw long before the war and settled in Switzerland, dealing in watches. His partner was a French woman – they never married – and he sent her to us in Paris. She took us out for meals in kosher restaurants a few times, always asking 'What can I do for you?' and 'How are you?' She was so nice. Her visits were one of the ways that Roma's father tried to help us during that time, to see that somebody looked after us.

Roma and I were living life! Going to museums, to the Louvre, at night to the Opera. We walked freely with our number tattoos showing – we didn't hide them. Of course we met Simcha Sneh who had our beautiful suits made so we looked the part. We loved going around Paris, visiting the big church Notre-Dame. We were alive! We wanted to see what goes on in this big world! We were carefree; we didn't think of the future, we lived from day to day, just enjoying it.

It's amazing how one comes back to normal life. We adapted ourselves, became like the next Frenchman there in Paris. Of course we spoke to one another about what happened during the war – we couldn't help ourselves, we had just lived through it and of course we talked about incidents and memories. But we couldn't stay still or go backwards – we had to go forward. We were alive; we lost everybody so we didn't want to bury ourselves. We had to go forward.

* * *

Meanwhile in Palestine, Roma's father went to the British consulate in Jerusalem and said: 'I found my daughter! Here is my certificate for my wife and four children. Only one of them is alive; please let her come from France.'

I didn't have a certificate like that – it had been for my sister and her four children – so he could only apply for a renewal of the visa for Roma.

He immediately got her a permit and Agudas Yisroel arranged for her to travel by boat to Haifa to join her father. This was after we had been in Paris about six months.

One strange thing I remember: when Roma's father sent her permit, which came to the Agudas Yisroel office, they actually received two permits for entry to Palestine. One was in Roma's name and the other, I'm not sure. We begged Dr Seidman, who was in charge, to give me the other permit. But he said, 'No, it's unfair to give two certificates to one family.' So Roma got the one and the nephew of the Gerrer Rebbe, the famous rabbi from Gur[109], got the other certificate.

---

109 The Gerrer is a large sect of the Chassidic movement – the religious Jewish spiritual revival group that arose in 18th-century Eastern Europe. Chassidic dynasties are usually named after the town where they were founded, e.g. the Gerrer/Ger sect from Góra Kalwaria (now in Poland). Their leaders are esteemed rabbis and the dynasty continues through familial succession.

Separation

He went with Roma on the same boat. I remained alone in Paris for another year or so.

Roma and I had never been separated since she was born. We lived together always. Maybe the only time we were apart was for a certain period in the ghetto but not for long. When it was time for her to leave, she had to depart from the port in Marseilles. I remember that day, and how hard it was for both of us. Roma herself writes:

> The final parting from Hela draws near. She has been my sole support, my loving, devoted solicitous mother in those terrible dark days of misfortune. Hela, who was as hungry as I was, still had the fortitude . . . to take the last morsel of bread out of her own mouth to put it into mine . . . Hela had stood behind me in the line for selection and tried to lift my morale by whispering in my ear: 'Hold your head up high, stand straight, walk firmly, I promise you that I won't let you go to the gas by yourself. If he tells you to go to the left I will go with you; I swear it to you.'[110]

I was devastated when Roma left. It took me a long time to find my feet on my own. I held on to one special picture that I had of her. We had met a girl in the street who we knew from Auschwitz. She said, 'You were so good to me, I am now the owner of a little hairdressing salon, come and I'll do your hair for free.' So she did our hair and then we went to a proper photographer, but that was on a Shabbat and I didn't want to have my picture taken on Shabbat. Roma did it and got a beautiful picture. I kept that photo with me in Paris all the time. I still have it, in the same frame. It was my support then and even now.

Until I got married, Roma was everything I had in my life *[tearful]*. It was like we breathed the same air. We were not two separate people, we were like one soul. And, although we each went off and

---

110 Roth, R. 2002. *Here There is No Why*. Rachel Chencinski Roth.

created our own lives, away from one another, we remained so connected. Now, we the survivors, can value the wonderful gift of motherhood and grandmotherhood and great-grandmotherhood that God has granted us. I would fight for my child; if I had to, I would give my life *[very tearful]* – to me it's unbelievable that I brought a new generation into the world! They say that six million Jews perished. I say it's more like 60 million because from only me, one survivor, one person, I have got *Baruch HaShem*[111] four children, eleven grandchildren and eleven great-grandchildren. So can you imagine the number of Jews the world would have had if there wasn't that terrible sacrifice!

I always looked after Roma, stood behind her, gave her courage, as she says. This was my aim: I must try to help her because she was very weak. As a young child she was not strong. I have mentioned that in wintertime they used to send her to the countryside so that she should rest and be fed properly and have fresh air. I fought for her life. She wasn't my niece, she was like my child. And at times that she was better off than me – like in Auschwitz when she worked at the *Bekleidungskamer* sorting clothes and she got me a pair of panties or when I had a problem with my leg and she managed to get some medication – then *she* helped *me*. At those times, the roles did change. But mostly, it was me looking out for her, 'organising' (not 'stealing' or 'smuggling' – *Ella winks*) extra food and things.

But now, Roma had the chance to go to Palestine. And although I was devastated to say goodbye, I was happy for her. She was going to her father who had lost his parents, siblings, wife – my sister – and three children; only one brother had travelled with him. He lost everyone else. So I was happy that Roma was going. With my whole heart, my wish was that she should join him, to give him *nachas*[112] and love.

---

111 From Hebrew this translates to 'Blessed be the name [of the Lord]'. Observant Jews use it to indicate gratitude and commitment, in place of the English, 'Thank God'.
112 Hebrew/Yiddish for 'pride', especially at the achievements of one's children.

Chapter 11

Paris

Ella's ardent excavation through her papers continues unabated, but today, rather than seeming buoyed by the affirmation of this corroborating material, she seems a little shaky. Where before, the extracts she read to me were complementary to her narrative, serving only to illustrate or elucidate, today she seems to be using them to check herself, distrustful of her own memory. I find it interesting that the arm's-length objectivity of a published article or book does not necessarily make me feel more confident in Ella's recollections; I never lacked confidence in the strength of her mind and memory to begin with – such is the energy she exudes even without trying. But today she is hesitant and needs my prompting as she becomes lost in the tide of memories, uncertain which are hers alone and which are ones she has read. It strikes me that this inability to distinguish between private and public, between the individual consciousness and the collective, is itself an aftermath of the Nazi terror. Stripped of even the most basic of human rights, Holocaust victims were quickly denied privacy and autonomy; from sharing a tiny ghetto apartment with four other families to communal ablutions and standing naked in a crowd, privacy quickly became not a fundamental right but an elusive luxury, even a crime. Jews were not individuals, not even individual humans – the Nazi strategy of dehumanisation of victims was comprehensive; whole ethnicities, races, classes were lumped together as 'other', Jews worst of all, portrayed as senseless vermin who would not bleed if pricked.

Now, years later, as Ella stops to record her story and sifts among her own and others' memories, she hears the echoes of her own trauma in every word recorded by her fellow sufferers[113]. *The Holocaust was a private ordeal lived publicly; and a collective nightmare suffered, uniquely, by each individual. Now, years later, and today especially, she greets these echoes and repeats these stories with a tone of utter incredulity – that she suffered as she did, endured as she did, survived as she did. And she says it again, 'No wonder people ask me for a brocha.'*

ELLA:
Roma left Paris and I remained. This was the middle of 1946. I became independent. I had to. That's me; I land on my feet. I knew I had to look after myself.

I used to go to eat on the Pletzl where survivors met – young men and women, not only from Auschwitz but from other camps. And we spoke . . . about the camps. It was always with us, you couldn't shed it. Even now, after so many years, I still live with it. I read, I live through literature, I cannot wipe it off me; it's impossible. And those people understood, they felt the same way.

When I moved to South Africa and was working with my husband and bringing up the children, I was busy and did not speak about the Holocaust. I was a strong person, trying to be like everybody else. But I never really mixed with the South African Jewish women – I never liked to go for tea with the ladies; I had nothing in common with them. Even now I find it difficult, although it's different here in Cape Town; I've found good people that I really love and who I find are genuine. But when I lived in Brakpan, never, never did you see me out. First of all, I was always busy. But also, I was never invited –

---

[113] Richard Freedman comments that, because so much has been documented about the Holocaust, these memories become the individual survivor's memories too. 'Ella never misses any events at the Centre as they seem to her as confirmation of her story. There is almost a need to relive her story through others.'

Paris

I used to greet the people in the car, I was in shul over *yom tov*, but otherwise nothing. I couldn't understand them and they didn't understand me – it was like a different world, their upbringing and way of thinking. But there, in the Jewish quarter of Paris in that year immediately after the war – there I found people who understood me.

I became very friendly with another Auschwitz survivor, Gina Fernebok, a Polish girl who had lived in Belgium and I think was sent from Belgium to Auschwitz. She had found relations who were born in Paris. They had a tiny, two-seater Fiat car with hardly any space to sit, and they used to pick us up and take us to their home. As it happens, they became very wealthy. After I was married, when we visited Paris, we were invited to the family for dinner. They lived next to the Place de l'Étoile, very expensive, and I didn't realise how posh it was. You had to 'report' – a person downstairs would ring up to the flat to announce you! I remember a minister of finance was also there and a lady walked around serving little pieces of toast in a basket with a white serviette and *pâté de foie*[114]. I didn't know it was not kosher; now I realise it wasn't. It was very elegant, very smart. After the dinner they sat in the parlour and they spoke French so fast! My husband couldn't speak French and they talked about business; they had big connections. I'm not in touch with them now but when one of my sons went to Paris for the first time, I gave him their number. He called them up and asked, 'Can you recommend a hotel around here?' *Ella laughs.* They probably thought he was wanting to stay with them!

Another very good friend was Paula, her maiden name was Schwartzmann. She was French-speaking because she had lived in Belgium. I was always with her and her family, who were also very kind to me. I got myself a place to live that was close to them. Paula lived with her family but she used to stay over with me sometimes. After I left Paris, she married a Polish man, I'm not sure if he was also

---

114 French: liver pâté.

a survivor, and they moved to Florida in the United States. I visited her when I went there; she was living the don't-care-life –*'Do you mean carefree?' I ask. Ella laughs, 'Yes! That's the word! Carefree!'* – with her husband in Sarasota, Florida; they played tennis every day and stayed in a beautiful condominium on the ocean. But what I remember most clearly is that the *mezuzah* was on the inside of the door, not outside. Nobody knew that she was a survivor or that Jews were living in that house.

Gina, Paula and I would get together with other survivors; so I did have company after Roma left but of course I missed her terribly and I still had no relatives of my own.

One Sunday morning, I was on the train, which was very empty, and I recognised a familiar face. The man was sitting at the end of the carriage and he came to stand at the doors in the middle, waiting for them to open at the next station. As I looked at him, something clicked. I went up to him and I said, *'Parlez-vous* Polish?' – do you speak Polish? He nodded. *'Du redst* Yiddish?' – you speak Yiddish? He nodded. 'You are from Warsaw,' I said, 'from Praga. You are Marcel Torstein.' At that moment, the doors opened and I told him who I was and we just fell out of the carriage to the platform at the next station. The joy!

Torstein's father was my mother's half-brother. I remembered walking with my mom sometimes on a Friday to his flat to give some money for Shabbos; my mother used to help them. I remembered the winding staircase to the flat where he lived. And I remembered his face; he came to us for Shabbat.

Marcel had been living in Paris for many years. He was already married to his second wife; I think he was divorced from the first one but she was caught, deported, lost.

He made me come and stay with them. He had a grown-up son from his first marriage. I used to have breakfast with him: coffee (in a bowl rather than a mug) with baguette. I brought tins of food with me from the place where I was staying, tins that the Joint Distribution gave us, and he put it in his attic. When I left, I took half the tins with me! I didn't stay there long because they lived outside Paris and I had to take the Métro to the end of the line and from there take a bus.

Marcel Torstein became a very wealthy man and they moved closer to the Côte d'Azur. We kept in touch. As a matter of fact, when I went to Monte Carlo on holiday, he assisted me; he took me to the Gare du Nord or Gare de Lyon, I can't remember from which station I left, and I travelled on Wagons-Lits du Cook. I had a bed on the train – I travelled like a real lady! I stayed in a *pension* between Nice and Monte Carlo where I met two lovely Jewish girls from Paris. We met and talked on the beach every day. I also met a Frenchman who had a car and offered to take me driving south; we stopped in Monte Carlo and he took a picture of me. Then we travelled on a road just like Chapman's Peak in Cape Town; a narrow road, winding through the mountains to a town called Menton, on the border of Italy. We travelled back the same route to the Cote d'Azur. It was beautiful: a free world.

Simcha Sneh sometimes used to come from London to visit me. I suppose you could say we were dating. He wanted to marry me and to settle in Buenos Aires, Argentina. But I wasn't ready. Not yet. I wanted my independence; I was happy to be responsible for myself. I had to be wide awake and know what's going on. I used to meet people who were helping with the illegal arrangements to send survivors to Palestine. This was usually done by sending people through Italy on illegal boats. I used to meet those organisers, talk to them about how they were operating, help them gather people. I was not tempted to take the illegal route to Palestine myself though. Why should I put my life in jeopardy? I was happy, doing well, and although I missed Roma, I used to correspond with her often. And I was working and earning good money.

Ella is quiet for a while, thinking back through a thick and murky wad of time. About her early years, the ghetto, the camps, liberation, and the general theme of survival, she has truckloads of material and various prepared speeches; but it seems that she has not really plumbed the depths of daily life thereafter. Ironically, the greatest detail belongs to the smallest portion of her life, and she stands now on the cusp of opening the taps to the lion's share.

For this first bit, she speaks hesitantly, without full sentences, definitely holding something back.

Somehow, I was recommended to a religious Jewish man – I will call him Mr Z – who was dealing in the black market, a big business after the war. I also met his young, pretty wife; while I was working for them she had a son. They lived in an apartment in a very quiet neighbourhood of Paris.

Practically every morning, I used to phone his home and he told me where to go. Sometimes it was to meet him or his wife at a certain location, always away from his home, and I'd get an address to go to. He would go another way and I realise now that he would go and do his black-market trading, all to do with *valuta* – currency. I was given the task of delivering it, or picking it up from somewhere. He also received packages brought from overseas by ambassadors or representatives of different countries. I used to fetch the packages from them at a very grand hotel in the Place de l'Opéra. Little packages I never opened. And I took other things to them: foreign currency, gold coins, Russian coins, English coins, American coins. Also between other Jewish people. I told you that the Russian coins we called *chazzerlach*. Even in the ghetto there was a black market. People used to walk in the streets, looking down, and saying, '*Harte! Veyk! Harte! Veyk!*[115]' – hard for coins and soft for paper money; this is how you knew someone was dealing in currency. In Paris, it was not so obvious.

Mr Z never did a delivery himself; it was too dangerous for him. He was the big dealer so he only organised it. I got addresses to go here, there, stashing small things in my underwear. I never used

---

115 Yiddish for 'Hard! Soft! Hard! Soft!'.

taxis and I had to make these trips with the Paris Métro so I was inconspicuous. I didn't buy tickets each time – I had a pack of ten journeys. And I got to know Paris so well. I didn't even have to check the map or which line to take, where to change. I was a real Parisian already.

I got paid nicely. I went out to eat at the Place de l'Opéra, and I would also order *une carafe de vin*.[116] It wasn't expensive and it was very beautiful there. I didn't worry much about going to the Warmans any more. She used to come and look for me, Mrs Warman. She knew I was alone but I was already quite a big shot so . . . *[chuckles]*.

I also used to buy clothes. There was a big *magasin*[117] where I went – Printemps, I think it was – with very smart stuff. I knew exactly what to buy and what to wear. I even brought things with me when I came to South Africa; beautiful shoes – people are wearing them even now – with the heel high. I nearly killed myself when walking with these high heels on the streets of Paris! Yes, I was very smart. You can see the way I'm dressed here in this picture taken when a famous French artist, Emmanuel Mané-Katz, came to South Africa for an exhibition in 1950: I'm wearing the big, beautiful hat I bought in Paris and kept with me. I still love hats – until today.

One time I decided I'm also going to do this currency business.

I already had a couple of gold pieces of my own; I must have bought cheap. But where do you keep such things? At this time, I was living in a room, not even a hotel. The owner and his wife lived downstairs and I had a room on the fourth floor; no toilet, just a little basin – the toilet was outside for everyone to use. And the telephone was in the owner's room at the entrance. I used to pay to phone my boss.

There was a street near Rue Poissonnière (where the Warmans lived) where these dealers were walking up and down but they

---

116 French for 'one carafe of wine'
117 French for 'shop' or 'store'.

didn't shout like in the ghetto. You just knew they were doing business. There was a flat in that street where I would sometimes deliver parcels; it was on the first or second floor and it was like a market in there. *Valuta*. Currency trading. I knew that if I wanted to buy or sell a piece, that was the place.

So one day, I walked up the stairs to this flat and went in. There were lots of people, men, all Jewish people – some very *frum*, some with hats, some without. As I came up, the main door slammed shut. The police! They were never there before! Just my *mazel*[118].

Two detectives dressed in plain clothes arrested everybody.

'What are you doing here?' they asked me.

'I don't know,' I said. 'I saw people walking up here from the street so I followed them.'

'What is going on here?'

'I don't know myself! I really don't.'

'Where do you live?'

I gave the address and they put me into the car. I had to take them up to my room. The owner stared as we came in – he could tell these were not friends of mine.

They searched my room, looking here, there. I had a bed, I don't even think there was a cupboard (I can't remember where I kept clothes), and next to the basin was a fireplace with a mantelpiece. I kept quite a few basic things there. I had two or three jars where I kept the parcels from the Joint Distribution. One jar had beans, one had fresh and dried fruit, one had proper food. Inside the jar with the beans, I kept two gold pieces.

When they checked my pockets, they found nothing – I had wanted to check out that place first, before I did any business, so I didn't take anything with me. And they found nothing in my room either. So they gave me a warning, and they left. But it was there – in the jar on the fireplace, staring at them!

I carried on working for Mr Z in Paris after that. Luckily he did

---

118 Hebrew/Yiddish for 'luck'.

not find about this incident with the detectives. The police were sniffing around though; they knew of him and his dealings – how long can you carry on with this? They couldn't find evidence because he never had anything on him or in his flat. Eventually they dug up his cellar. And they found . . . nothing. But it was burning on him: in Yiddish we say *de hitl brent afn ganef* – the cap burns on the thief's head. It was closing in on him; he knew they were digging up everything, probably looked at how he lived, what he was paying. He left for America with his wife and child.

That is not the last I would hear about the Z family. After Paris, I went to Palestine and then to South Africa. Soon after I arrived in Palestine, I contacted Mr Z; I told him I had no means of sustaining myself, would he kindly send me something? And he did.

I heard nothing about him for many years after that. All our lives moved on and around the world. Roma landed up in America herself – she lived on Staten Island and she had a business in Borough Park. All three of her children were born in Israel where she lived for almost 30 years before moving to America. I used to travel often to visit her.

When her youngest son, Rami, was going to become Bar Mitzvah, I had to go for the occasion of course. I took my daughter with me – Evy was 14 at the time, she's a year older than Rami. We arrived two weeks before the Bar Mitzvah and, as Roma couldn't get away from her business, she arranged for her older son to hire a mobile home. We travelled from New York to the border of Canada; we saw the Niagara Falls and drove through Canada for maybe two weeks. Just wonderful!

Somehow, we connected with a Jewish group – I can't remember if it was other survivors – but it was in a home of sorts with a committee of people who gathered and talked Yiddish. For some reason, I mentioned the name of Mr Z to these people and one of them said, 'I know them! Mr Z passed away but Mrs Z lives in New York; she's remarried,' and they gave me her phone number.

After the Bar Mitzvah, I told Roma about Mrs Z and that I wanted to meet her. So I phoned, and spoke in French of course. She said she didn't remember me! I told her if she saw me she would remember, and begged her to meet with me. I even asked how old her son was.

Eventually, we met for tea. Roma came with me of course. I reminded Mrs Z who I was and told her, 'I don't need anything from you. I am married, I live in Johannesburg, South Africa and, *Baruch HaShem*, I don't need anything from you.' I thought perhaps she remembered that I had written from Palestine all those years before asking for help and maybe she was worried I was going to do the same again. Or maybe she was worried that I would report to the police what they were doing in Paris, perhaps she was scared of the American authorities. I didn't know who she was married to – maybe she was still doing it with this new husband!

Do you know that she never ever admitted that she knew me? I worked for them for over a year, in 1946 and 1947. This was 30 years later. And it was definitely her! Remember she was much younger than Mr Z, a beautiful woman. I knew her immediately. But she would not admit that she knew me.

Anyway, *c'est la vie*, my dear. And that is the story of the Zs.

So I looked after myself!

I earned good money. I even decided to buy a pure gemstone and have it set in a ring. I gave Simcha Sneh the money to buy the stone overseas and the family of my friend Paula took me to a jeweller and picked out the setting. It was beautiful. And it came with me to South Africa. My husband never gave me an engagement ring. When I met him, I was wearing my own ring, and that is how I came to this country! *I glance at Ella's hands and she sees me looking for the ring.* You want to know where it is now?

Years ago, in the early sixties, I went on holiday with my husband to the Beverly Hills Hotel outside Durban. I love swimming, as you know, so every morning after breakfast we used to go and sit at the pool. But should I go with a diamond ring? I swam most of the time while my husband was sitting in the shade. So I left my precious ring hidden in the room, mixed up among other things, and I wore artificial jewellery instead. But when I came back to the room one day, it was gone – only the ring, nothing else. The hotel told us to report it to the police; they said they'd had other similar complaints and they suspected that people were dressing up as cleaners, then searching for valuables rather than cleaning the room. I don't really believe in insurance, so I think it was only insured for a very small amount, if at all. *Seeing my horrified face, Ella waves her hand dismissively.* It's nothing; just as long as I was fine – a stone is a stone, we can always buy one, it's really not a tragedy.

Ella has an intrinsically comical way of shaping a facial expression to suit a turn of phrase; her manner of storytelling makes me laugh out loud at its apparent preposterousness, even if the circumstance itself is quite serious. Like this one, about the vanishing gemstone. And another, about the French delicacies to which she had to quickly become accustomed during her time in Paris after the paucity and plainness of her war-time fare. We had similar banter early on in her story when we both struggled to find the correct word for 'goose' while discussing her childhood Shabbat meals (Turkey? Chicken? Peacock? Swan? – No, like a big duck!). So when it happens again, it is too hilarious to edit because this is just . . . so . . . Ella.

This reminds me of something else that happened in the sixties, when I was travelling with Roma to Europe. We stopped in Nice and went to visit her husband's relations in Monte Carlo. We slept over for a few days and the wife was a wonderful cook. She made . . . not a bird, bigger than a bird – what do you call it? It was flying, I don't know.

   A turkey?

No, no, no. Like a big bird or—

   Not a duck?

No, a duck doesn't fly. It was a very special dish in France.
Oh, like a quail?
I don't know what a quail is.
You get the quail eggs.
I still don't know it.
A fancy bird.
A big bird, but it flies. *Ella flaps her arms and bats her eyelids as if in a game of charades.* It was a fancy French food, she cooked it for us. *[Chuckles]:* I couldn't look at the poor bird.
So what did you do?
We didn't eat it, we just looked at the space next to it. It was a lovely plate.

* * *

I had been living and working in Paris for about one-and-a-half years. It was now 1947.

Simcha Sneh still came back and forth from London, talking about marriage. I must tell you, though *[Ella lowers her voice]* – this Simcha Sneh was older than me and also . . . very . . . ugly. *We laugh.* 'Well no wonder you didn't want to follow him to Argentina!' But he was very educated, an intelligent man; it was a pleasure to be in his company. And he was full of life.

Early that year, I got a visit from my brother-in-law Samuel Rothstein. It was the first time I had seen him since the war broke out. He travelled from Palestine to the Zionist conference in Basel – he was a correspondent for one of the papers – and he came from there to see me in Paris.

At the time, this Simcha Sneh was stationed in London and I told my brother-in-law he wanted to marry me. So Shmuel went there to meet him. When he got back to Palestine, he wrote to me: 'It's not for you, you cannot marry him.' Sneh was definitely not religious because he was a socialist, almost a communist. And my brother-in-law did not approve.

So eventually I persuaded Sneh, exactly like I did with the Russian man in the camps. I said: 'You go and I will follow you.' I went to see him off at Orly Airport. We kissed. He left.

I got correspondence from him, but I didn't even answer. It was *finito*.

I did not ask about him for a long time but Roma told me once that she heard he was a journalist on a Jewish paper in Buenos Aires. Some years ago, I did make some inquiries but nobody knew him; I thought they would.

So this was the beginning and the end of Simcha Sneh who found us in Paris.

When my brother-in-law returned to Tel Aviv, he decided that Paris was not a place for a young woman to live alone. So he came up with a plan to bring me over.

He went to the British consulate and said, 'I found another daughter alive! She is in Paris!' Roma had had a sister called Rywka (in Polish, you would say 'Rivka') who, as you know, had died along with her other siblings and mother. Well now Samuel claimed to have found one of them alive. So the British consul gave him a permit for Rywka Rothstein. It was sent to me in Paris; meantime I got papers from the Polish consul to say that I am Rywka Rothstein born in 1927 on the 12th of April. I got my travel documents and travelled to Palestine under my late niece's name.

Ella often mentions that there is a long story associated with her name and she reveals it piecemeal – the Rywka Rothstein component is only one part. But right now, the question that bothers me is why it took Samuel Rothstein one-and-a-half years to bring Ella to Palestine. Why not claim to have found both his daughters alive at the time he applied for Roma's visa renewal, and assign Ella the name of Rywka Rothstein then? Ella is indignant in her response:

You couldn't think of doing crook business then! It wasn't legal, what he has done. Only when he came to see me in Paris and realised that I had helped save the life of his daughter Roma and that I'm one of only two relatives who survived, did he come up with a way to get me out. Maybe somebody advised him, you never know, but not before. It never dawned on any of us that I could go illegally to Palestine under his other daughter's name. And travelling illegally on *Aliyah Bet*[119] was very dangerous. Perhaps, when he went back, he thought about it differently. Whatever the case, it was now time for me to leave Paris.

---

119 Code name for the clandestine immigration of Jews to Palestine between 1920 and 1948 when the country was under British mandate.

Paris

Translation from the Hebrew Language

CERTIFICATE OF MARRIAGE   No. H 93847

DISTRICT: 966/708   LOD   TOWN: TEL AVIV

Marriage solemnised at TEL AVIV on Tuesday the Second Day of the month Shvat in the year 5708, on 13th day of January 1948.

	HUSBAND	WIFE
1. Name and Surname in full	Yitzchak Isaac Blumenthal (sgd) Isaac Blumenthal	Rywka Rotstein (sgd) Rywka Rotstein
2. Age	32	21
3. Calling (occupation)	Deputy Manager	–
4. Community	Jewish	Jewish
5. Residence – Place of his or her residence	Tel Aviv	Tel Aviv
6. Name and Surname of Father and mother	Yehuda Idel and Hena Blumenthal	Shmuel and Golda Lieba Rotstein
7. Calling of Father and Mother (occupation)	–	–
8. Residence of Father and Mother	–	–
9. Name and Surname of Witnesses	Y Y Frankel	B S Wilner
10. Calling of Witnesses (occupation)	–	–

Certified that the above is a true extract from the Register of Marriage kept at the office of THE CHIEF RABBINATE OF TEL AVIV (OFFICIAL ROUND SEAL OF CHIEF RABBINATE TEL AVIV APPEARS OVER PALESTINE REVENUE STAMP Value 10 MILS).

No.708/35453 in the District.

I, hereby testify that the above Certificate is a true extract from the Marriage Register kept at the Office of this Chief Rabbinate in the Town of TEL AVIV, District of LOD.

Date: 13th January 1948

SIGNATURE Yaakov Moshe Toledano
(Appears)

One of two marriage certificates that Ella and Isaac Blumenthal received in Palestine, 13 January 1948. This one is in the name of Rywka Rothstein – Ella's late niece whose name she assumed when given passage to Palestine from Europe after liberation.

Chapter 12

Palestine

We move from the threat and gloom of wartime to the hope and bloom of post-war, and there is a noticeable shift, not only in the tone of Ella's narrative but in the pace too. The slow crawl through the Holocaust years becomes a lope through liberation and Paris, and a canter to Palestine. I imagine we'll be in full-blown gallop by the time we reach South African shores.

She has coughed up the darkest pieces of her past; dislodged them though they threatened to choke her. Now Ella opens the taps and the flow of memories runs faster. At one point she stops, mid-sentence, and comments with amazement: 'Can you see how it's pouring out of me?' Again, she marvels at the ease with which she talks to me. I jokingly put it down to the frequent snippets of Yiddish I throw into our banter and to which she always responds with delighted disbelief. 'Maybe,' she laughs, 'and I still don't know how you are going to put it all together because I keep jumping around. But I can't stop. It's just coming so easily now.' I reassure her, once more, that that puzzle is mine to solve. Now is not the time to slow her down or force chronology. Now I must let the river run.

ELLA:
The papers were fixed up, I had a permit to travel and a permit to arrive in Palestine. I was ready to leave Paris.

Roma was engaged! I was leaving in July and she was getting married in November, so I would arrive before the wedding. Her future husband, Shlomo, worked for his father. They had a business in Shenkin Street, Tel Aviv, where they were manufacturing duvets. Do you know what a duvet is? You don't get them here. *Ella is quick to disabuse me of my understanding of the word.* Here you get duvets filled with artificial fibres. What *they* made were proper silk duvets filled with pure down. They had big wooden stands and a long table, and the machine used to go along stitching, this way and that way, to make squares. I'll show you one of my duvets just now. *I comment that I'm sure I have a down duvet just like the ones she is describing. Once again, she puts me in my place.* No, I can tell you, it's not like the ones I have!

So anyway, Roma wrote to me before I left. She asked: 'If you can bring with you a sewing machine from Paris, it would be a wonderful gift.' Well, I had the money, so I instructed the neighbours, Mr and Mrs David – the people who owned the flat with the clattering sewing machines, where the Warmans lived. I told them: 'I'm going to Palestine and I want to buy a sewing machine. Send me a good one.'

A machine was sent to Palestine, but it never arrived! I sent a fridge too, you know; Roma wanted a small one for her father. Owning a fridge back then was like owning a Mercedes-Benz. For love or money I can't remember how I sent them. Roma gave me the address in Tel Aviv but they never arrived. I looked today at letters that I sent to claim for them, one in French and one in Hebrew, but nothing came of it. I paid good money but I came with bare hands.

Remember I had permission to travel to Palestine as Rywka Rothstein.

The Agudas Yisroel office fixed it all up, they knew what to do. I didn't have a proper passport; it was just a travel document to get through borders – I still have one page from it. And I even put on glasses and tried to change my appearance a little so I wouldn't look as old, I would look more like my niece whose name I took over.

I went on my own to Marseille and boarded the ship. I don't remember the name of the boat I travelled on, though everybody asks me.

On the boat I met two or three young Israelis who had been studying in Switzerland and they were going back home after their studies. They were not Ashkenazi Jews, they were Sephardi Jews from Persia. I was not used to everybody mixing freely. Nowadays there is a wonderful melange in Israel: Ashkenazi, Sephardic, Yemenite... Jews of all types and colours living together. But back then, it was totally strange to me.

I remember arriving in Palestine, or *Eretz Yisrael* as we preferred to call it – even before the state of Israel was established. The idea of coming to Israel was always a dream of the Agudas Yisroel group. This is of course different from the Bundists[120], who were against Zionism. The Agudas Yisroel were young people who wanted to eventually get to Palestine to form *kibbutzim*[121].

So now, here I was, about to reach the Land of Israel.

We arrived at the port in Haifa. There were Arabs working at the border offices. Very, very strict. 'Have you got anything to declare?' I said no and kept walking. I thought I was finished with customs, so I started fiddling in my case. I had brought silk stockings with me for Roma but that was not allowed. Somebody saw me fiddling and they opened up my suitcase. They found the stockings and I had to pay a fine for bringing them in – I suppose because they were new items. I had no money to pay a fine! Roma and her father were waiting for me; I had to leave my case and go out through the border to ask Samuel for money to pay the fine. It was a very stupid thing I did.

At first, I stayed with Roma and her father. They were living in a small flat. On Friday nights we'd sit on the little balcony, and I'd ask them to sing the *zemirot* and remind me...

I was so happy because I was with Roma. I remember watching

---

120 Bundism was a secular Jewish socialist movement, popular within Polish Jewry and active in the struggle against Nazism but opposed to Zionism and immigration to Palestine.

121 Collective, voluntary communities in Israel, traditionally agriculturally based.

Palestine

my brother-in-law walking to shul and thinking that it was such a beautiful thing to see – walking freely to shul. But life in Palestine in 1947 was a struggle. Samuel was a reporter at one of the Hebrew papers and he hardly made a living. We cooked very basic meals on the tiny stove that he had and made do with very little. Still, I thought life was beautiful.

I had no idea what I would do once I got to Palestine. I had taken Hebrew at school so I knew a little bit, but only a little. There was one boy, Mulka, who used to take me out sometimes to have coffee in a tea-room or a restaurant. He was trying to teach me Hebrew, bit by bit. I've even got a silver cigarette container with my name Hela in Hebrew letters – *hey lamed hey*[122]. Everybody smoked so I also smoked sometimes, like when we'd sit and talk, drinking coffee, smoking a cigarette. This boy Mulka used to come and fetch me from Roma's flat at Hadar Am *moshav*[123]. By the way, we never kissed; it was just a friendship.

Across the road from Roma's flat was a grocery shop. The owners were always outside, watching people come and go. They told Shlomo, Roma's future husband, that I must watch out for Mulka. They said, 'This man that keeps on coming to fetch your aunt belongs to the Underground and the English are looking for him; just tell your aunt about it. He belongs to the Stern Gang!'[124] Well he never told me anything of the sort and to me he was so kind and nice, a lovely boy.

I tried to get a job; somebody recommended me to a business similar to what we had back home, with textiles. I spoke Yiddish well and I remember standing behind the counter on a business street in Tel Aviv, trying to make myself understood. I was trying to become an Israeli.

---

122 Referring to the 5th, 12th and 5th letters of the Hebrew alphabet.
123 A cooperative agricultural community of individual farms in Israel.
124 A Zionist paramilitary organisation in Mandatory Palestine. Their aim was to evict the British authorities by use of force and by allowing unrestricted immigration of Jews to support the formation of a Jewish state.

Most of my time was taken up with Roma's wedding preparations and meeting people through Roma's father. He had made a life for himself and he was ready to remarry, but he did not want to get married before a daughter that is of eligible age. So he arranged a *shidduch*[125] for Roma.

I was still in Paris when Shlomo and Roma met and she told me that when she met him the first time he had a car already – to have a car in those days was a big achievement; he clearly wasn't *schnorrer*[126]. And he brought his father with him – I don't know if it was their first or second meeting – so he was sitting there in the back seat! The groom told Roma that he had lost his mother not long before so he couldn't leave his father at home alone. His siblings were already married, he was the youngest, and Roma's father told her: 'He's going to be a good husband because he's a good son.'

He was right. They were married 60 or 70 years I think. They were wonderful, the two of them. I have never come across such a happy marriage. I never found them fighting or getting cross with each other. If he ever made decisions that were not so smart, Roma never picked him out. He was very devoted to her, and she to him. He worked for his father in that duvet business. Years later, when they left for America, he worked this trade in a factory and eventually opened his own business and bought the building. They built a house, where they lived for many years – I called it the White House. It was beautiful. So they did very well and were very comfortable. But back in Palestine in 1947, we were not yet comfortable. I told you that I even wrote to my old boss, Mr Z, to help me.

That reminds me: during the first part of the war, some wealthy and powerful Jews managed to get out of Poland. Quite a few important rabbis were saved, such as the Gerrer Rebbe who had the biggest following of Chassidim, and the Amshinover Rebbe who was taken to Shanghai with his whole family.

Now remember my brother Froim's wife came from a little town

---

125 Yiddish for 'love match', essentially an arranged marriage.
126 Yiddish for 'beggar' (someone who leeches off others) or 'stingy'.

next to Lodz. Her family manufactured textiles – very wealthy people – and one of her uncles, a Shapiro, was one of those whisked out of Poland. He came from Lodz ghetto to Warsaw and, even though I wasn't supposed to know exactly what was happening, I must tell you what transpired.

This uncle told Froim that they were going to get him out – he must have paid a lot. So my brother gave him money and wrote a note that he must buy him land in Palestine. Of course Froim and his family were murdered in the Holocaust.

Now when I arrived in Palestine from Paris, my brother-in-law found this uncle Shapiro in Jerusalem, and I went with Shmuel and Roma to present myself. I told him I was Froim Frank's sister and asked where he'd bought the land that my brother gave him money for. 'I don't remember,' he said. I asked again but it was no use; there was no land. He then gave me some money to get rid of me and made me sign that I had no claim against him. I've only just remembered this! I never saw him again, but I do know that I needed every penny, and this was at least something.

In November of that year, Roma got married and I moved to living quarters for refugees. It was a big hall with iron beds on each side for the girls, quite a lot of them. Then after Roma got married, I used to stay sometimes at her home. It was from this flat that Mulka fetched me on the 31st of December 1947 to go to an Old Year's Eve dance with another couple – a South African man who was taking out an Israeli girl, a friend of Mulka's. We met them at Club Eden.

There weren't many people there, a few men sitting at the bar and drinking, music coming from the ceiling, one or two couples dancing. We danced too, and we changed partners: I was dancing with Mulka and then with the South African boy, and the Israeli girl was dancing with Mulka.

We were sitting at the bar having drinks and suddenly the men at the bar announced that a British officer had been shot at the Park Hotel. And this South African man said, 'I am staying at the Park Hotel!'

It was already getting very late and I said to him, 'You shouldn't go back to the hotel because it must be dangerous now!' Remember Palestine was under British control still. He ordered a taxi and said he would drop each one of us off. When he dropped me in Hadar Am, at Roma's place, he said, straight out: 'May I see you tomorrow? Can I come and fetch you in the morning?'

And I said, 'All right, be my guest!'

After that, he came at nine o'clock every morning to collect me, and he brought me back in the evening. For twelve days. His name was Isaac Blumenthal.

Where Isaac stayed was quite central, the Park Hotel – it was the only decent hotel and quite expensive. We used to walk and talk from morning 'til night, up and down Allenby Street and along the beachfront, which was still sandy back then. He couldn't speak Polish and I couldn't speak fluent English. But with my bits of broken English and his bits of Yiddish, we understood each other. He mainly used to ask me about shares, if I knew anything about the stock market. He kept referring to it as the 'stock exchange' and I had no such phrase in my vocabulary. To me, in Polish, it was *berze*. And in fact, I knew quite a bit about *berze*! You remember I bought my own ticket to Froim's wedding? Well, when they got married, he left our home and went to join his wife's family. Now these wealthy people were playing on the *berze*, so my brother did the same and in no time he lost a lot of money. He used to write to us saying it's up or the next time he says it's down. My parents gave a dowry and her father also gave a dowry; so together they had quite a bit. When he was losing so much, my father said, 'Come back,' and they did, with whatever he managed to save. They stayed with us in that big flat with one baby. I can still see her standing washing the napkins.

Anyway, this is what I knew about the stock exchange, as Isaac called it.

He even took me to his sisters! He had five sisters in Israel, in Palestine. One of them was living in Tel Aviv, one in Petah Tikva, one outside Petah Tikva, one in a *moshav*, and one who had been in hospital for some time. I suppose he wanted to hear what they thought about me. It looked like he wanted me to become his wife.

'But what about the girl that you brought to the Old Year's Eve party?' I asked.

'You know,' he said, 'Every time I took her out, she wanted me to take her back by taxi. But you! You don't want that. You say, "let's take a bus!"' That's me. I was really tight. I still am.

He fetched me at nine o'clock for those twelve days – and on the thirteenth day, we were married.

I got married as Rywka Rothstein. Do you know that I still live under this name? My passport says Rywka Rothstein, born in 1927.

Roma always called me Hela. But when I met my husband and told him my name was Hela, he said:, 'In South Africa there isn't such a name as Hela. We're going to call you Ella.' And that was that.

You know, his family advised him not to marry a girl from the concentration camps. Nowadays, we survivors are quite sought-after. Back then, I wouldn't say we were scum but we were poor, and certainly not sought-after; we were struggling to become normal people. He knew I had survived the Holocaust – I still had my number tattooed on my arm – but we did not speak about it.

I asked Roma: 'Can I marry him and go to Africa?' What did I know? I didn't say *South* Africa – just Africa. 'Will you allow me?' I asked her. Since her birth, we had been together except for the year or so when I was in Paris and she was already in Palestine. Our families were so close. As I've said, she wasn't like my niece, she was like my sister. I had nobody else to ask. 'Can we part now, after we've been together all our lives and now reunited?'

Roma was married already. Her father wanted to remarry too. He had lost his wife, my sister Golda, yet he was still a young man and a religious man needs a wife. Now that his daughter was married, he could remarry. He actually landed up going to New York and marrying the daughter of a Chernobyl *rebbe*. He continued writing – in Yiddish and Hebrew, not in English – and became a famous author and journalist.

So Roma says, 'How can I say no? I am married myself. I have no right to refuse.'

Roma had only met Isaac once, that Friday night for Shabbat dinner when she served him the head of the fish! The next time was at the wedding.

On the 13th of January 1948, after thirteen days of walking up and down the beachfront, we were married under the *chuppah*.

I didn't have time to buy a new dress or even a little white suit. The wedding was arranged so quickly that I just wore a dress I had brought with me from Paris, a white, calf-length dress with a print on it. It was good enough. And they made me go to a hairdresser to do my hair – it was made curly and terrible. I never used to go to the hairdresser! Too terrible.

We got married on the flat roof of a building in a suburb of Tel Aviv called *shchunat*[127] Montefiore, where one of Isaac's sisters lived. Roma's husband's family was very close to the Frankel family and Shlomo asked Rabbi Yitzchak Yedidya Frankel, the rabbi of a small district, to marry us. Roma and Shlomo used to go sometimes on a Saturday afternoon to Rabbi Frankel's home to visit for Shabbos, and I would go with them. He had six or seven children and we would all be together for those afternoons. The rabbi married us as a favour to his friend.

Rabbi Frankel went on to become the chief rabbi of Tel Aviv-Jaffa. And one of his daughters, Chaya Ita, with whom I spent time on those Shabbos afternoons – married Yisrael Meir Lau, one of the youngest survivors of the Buchenwald concentration camp who became the Ashkenazi chief rabbi of Israel. So I was married by a chief rabbi who was the father-in-law of *the* chief rabbi. Isn't that amazing?

So on that rooftop in Montefiore, I walked around my husband seven times, with my brother-in-law Samuel making the prayers right next to Rabbi Frankel. He had a big *mitzvah* in this, Roma's father.

---

127 Hebrew for 'neighbourhood'.

Someone took a film and I kept it with me for many years afterwards; I believe that one of my children eventually made something out of it. You can see me dancing with my husband in my white printed dress, terrible curly hair, and a big plaster on my arm where I covered up my number tattoo. Up until then, we had walked freely with our numbers, we didn't cover them. But I wanted to keep Auschwitz hidden on my wedding day.

We spent our wedding night at a hotel in a very small room where the beds were squashed against the wall, more like a sofa bed actually. The day after the wedding, my husband went to Rabbi Frankel to get the *ketubah* – the Jewish marriage certificate. In fact, he got two. One said that the bride was 'born Rywka Rothstein' just like my passport, and the other one said 'born Nechama Frank' in case I needed it, because I was going to South Africa. This second one had exactly my father's name – that I was Nechama, daughter of Naftali haKohen; that's the one that I consider the proper Jewish one.

The next day, my new husband left for South Africa. I could not go with him because I still had to have inoculations and needed a vaccination certificate to travel. But Isaac fixed up the flights – I took Swiss Air about two weeks after he left.

The security situation in Palestine at the time was terrible. When I arrived in July 1947 it was not so bad, but soon afterwards there were riots and the Arabs were hiding in the mountains along the road to Jerusalem and they were shooting at travellers. When we went to Jerusalem to get my passport at the British consulate, we had to go in convoy, in an armoured car. We had shooters defending us through the windows.

I even remember being stuck in Jaffa one night, not being able to get back to Roma's place or my place because the Arabs were shooting and we were under siege. That was the end of 1947. Nevertheless, I still loved Palestine and felt at home there. I never thought I would leave; I thought I'll be like Roma – meet somebody and live there. I didn't know that I would meet a South African and land up in Africa! And we didn't know yet that *Eretz Yisrael* would become independent – that all happened a few months after I got married. I had been in Palestine for six months, and married for only two weeks, when I said goodbye to Roma once again.

When it came time for me to depart, I couldn't get to the airport. I had to spend one night in an empty room along the way because of the firing; I could only leave in the morning at dawn when the shooting subsided.

Roma and her husband saw me off. They took me to an open space where a small plane then took me to the airport. It was five sterling to travel from Tel Aviv to the airport – very expensive.

This was my first time on an airplane! I travelled for two days, two nights – the plane didn't fly at night. The first night I slept in Khartoum and the second in Nairobi – we had those beds with mosquito net curtains around us.

I made friends on board. I was sitting in the front row with a very smart woman named Silla Eveleigh, wearing a beautiful hat with a bird or something on it. She was an Israeli girl who had married a non-Jewish British soldier. They lived in Bryanston, Johannesburg (no Jews lived in Bryanston then!) and she was coming back from visiting her mother in Palestine. In Nairobi she put through a phone call to her husband; I was sitting next to her and was amazed to hear her fluent English – she spoke so nicely with him. I also telephoned my husband, but of course I couldn't converse with him the way Silla could. It would be a little while before I could speak English well; first I had to start my new life.

Chapter 13

Johannesburg

Interviewing Ella over the weeks is like watching the images of her life story develop in a photographer's darkroom. Slowly, her black-and-white narrative morphs to sepia and then starts to take on the faded hues of modern life. It is of course fitting that history, especially Holocaust history, is devoid of colour, or that black and white are, technically, not even colours at all. When we picture Holocaust scenes, we imagine them as we have only ever seen them depicted in early photography or cinematography – that is to say, in black and white. I often wonder how Ella views her own history in her mind's eye. Life is lived in colour; is it remembered in colour, even if not portrayed that way due to the limits of the technology of the time? Steven Spielberg famously played on this concept in the movie Schindler's List*; a Jewish girl's red coat, the movie's most poignant symbol, is the only colour object in an otherwise entirely monochromatic film. In this case, it is the colour that is the emphatic literary device. But lived experience is in colour – not muted by time or technology but with all the brightness of the full spectrum. And as we move through Ella's life story, I find that my personal red-coat moments are the ones I can touch, more than envisage. Like today.*

I arrive expecting to continue our discussion about moving from Palestine to South Africa but instead I am greeted by a highly animated Ella who has just rediscovered one of her own red-coat relics. 'Look!' she cries, as soon as I walk through the door. 'It's an actual piece of the Haggadah[128]. *A real piece of the book. I may have hidden it and kept it with me as a lucky charm.'* I notice that she uses the word 'may' and I probe further. *'I don't remember where I got it – maybe I found it in the sauna when we were changing – you know when we had showers or when they chased us for delousing. It could have been that I saw it lying and I couldn't believe it and I kept it with me always. I was just lucky that they never found it on me.'*

The story of Ella saving a piece of Hebrew text rings a bell and I check back. Some time ago she talked about a snippet of 'parchment' with Hebrew writing that a Greek girl gave her. While recounting the memory, she could clearly see the paper in her mind's eye and suggested that it came from a siddur or even a mezuzah. But that was before she found it among her papers. Now that she holds it in her hands, she sees the words 'Ki lo naeh ki lo yaeh . . .' – a distinct melody sung at the end of the Passover meal and most certainly from the Passover text, the Haggadah. *'I put this here among the papers myself, this was saved from the camps. I must have kept it on my person because there was nowhere else to keep it. Isn't it wonderful to see this artefact? It's the real thing.'*

That Ella is finding this relic only now reinforces just how recently she broke her understandable silence about her Holocaust past and began speaking publicly; she famously began doing so only in her 80s and she is now in her late 90s. But this red-coat moment means even more: that she has discovered this relic now means she must not have combed her personal archive of keepsakes either, or at least not thoroughly. The fervour with which she has been pulling out articles, journals and photographs over the course of our interviews has grown with every visit, and I am only now coming to understand just how deeply her Holocaust history is buried.

Ella's excitement is almost as tangible as the paper itself – further proof, as if she needed any, that she was there, then. And that she is here, now.

---

128 The Jewish text which outlines the order and prayers of the Passover meal and tells the story of the exodus from Egypt.

ELLA:

South Africa was Africa to me – I knew nothing about the country; I didn't even know where it was located, that it was right down at the bottom of the continent.

My husband had five sisters in Palestine and two brothers in South Africa. His plan was to return to South Africa and work for his brothers.

At the time of our marriage, he must have told his family that he was coming back from Israel with a bride. They expected me to be on the plane with him, so they arranged an enormous family dinner at his brother's house in 6th Avenue, Lower Houghton – a beautiful house with a swimming pool. When Isaac got off the plane without me, they couldn't believe it! He came alone to the dinner – no, not a dinner, a banquet! They couldn't cancel or change it since everything was prepared. So when I arrived some weeks later, it must have been an anticlimax.

I landed at the Palmietfontein Airport. I saw a thin figure waiting – my husband was there to fetch me. He had come alone in a big Buick car and we went straight to 77 Essenby House, Jeppe Street, in central Johannesburg. Downstairs was a well-known furniture store called Shepherd & Barker, right near the post office. The apartment itself was a one-room flat on the seventh floor. There was an entrance hall, kitchen, bathroom and a settee, which we used to open up at night. In the corner there was a radio and a carpet – that very carpet *[Ella points]* that is still lying here today. This was my husband's flat, and my new home.

The first thing my husband did was arrange an elocution teacher for me – Mrs Lutrin. It was already set up, so the morning after I arrived, as he left to go to work, he just gave me some money and said, 'You will walk down and get the tram, not to the left but to the right as you come down Eloff Street. Wait at the stop around the corner for the B2 to arrive. When you pay for your fare, you will ask the conductor to let you off at Francis Street in Yeoville.' He gave me a piece of paper that said Mrs Lutrin, Francis Street, and the number of the house. And off he went.

It sounds daunting but it wasn't very difficult for me because I had lived in Paris and found my way around easily. So there was no problem getting around Johannesburg. I took the tram, got off and found the house. Mrs Lutrin worked with me for many lessons – I don't remember exactly how many times a week. And I was improving but she had one problem: she couldn't get me to say the long 'o' sound. In Polish, there is no sound like the 'o' in 'nose'; the sound is shorter, more open-mouthed – like the o in 'bore' or 'boy'. Like in Hebrew. Or Yiddish. Eventually she said: 'I'm going to give you some homework, that's the only way to do it because we're trying so hard every time. You're going to sit down at home, hold a mirror in front of you and repeat what I'm giving you.' And so I did. *Ella enunciates in a slow, exaggerated fashion, which makes me giggle*:

Oh. No. Rose. Don't. Go. Home. Alone. *We both laugh.*

And again: Oh. No. Rose. Don't. Go. Home. Alone.

And it helped! It was brilliant! I practised in front of the mirror over and over: Oh. No. Rose . . .

Bit by bit, my English improved and I continued with Mrs Lutrin until my English was bearable, until I understood. I do still have an accent and sometimes still make the Polish 'o' sound instead of 'oh'. But in general I think my English is better than other Polish-speaking people – at least a little. And the way I speak makes me recognisable. People often tell me: 'Oh, Mrs Blumenthal – I recognise you by your accent.' *Ella chuckles again*: Oh. No. Rose . . . people become hysterical with laughter when they hear this; my daughter Evy loves this story.

When I came here, my husband was not religious at all, but I was. Since I was now a married woman, one of the first things I looked for was a *mikvah*.[129] Somebody told me there was one in Fox Street. When I got there, there wasn't a soul inside; the door wouldn't even close properly. I went once but I was too afraid to go back. Luckily,

---

[129] In Orthodox Judaism, the laws of family purity require married women to immerse in the *mikvah* after menstruation as one step in the cycle of reunion and separation between husband and wife.

not long afterwards, they built a *mikvah* in Yeoville – the first decent *mikvah* in Johannesburg.

My husband's family decided that I should have my number tattoo removed. 'You can't walk around with it,' they said. 'You must forget about the Holocaust, about your life before – the best thing would be to take out the reminder.' So Dr Jack Penn, an amazing plastic surgeon, removed it. Three times he had to go back and fix it because the keloids kept forming. I was walking around with a sling for quite a long time because it just didn't want to heal.

I arrived in Johannesburg in early February 1948 and this was now April or May of that year. Dr Penn removed the tattoo but he wouldn't accept money from me. I know I was the first person he saw with a number.

As a matter of fact, Dr Penn was one of the first who volunteered in Israel when the state was born in May 1948. There were a lot of young people, doctors, military, who went to fight and help; he was one. A wonderful man.[130]

How did I feel about having my number taken out? I tell you, I was so dependent on my husband's family, I wasn't myself. But most of the Auschwitz survivors who lived here in South Africa had the number removed. Roma and others who stayed in Israel or the United States, they left them. But here in this country . . . I don't know why but I couldn't have gone through life here with the number.

As a matter of fact, until I had the number taken out I used to wear a plaster because people didn't understand! Even our own Jewish people didn't realise what a tragedy it was, that they lost their families in Lithuania, Latvia, Russia or Poland. Nobody realised the enormity. In the beginning, not even those of us living in Europe

---

130 Dr Penn is a notable character. Born in Cape Town and educated in Johannesburg, he became a pioneer of plastic surgery and a talented sculptor and writer. He served in London during the Battle of Britain and helped to initiate plastic surgery in countries such as Israel, Zimbabwe, Kenya and Japan (where he assisted victims of Hiroshima and Nagasaki). His sculptures can be seen in South Africa, England and Europe.

knew what was happening. I didn't even know that I was in Germany – that Bergen-Belsen was in Germany! By the time we were loaded onto cattle trucks, we didn't care where we were going. So if we, who lived through it, did not realise the extent of the Holocaust, how much less so the people living overseas? It was only much, much later that people came to understand what happened to us. During the war itself, they didn't realise what was going on, or they didn't want to know, or maybe they didn't comprehend. From what I understand now, a man named Jan Karski – a Polish Resistance fighter and diplomat during the war – tried to report on what was happening in Poland and the death camps, but President Roosevelt of the United States didn't want to listen to him. The British neither. I suppose they were busy fighting a war, they couldn't think of the Jews that are being killed en masse.

All I know is that when I came to South Africa, people didn't know much about the Holocaust; it wasn't yet put on paper and people didn't understand the full extent of the tragedy. I lived in Johannesburg for 30 years, and for most of those, nobody even knew that I was a survivor. I never spoke about it.

My husband knew, of course. I told him before we married, and you remember that his family told him not to marry a girl from the concentration camps. My husband never wanted to hear my story. He was devastated if I ever opened my mouth about it. Even years later, when we would meet survivors, I didn't speak about my experience.

I think for me, and perhaps survivors or immigrant Jews in general at that time, it was important to blend in to our surroundings – not to make a big noise or a splash, not to be noticed by authorities.

Shortly after my arrival in South Africa in 1948, the government changed. The Nationalist Party won, and we got a terrible fright – my husband and myself and other Jews. My husband knew about the Greyshirts[131] and we were worried. This was soon after Israel became

---

[131] Greyshirts refers to the South African Gentile National Socialist Movement, a South African Nazi movement during the 1930s and 1940s.

an independent state, and we thought about returning there. We started to learn Hebrew – I've still got the little booklet – and we sent money away to a bank in Israel. You know that we never got a cent out of that account! The bank went under or the money was lost, but we never got it back.

I just can't remember why we decided to stay on here, but we remained. We could see that you've got to just fall in with the new government. We were afraid, but they didn't touch us Jews in those first few years, or even afterwards really. Jews carried on, some even prospered; many did fight against the regime because we understood what it is like to be persecuted. My family chose to go with the flow, not to stand out. And look how long it took for the government to change. It wasn't until 1994 that things changed, thanks to Nelson Mandela. He was a great man, strongly supported by Jews. As a young lawyer, he worked for a Jewish firm and he showed, while he was president, that he wasn't against us. He didn't pass any laws that would diminish us, that would make us feel that we Jews are different to other Africans. But anyway, that was a long way off still. Until then, we just kept our heads down and worked hard.

My husband Isaac's two brothers were very wealthy and they brought him to this country when he was a little boy. When he volunteered for the Israeli army, they were so proud; it was a big honour to have somebody in the army fighting the Germans. When he came back, he joined them in their business.

They owned a big dress factory called Johannesburg Dress – 187 Pritchard Street. The five-storey building is still there now. As for where they lived, it's still a fancy suburb: one lived in 6th Avenue, corner 4th Street, Lower Houghton, the other one subsequently lived in number 52 2nd Avenue, opposite the golf course in Lower Houghton.

The first brother, Jedidiah, was a well-known Zionist, chairman of the Revisionist Party and editor of their paper, the *Jewish Herald*. Israel was his life. We even have a picture that Menachem Begin offered him at one birthday: a big photo of Begin with the inscription 'To my dear friend and mentor'.

The second brother, Adolf, was quite a character. He loved women and whiskey. He was married to his third wife by the time I arrived – a beautiful woman from Berlin. They built a billiard room and a cinema next to their very elegant house; when there was a dinner party, my sister-in-law had a bell by her feet, under the carpet, to ring for the staff to come in.

Very often on a Sunday we used to go to my eldest brother-in-law for tea parties and we'd see lots of big shots: the Cohens from OK Bazaars and the Herbers from Greatermans, Rabbi Rabinowitz, the chief rabbi of Johannesburg . . . My sister-in-law was always entertaining and she was a wonderful cook – or – she had a wonderful cook. I remember those parties and seeing all these women with diamonds, Mrs Cohen, Mrs Herber, all those *machas*[132]. And there I was, the poor sister-in-law, wearing a white blouse with a black skirt, sitting quietly. Nobody spoke to me, nobody took notice of me [*laughs*]. And my husband was the quiet type, not a big talker.

Isaac's family was originally from Libau in Latvia. The father and two older brothers came to Durban in the 1920s and brought my husband over when he was 13 years old. He barely had any schooling. The mother and five sisters went to Palestine so when Isaac was in the army during the war and was stationed in Alexandria, he used to go from Egypt to Palestine to visit. My mother-in-law, whom I didn't know, passed away in Palestine and is buried in Nahalat Yitzhak Cemetery, outside Tel Aviv. Isaac's eldest sister is also buried there; she passed away after we were married. I go to the graves every time I am in Israel, to put a stone. This is one of the oldest cemeteries. I wanted to be buried there, my husband did too, but you can't get a place. It's packed, packed, packed. I once even tried to ask about buying a plot – they quoted me some hundreds of thousands of dollars, so I left it.

My father-in-law died while travelling by boat between Durban

---

132 Yiddish for 'big shots'.

and Latvia in 1926. I think he was going back to Europe to fetch his wife or the children when he got ill. They took him off in Belgium and he passed away in the hospital there. The queen of Belgium did not allow Jews to be buried in that country, so they used to bury them across the border, in Holland. I've visited that cemetery; my husband and I had the stone redone. There was a Jewish stonemason who helped us; his wife would pick us up from the hotel in Belgium and take us to visit the grave because their workshop was across the road from the cemetery. That's how I know the year he died – 1926 – because it is on the stone.

So I did not meet either of my parents-in-law.

My first child was born just over a year after I came to South Africa. I arrived the 9th of February and he was born the following year, in April 1949. We called him Norman Julius, after my father Naftali and my husband's father Julius – in Hebrew, Naftali Yehudah. He was a beautiful child. And it was a miracle that I should survive to bring a child into the world: a new soul. I had looked in the face of death so often, yet now I was looking in the face of my own newborn baby, safe from harm. It was a miracle.

When I was expecting, we realised we couldn't stay in that little bachelor flat, so we advertised to exchange the flat for a bigger one. We had a reply from someone in Broad Windsor, corner Quartz and Plein Streets. I could see Joubert Park from my window. It was a beautiful flat and we ordered curtains right away. I got beautiful furniture similar to my sister-in-law's in Lower Houghton: a dining room suite which today would have been an antique worth thousands – if only I hadn't had the auctioneers take it away when I was moving to Cape Town years later – and a very nice bedroom suite which lasted me until I came to Cape Town.

Dr Rachel Getz was the doctor who confined me. I had no problems in the pregnancy, I had a normal birth without any stitches or any problems. Norman was born in a private nursing home and the *bris*[133]

---

[133] Ritual circumcision of Jewish male babies, usually at eight days old.

was in the building where we lived, in a special room on the ground floor. I had no family, so the people who came were my husband's family and their business acquaintances.

The first day I brought the baby home I had a nurse who came with me, but at five o'clock she left and my husband had people coming for a poker game that night. I managed to get up and prepare tea and biscuits. But I had big problems because the nurse didn't show me how to look after the baby and when he cried, I did not know how to change him or what to do! Luckily I was breastfeeding him. I managed through the night and she came the next morning. Eventually I got used to it.

My second one arrived 22 months later.

I remember calling the doctor to say I've got pain and she asked my husband to take me to the same nursing home where I had Norman. They had special rooms for women in labour, tiny little rooms where you could hardly move; there was just a bed. They kept me the whole night and the pains disappeared, so they phoned Isaac to take me home. False labour. And exactly a week later, he was born: 22 February 1951. That's Alvin – in Hebrew, Elchanan. I was now the mother of two beautiful sons.

* * *

During the war years, my brothers-in-law had built a successful business. They had an enormous factory – five storeys – and they employed a lot of people. There was limited supply of cloth during the war yet they somehow got hold of it and manufactured dresses. Their business, Johannesburg Dress, was a public company. When my husband came back from up north, he got shares in it. They also had retail businesses in Johannesburg, Springs and Benoni. When Isaac joined them in the business, he worked at the factory and was a sleeping partner in the shops. The main shop was the Johannesburg branch – I got a blouse there once – which Abe Donan ran with his wife, who was a relation of my husband's family. They eventually sold the big factory and bought a small underwear factory called Continental Lingerie, in Pritchard Street, just at the corner of End Street. My husband was also a partner in this.

At this time, my two boys were still small, around three, four years old. Unfortunately, things went wrong in the family business and my husband lost his position; his brothers sold this small factory too and Isaac did not have a job or a steady income. To support our family and preserve the money, I went to work.

I saw an advert in the paper for Harrows – a small department store owned by Jewish people – the Jacobson brothers. I went to see the managers – the one's name was Goldblatt or Goldstein, and the other one was Unterslak – and I told them I'd worked in Paris in big stores and that I knew a lot about clothing. My English wasn't so good yet and you could hear that I had an accent.

Goldblatt put me in as a sales lady.

It was not a big store like Edgars, so the ladies' outfitting was all together in the basement. An Afrikaans lady was in charge and I was one of the sales ladies under her. I had been working there for three weeks when the Afrikaans woman was fired and I became the manageress.

One day, one of the managers picked me out, saying quietly: 'You must be careful not to offend our customers, they are our bread and butter.' Apparently I was a bit offish. I imagine I was a bit offish to everyone!

There was a winding staircase up to the owners' offices. We used to meet on the steps and the one Mr Jacobson would say, 'Carry on your good work, carry on.' One day I had the nerve to knock on his door and ask to see him. I told him I had been offered another job with a bigger salary but that I didn't want to leave him.

'How much?' he asked.

I can't remember what I told him.

He responded: 'Don't worry, it's quite in order, you're not leaving us, you're getting a raise.' Of course there was no other job.

I stayed there for two or three years.

In this time, my husband was not working. He would come and fetch me with the car, or sometimes I took the tram. He helped me out a lot by looking after the kids, he used to take them to nursery school, or fetch them. And the whole time, we were on the lookout for a business to buy.

In *The Star* newspaper there was a column 'Business Opportunities'. I was the one who used to reply to them: 'I'm interested in your advertisement, please call me or write to this address.' One of them was for an old, established business called CD Lamb in Brakpan, 40 kilometres outside Johannesburg. The owner was a Scotsman – Mr Charles Dickson Lamb – an honest and straightforward man who had run this department store for twenty-odd years. It had a good name selling linen, materials, dresses, haberdashery, wool and ladies' hats made by an old English lady who was a milliner by trade. His clientele were mining families – the Afrikaans and English people from all around – and they could get dresses on appro, which he would have delivered to them by a man on a bicycle. The business ran on cash and on accounts – there was a big book listing all their clients – and Mr Lamb owned the whole building and employed about ten staff, including one who made tea and the one on the bicycle.

We made arrangements to go and see CD Lamb. We liked it very much but we weren't sure if buying it was the right thing to do. So we asked for advice. My brother-in-law was friendly with the Mincer family – Mr Mincer was mayor of Johannesburg and his brother-in-law was a Mr Shapiro, an auctioneer who we thought would have good advice. He came to see the store and Mr Lamb opened for us one Sunday, when the shop was otherwise closed. Mr Shapiro looked around, went behind the counters, and on the way home to Johannesburg, said to us: 'If you don't buy it, I buy it.' That was good enough for us.

So we packed up and moved to Brakpan. It was April 1956. Norman was 7 and Alvin was 5.

We took over CD Lamb and did well. Mr Lamb stayed on for about a month to help us; my husband worked with him to learn the ropes. There was a man in the office named Mr John who did the accounts and the banking, so I worked closely with him to learn about the financials; I remember he used to put a rubber thimble on his finger to count money. Of course we had a professional auditing company, Levitt Kirson, doing our books but there was also a lady named Maude Norman who helped with daily accounting, and she stayed on after we bought the business; she worked with us for many years.

After handing over the business and seeing it thrive, Mr Lamb left. I think he took a good holiday. Not very much later, he fell ill and passed away. We shut the shop and went to the church where we saw him lying in his coffin. Catholic he was.

I did a bit of everything in the business. Firstly, I did the buying, initially with my husband and then with one of my sons. The buying is the essence of the business – you need to have good stock to sell. Secondly, in the running of the business, I was supervising everything. There was a big staff and I was very strict with them; when they needed something like a loan or special time off, they waited until I was not around and asked my husband! And then of course there was debt collecting. We had a big, heavy book with all the customers' names, the amount that they bought for and when they paid. This ledger was the life of the business. It listed who had paid cash, or who put their purchases on account and owed us money. I'd say it was about 80 per cent buying on the book and 20 per cent cash, or maybe 70/30. I was the one who looked after that book. In other words, when people didn't pay, I was the one who went after them. I phoned, I drove around, I used to go knocking on doors and neighbours' doors, looking for customers. Once a dog bit me terribly! But I carried on. I had been through far worse.

Mr Lamb's wife was an Afrikaans teacher; she had taught all the time while her husband was running the business. She decided that her husband had given the business away too cheap when he sold to us. One day, after he died, she came into the shop. The staff all knew and respected her, and helped her out with a whole lot of small things she was asking for. After she left, we realised she had taken that big book with all the customers' information. She had asked to see it but had not given it back! Without it we couldn't carry on. Turns out she wanted more money. Can you believe? She would not release the ledger unless we paid her. And we had to! We simply could not run the business without that book!

We took over CD Lamb in 1956 and ran it for more than 30 years, during which time we changed the name to Lamb's. For the first year, we paid rent to Mr Lamb because he owned the building, but soon we negotiated to take that over too. So we now owned the property.

That lady who helped with the books, Maude Norman, was with us the whole time. I even have a newspaper clipping about her. *Here comes another red-coat moment as Ella pulls out the news clipping; her face lights up and she exclaims 'ooh, ooh' as she shows it to me and asks me to read it aloud:* 'Maude Norman is congratulated by Mr I Blumenthal and Mrs E Blumenthal on having completed 45 years' service with Lamb's in Brakpan.' *I too am amazed – at the length of service! One place of employment for 45 years: virtually unheard of these days. And it seems that Ella and Isaac gave Maude Norman a two-week holiday for her and her husband 'at a Durban hotel all expenses paid and travel by means of a luxury bus . . .' Isn't that wonderful? I'm so pleased I found it, I need it for my children!*

Maude Norman was with the business for 45 years and we owned it for 34 of those. We eventually sold it to Miladys in 1990. It was a discreet sale. When the buyers came in and looked at the book, they were amazed at the minimal amount of bad debt – I think it was only about 2 or 5 per cent. My husband pointed at me, that I was the one looking after the ledger and chasing after the money owing to us. That big book was very important!

My third child, also a son, was born in 1959. We named him Henry Errol – in Hebrew, Chaim Ephraim – named after my brothers Chaim (Heniek, the one who wasn't religious) and Ephraim (Froim, the eldest). By this time, I was full-time in business, from early in the morning until late at night. I even did some of the books at home once a month when we sent out the statements. So a few months after Henry was born, I got Maude West, who helped me with my children for years, until she died. Maude worked for my brother-in-law Adolf in 2nd Avenue for many years, brought up their daughter Cora. I managed to get her when Cora was big enough. She was the most wonderful woman, a devout Catholic who made the most beautiful bread-and-butter pudding, but otherwise couldn't cook. She used to get up early and switch on the stove plates so they would be warm to make a cup of tea for the milkman. She was like another mother to everybody – not just my children. All the maids in the area came to her for support; she even kept their money safe for them, and every week a truck would come from the bakery and she would get cakes for them all.

Henry was the first of my children to get a Jewish education. There was a beautiful shul in Brakpan, and we always had a rabbi and a roster to make a *minyan*[134], but no Jewish school. For primary school, my kids all attended the local school – Brenthurst Primary School – which was right next to our home. By the time Henry came to high school age, a Jewish school called Hillel had opened in Benoni, about 25 kilometres away, and we decided to send him there.

Although they did not all have a Jewish education, my children grew up in a traditional Jewish home and I was always observant. I feel that the home is more important than the school for a Jewish upbringing, although of course school helps. I mentioned that when I married Isaac, he was not religious. He was brought up mainly without parents, arrived in the country as a teenager and worked since then. So he did not know much. When I arrived, I went to OK Bazaars in Eloff Street and bought a few extra pieces of crockery and cutlery to separate meat and milk. Also a few separate things for Pesach. I lit candles, I made *yom tov* whenever possible. We used to go for Pesach and maybe other festivals to Isaac's eldest brother – it was always a

---

[134] The quorum of ten Jewish adults needed for certain religious obligations.

big dinner. The other brother was not religious at all. And slowly, slowly, my husband joined me.

We spoke English at home but I still sometimes spoke to Isaac in Yiddish and my children picked it up. Even now, when they speak to me on the phone, they put in a lot of Yiddish expressions, and I'm amazed at how much they know. If I'm with Evy and I don't want somebody to understand, I speak to her in Yiddish. I love talking Yiddish – I look for any opportunity. I don't want to forget; I don't want the children to forget. I don't know whether they can converse, but they're not lost in Yiddish. They know a lot of expressions and especially my songs that I sometimes sing.

Food is of course a big part of a Jewish home. There was a woman in Brakpan named Goldie Shapiro, who was from Lithuania. She was the most wonderful cook, unbelievable in fact, and she had these tiny little hands. She had a black man working for her for many years and he was her right-hand man. She used to buy a whole case of live chickens at the weekly market and keep them in her back yard; sometimes she used to buy for me too. She'd go off to the rabbi and he would *shecht*[135] them, and then the man who worked for her would pluck them.

I used to go and watch her cooking for Pesach. She made stuffed *teiglach*[136] and her *kneidlach*[137] also had a filling – she used to call them *neshomele*[138]. Just beautiful. She made jam from cherries, and different treats. And every time I came back from an overseas trip, there was always a cake waiting for me on the table – a beautiful round cake with raisins in it. You know, I couldn't make a cup of tea when I arrived in 1948! Even that I had to learn from the tea lady who worked for my husband. Whatever I know to cook, I learned from Goldie Shapiro, though I could never do what she did with her little hands.

---

135 Slaughter in the kosher manner.
136 Traditional Jewish pastries, boiled in syrup – sticky and sweet for holidays.
137 *Matzah* balls – dumplings traditionally used in chicken soup.
138 Yiddish: 'little soul' (diminutive of 'neshama' meaning 'soul').

Johannesburg

My daughter Evelyn was born in 1963, four years after Henry and fourteen years after my first-born, Norman. Evelyn's Hebrew name is Chava, after my late mother. The English translation of Chava is 'Eve', as we know her in the bible, or Evelyn. My daughter couldn't forgive me that I called her Evelyn *[laughs]*; I suppose she doesn't like the name. But we call her Evy for short.

Before I went into the nursing home with my fourth child, I called my two big boys (Henry, my third one, was still very young) and I pointed to the cabinet: 'Here, in the last drawer, is the robe for the *bris*.' It was the robe that all three boys had used. My sister-in-law, Jedidiah's wife, bought it as a gift for my first-born. I've still got it: a long, white, satin robe, almost like a nightie dress, with a white cap. My grandchildren wore it too, and I even used to lend it to people who wanted it because they said it was *mazeldik*[139]. So I showed them this robe and I said, 'When this baby is born, please God, you must bring it with you when your dad comes to the hospital.' After three boys, I was sure I was going to have a fourth.

It was a girl.

Roma was there when Evelyn was born, though of course it was not the first time she had been to visit. We moved to Brakpan in 1956 and as soon as we got settled and were on our feet, my husband and I brought Roma and her three children to South Africa. I remember waiting for her at the old airport, my two sons so excited. In those days, there was a big balcony at the airport where you could see the planes landing and we watched for them and called when they got off. It was precious time together.

She came again and we used to go to Israel to visit her too. And then, when I was expecting my fourth child, Roma came from Israel with her little daughter. We were longing for each other; we needed each other, although we also had our own families already.

So when Evy was born, Roma was there. With the boys I had natural births but with Evy I had to have a Caesar, with full anaesthetic. It was July, freezing cold, and I was like ice. The baby was born in the

---
139 Yiddish for something that will bring good fortune, a good luck charm.

middle of the night. Roma stole into the nursing home to stay with me but when they found her, they chased her out.

The next morning, she came in as a visitor and told me it was a girl. I was in terrible pain, terrible, but we were so elated – all of us! We were so happy! Roma commented that it was so wonderful to have a baby. So you know what I said? 'Why don't you have another child when you go back to America?' And she did. Just less than a year later, she had a boy, Rami, who is now an anaesthetist. He lived in New York with her after he qualified, but the other children are all in Israel. So then we both had four children.

With my first three, I always worked until the last minute – I almost had the baby on the shop floor! Except with Evy – I took off a little bit at the end because my legs were swollen. I never complained because I always felt fine. Not like nowadays! I don't know what's happened to me. This is sore, and that is sore, and this is sore. I actually should have had a knee replacement, but I never complained. And then all of a sudden, I was too old and it was too late to have a knee replacement.

Maybe it's swimming that kept me fit. You remember I told you that I used to love ice-skating and swimming in Warsaw? Winter was the ice-skating and summer was swimming on the enormous Wisla River on the Praga side of town, our side. There were the two wooden structures – one for men, one for women – with benches around, and a wooden covering, and sunlight pouring in, and steps to go into the fresh, beautiful water. I enjoyed it.

When they were growing up in Brakpan, my children realised that I loved swimming because I used to go to the public pool. My husband and I would take the children on a Sunday afternoon. Then they built a pool at the house and I swam every morning. We all loved it. I still do.

Evelyn was adored by her brothers. Apparently Norman even used to take her with him on dates when she was small! They loved her so much. This little girl growing up in a house with three brothers was a real tomboy – I even kept her hair very short. She played soccer with them and was always keeping up. I think she even played more soccer than Henry, who preferred the whistle; he had the whole outfit but he preferred to be the referee than to play.

Evy also went along to arrangements organised by Betar – the Revisionist Zionist youth movement. Betar was very active in those days, and because of my brother-in-law Jedidiah's position as chairman of the Revisionist Party and being involved with the Zionist movement, we became Revisionist by marriage *[chuckles]*. Betar used to organise things for the kids on a Sunday to try and bring them into the movement. The boys had their navy shirts and blue ties, went out, played soccer . . . Evy would do the same.

That little tomboy surprised us in many other ways too. At the end of each year, there was the final meeting at the Hillel School, like a prizegiving. Evy was always fine at school, never needed help with anything and she worked hard so she usually got a prize or two, and always tops in Afrikaans, even though we did not speak Afrikaans. Every year, I went to the prizegiving. Except in Evy's matric year. I was so tired of going every year for the same thing. But that final prizegiving, her name was called out continually. Prize after prize after prize. She did so well, and I wasn't there! I've never forgiven myself.

I've often heard about the drive of survivors, and the deeply religious, to 'replace the lives that Hitler stole', to repopulate the Jewish nation. I'm intrigued as to what it was like for Ella to have a girl after three boys, and whether Evelyn's arrival brought a sense of completion because of those she had lost.

It took me a long time to come to terms with having a daughter after bringing up three boys. And it wasn't because I have lost everybody. I was so busy in business that I didn't have time to think, to understand how I feel. It took months, maybe a year, to fully realise I've got a child that I've given my mother's name. It was wonderful.

As for my family planning . . . I never planned any of my children. It just happened.

I'm sorry I never had more.

הגדה של פסח

די ערשטי נאכט פון פסח זאגט מען דאס

וּבְכֵן וַיְהִי בַּחֲצִי הַלַּיְלָה:

אָז רוֹב נִסִּים הִפְלֵאתָ בַּלַּיְלָה. בְּרֹאשׁ אַשְׁמוּרוֹת זֶה הַלַּיְלָה. גֵּר צֶדֶק נִצַּחְתּוֹ כְּנֶחֱלַק לוֹ לַיְלָה. וַיְהִי בַּחֲצִי הַלַּיְלָה: דַּנְתָּ מֶלֶךְ גְּרָר בַּחֲלוֹם הַלַּיְלָה. הִפְחַדְתָּ אֲרַמִּי בְּאֶמֶשׁ לַיְלָה. וַיָּשַׂר יִשְׂרָאֵל לְמַלְאָךְ וַיּוּכַל לוֹ לַיְלָה: ויהי בחצי הלילה. זֶרַע בְּכוֹרֵי פַתְרוֹס מָחַצְתָּ בַּחֲצִי הַלַּיְלָה. חֵילָם לֹא מָצְאוּ בְּקוּמָם בַּלַּיְלָה. טִיסַת נְגִיד חֲרֹשֶׁת סִלִּיתָ בְּכוֹכְבֵי לַיְלָה: ויהי בחצי הלילה: יָעַץ מְחָרֵף לְנוֹפֵף אִוּוּי הוֹבַשְׁתָּ פְגָרָיו בַּלַּיְלָה. כָּרַע בֵּל וּמַצָּבוֹ בְּאִישׁוֹן לַיְלָה. לְאִישׁ חֲמוּדוֹת נִגְלָה רָז חֲזוֹת לַיְלָה: ויהי בחצי הלילה: מִשְׁתַּכֵּר בִּכְלֵי קֹדֶשׁ נֶהֱרַג בּוֹ בַּלַּיְלָה. נוֹשַׁע מִבּוֹר אֲרָיוֹת פּוֹתֵר בִּעֲתוּתֵי לַיְלָה. שִׂנְאָה נָטַר אֲגָגִי וְכָתַב סְפָרִים בַּלַּיְלָה: ויהי בחצי הלילה: עוֹרַרְתָּ נִצְחֲךָ עָלָיו בְּנֶדֶד שְׁנַת לַיְלָה. פּוּרָה תִדְרוֹךְ לְשׁוֹמֵר מַה מִלַּיְלָה. צָרַח כַּשּׁוֹמֵר וְשָׂח אָתָא בֹקֶר וְגַם לַיְלָה: ויהי בחצי הלילה: קָרֵב יוֹם אֲשֶׁר הוּא לֹא יוֹם וְלֹא לַיְלָה. רָם הוֹדַע כִּי לְךָ הַיּוֹם אַף לְךָ הַלַּיְלָה. שׁוֹמְרִים הַפְקֵד לְעִירְךָ כָּל הַיּוֹם וְכָל הַלַּיְלָה. תָּאִיר כְּאוֹר יוֹם חֶשְׁכַת לַיְלָה:

די אנדרי נאכט פון פסח זאגט מען דאס

וּבְכֵן וַאֲמַרְתֶּם זֶבַח פֶּסַח:

אֹמֶץ גְּבוּרוֹתֶיךָ הִפְלֵאתָ בַּפֶּסַח. בְּרֹאשׁ כָּל מוֹעֲדוֹת נִשֵּׂאתָ פֶּסַח. גִּלִּיתָ לְאֶזְרָחִי חֲצוֹת לֵיל פֶּסַח. וַאֲמַרְתֶּם זֶבַח פֶּסַח: דְּלָתָיו דָּפַקְתָּ כְּחֹם הַיּוֹם בַּפֶּסַח. הִסְעִיד נוֹצְצִים עֻגוֹת מַצּוֹת בַּפֶּסַח. וְאֶל הַבָּקָר רָץ זֵכֶר לְשׁוֹר עֵרֶךְ פֶּסַח: ואמרתם זבח פסח. זֹעֲמוּ סְדוֹמִים וְלוֹהֲטוּ בָּאֵשׁ בַּפֶּסַח: חֻלַּץ לוֹט מֵהֶם וּמַצּוֹת אָפָה בְּקֵץ פֶּסַח. טִאטֵאתָ אַדְמַת מוֹף וְנֹף בְּעָבְרְךָ בַּפֶּסַח

A page of the Haggadah that Ella saved from the camps.

Chapter 14

Cape Town

The act of writing Ella's story, something I only begin to tackle some three years after we conclude our interviews, feels equal parts privilege and duty, and my work mode vacillates between swift and sluggish.

As is always the case with my projects, I try to remain sensitive to the matter of boundaries, wanting to neither over-identify with my subject nor blunt myself to the enormity of their experience. But as I drag myself through Ella's war years, I find my writing life reflecting my mood, or vice versa: glacial in pace, leaden in tone. Perhaps I've lost perspective, become too immersed in our traumatic past; perhaps my professional objectives have simply been swamped by the pitch-black Nazi night.

And then . . . South Africa, and the goldene medine *blazing bright. As Ella's story moves out from the shadow of the war, it gathers pace; I find myself eager to work, productivity soaring with this phase of storytelling. As Ella talks about her new life in South Africa, the relative levity in her tone and content marks a shift in me too.*

It is so much easier to write that which is easier to hear.

ELLA:
The children grew up.

Norman was an exchange student in America for a year after school. When he came back, he had to go into the army because there was conscription in those days. He took it very badly. My husband and I visited him one Sunday; we sat on a blanket on the grass and

I could see it . . . Norman wasn't meant for the army. But there was no other way, he had to go. I couldn't keep him back like in the olden days. While growing up in Poland, I was told that when my brothers had to go to the army, they tried to lose weight to become very thin – if you were weak or injured, that was a way of getting out of the army. None of my brothers was in the army, so perhaps it worked. At least with my boys, they were not involved in any conflict; Alvin and Henry were both officers and I think they quite enjoyed it – Henry was based in Pretoria and I would fetch him on a Friday to come home for Shabbat.

I know what you're going to ask me: did I feel it was wrong at the time, to be in the army? But you know, we had to fit in. We could not go against the country's laws; we just wanted to live freely and go unnoticed.

After the army, Norman went to Wits University to study medicine. Alvin also went to Wits; he did law. While he was studying, he helped us in the business. All my children had to help in some way, but Alvin was especially good in business – so good, in fact, that after he was sworn in in Pretoria as an advocate, he decided not to practise law but to join us in the business. He made a lot of improvements to Lamb's and he really modernised it; from the time he joined, the business thrived. We managed to buy the property next door, which was Cuthberts, the shoe people, and Alvin expanded into a separate division of carpets and curtains; even the ladies' section became much bigger. By the time we sold the business, it was a big enterprise with lots of good, clean stock.

Henry went to Wits University too and became a chartered accountant. Evy studied medicine. They all stayed in a little flat, well it was more of a room, in Johannesburg, which we got for them to use during the week so they wouldn't have to travel every day from Brakpan. I would send food for them to keep in a little fridge there.

We later bought a much nicer flat in Berea, where Henry and then Evy lived while they were studying. Evy was working at Coronation Hospital. She wanted to do paediatrics, but she did not land up finishing that speciality.

Norman was working at the Johannesburg Hospital in obstetrics. He married Caron from Johannesburg and about a year later, Alvin married Debbi from Port Elizabeth. Alvin built a house in Benoni – Brakpan's smarter neighbour – and had three children while he was helping us with the business.

Henry married Fran in 1989 and they lived and worked in Johannesburg. That same year, Evy married Paul, a Capetonian; they lived for a few years in Johannesburg while he was doing his MBA, and then they moved to Cape Town.

Our family was starting to move further and further apart, but the big break came when Norman and Caron decided to emigrate to Sydney, Australia, in 1982 when their first child, Lorin, was a year or two old.

By that time, none of my children were living at home so I was already used to not having them around, even though they would still come home for Shabbat, stay over, and we'd walk to our Brakpan shul. Only Alvin lived nearby. But they had to grow up and away; they had to lead their own lives.

As we approached the 1990s, Isaac and I were also looking to slow down and sell the business.

Alvin was actually responsible for the sale; he got Miladys involved and did all the work. We were very happy with how it was done: quietly, no fuss. But not long after that, my husband took ill. We thought he'd had a heart attack but it was a stroke. He had to go to a convalescent home in Johannesburg but he was not getting better. Once we were home in Brakpan, I had nurses to help but mainly it was me taking care of him. Norman was in Sydney, Evy in Cape Town, Henry in Johannesburg. Alvin was the closest, but he and Debbi decided to emigrate too, also to Sydney. He did not want to leave me in Brakplan with a sick man, so he said to his siblings: 'Now we've got one sick person; if we leave her, we'll have two.' They decided we should move to Cape Town where Evy was living and working as a doctor.

I came down to Cape Town with Alvin for a weekend to have a look. We went to the care facility in Mouille Point – Good Hope Park – but they did not take people who were immobile and Isaac could hardly even walk with a stick. So they advised me to go to the Jewish place, Highlands House, where Paul had some connections. Since Isaac needed to go to frail care, I was not going to live with him, so we looked at apartments for me and settled on this one, this very one in Bordeaux Flats, where we're sitting right now.

Alvin and I returned to Brakpan and made the arrangements. We negotiated with the agent for the apartment in Sea Point – funnily enough, the previous owner was an ex-Benoni man. We sold the house in Brakpan, packed up, and moved to Cape Town. It was the 31st of May 1995.

Isaac was in Highlands House, I was in the apartment in Sea Point, and I used to go every day to spend time with him. He was not in a good state. He had a few more small strokes, Evy told me, but he could still talk. We told him he was coming to Cape Town to stay in a hotel but the next morning, when I arrived, he said: 'I know I'm in an old age home.' He hated the place, couldn't take the food and the people. I used to bring him food and leave it in the fridge but I don't know whether they gave it to him, even though he had someone caring for him from morning until night. He was very unhappy. I still feel bad that we put him there, but I would never have managed to look after him in this apartment; even with staff it would have been impossible.

I believe that it's wonderful these days; I know people who are so happy there. But my husband lasted only eight months in Highlands House.

It was a Sunday afternoon, the 4th of February 1996. Evy had come with me to visit Isaac. I remember she said: 'Let's go out for some tea, you'll come back here later.'

I said, 'No, I'll stay.'

I was there, sitting next to him while he was going. I called the sister. It was seven o'clock, I could see that he was going. He was so thin: he couldn't eat or wouldn't eat the food. I was there with him when he passed.

* * *

When the children were small, I used to sometimes wake up screaming from nightmares. The Nazis would take the children away from their parents, so I had to get up and check to see if my children were alright in the middle of the night. Terrible thoughts came to my mind and I'd wake screaming.

My husband got used to it.

He never wanted to know anything that had to do with the Holocaust, even if it touched me. But he supported me without speaking.

One day in our early Johannesburg years, I was walking in Eloff Street. CNA was on the corner, and OK Bazaars was nearby. Across the road, on the opposite sidewalk, I saw two women. I noticed the younger one and called across to her: 'I know you... You were in Auschwitz.'

'Yes,' she said.

'You speak Polish.'

'Yes,' she said, 'How do you know?'

'I just remember your face.'

I still grow cold when I think of this. How could I remember? There were thousands of us and she wasn't even in my block. She had blonde hair now yet no hair at all in Auschwitz. How had I recognised her?

We became so friendly. Danka was her name. She was staying with her sister who brought her out to South Africa. They lived in Yeoville; they were so good to me, always took me with them to Crystals in Doornfontein when they went shopping.

This Danka was the first Holocaust survivor encounter I had during our early days in South Africa. But apart from realising that we'd met in Auschwitz, we did not talk about the Holocaust at all.

I never spoke about it.

First of all, my husband did not want to hear about such things. He never even wanted me to apply for the *Wiedergutmachung*[140] from Germany; he said, 'I don't want their money.' We were working together, trying to build something in our lives. I was by nature a leader and together we made a wonderful team. It worked, thank God. I was trying to come back to a normal life, which I'd lost, and I put everything into my children – the love, the upbringing, the education so that they should become *menschen* and get degrees. Each one of my children became a professional: Norman is a gynaecologist; Alvin is not only an advocate but a stockbroker too; Henry is a CA; and Evy is a medical practitioner.

I was not a neurotic mother, not at all, because I felt the world was so different to how it was when I was brought up. I poured my life into my children and their education . . . through the business too – we turned Lamb's into something big! So I had no time for dwelling on the past or speaking about the Holocaust.

There were Holocaust survivors clubs in Johannesburg, there must have been about twelve or fifteen of us attending the meetings, but I never spoke. I undertook to collect the small fees that each one of us paid; I don't know what we really did with it apart from the tea and cakes we had when we met. So I used to send out statements and collect the money. Don Krausz, a Dutchman, was our chairman, and we sometimes met at Vera Reitzer's, a Hungarian survivor; they were both running the club.

Those monthly gatherings were a chance to talk. But I was one of those who never spoke – not even to other survivors.

First of all, when I came into the open and free world, it was in Paris, and whoever I came into contact with, when they saw my number they felt sorry for me – the small, young deportee. Everybody was very kind to us and, because French people went through almost the same as we did in Poland, they understood and appreciated us. I never felt the need to talk to anyone other than Roma.

---

140 Reparations that the German government agreed to pay in 1953 to Holocaust survivors and other Nazi victims.

In Israel – then still Palestine – where many survivors landed, there was no time for talking; no need to talk. We were busy making a new life.

In South Africa, my husband's family never spoke about it and my husband never wanted to listen. But he used to drive me to Johannesburg from Brakpan for the group meetings. We had speakers coming to address us – rabbis and things, not survivors – and he used to stay there, listening. He never wanted me to drive by myself.

I did speak once or twice in Brakpan, although you can't really call it speaking because my thoughts were not properly organised. The first time was when Roma was visiting and we were invited by the rabbi of the Jewish school in Benoni. Roma and I stood next to each other, and I didn't say much. And then once in shul somebody asked me to speak. Most people in Brakpan did not even know I was a survivor; I remember sitting down and almost shivering while I said a few words. But nothing much.

The consequences I suffered as a result of the camps were more emotional than physical.

Physically, there was nothing wrong with me. It did take me some time to start menstruating again after liberation; for me it took about eight months to return. Even when I came to Paris, which was already six months later, I still didn't get it. They were going to do something about it but eventually it did come back to normal. So really, the only physical after-effect was for some seven or eight months.

But emotionally, it was very different. This took me a long time to recover. That's why I could never talk about it. Even my husband didn't know my whole story; he just knew I was a survivor and that only Roma had survived with me; he didn't know who or what or when: how many brothers, how many sisters . . .

I say that I lived for my children and the business, that I had no time to go have tea with women. And that is true. I helped the Women's Zionist Organisation to collect money, I paid my fees, but I didn't play a part. You see, it was very difficult for me to make friends, so I hardly had any. I couldn't open up.

In Brakpan there were a lot of Jewish families, young people, mostly South Africans, and I just could not connect with them. Even now it's difficult for me – I still find that people cannot understand me. They may say 'survivor, survivor' but I know it's just words. Nobody could feel with me; that's why I could never bring myself to talk, for years and years, until I came to Cape Town.

Although I did not grow up in Cape Town and only moved here in 1995, I cannot recall a time when the name 'Ella Blumenthal' was not a headliner for Holocaust survivor testimony. Along with fellow-survivor Miriam Lichterman (who, at the time of writing, had recently passed away just shy of her 100th birthday), Ella has 'always' seemed to be at the forefront of public commemoration. So I guess I just assumed that it has 'always' been this way – that Ella has been the long-time face and voice stridently honouring the six million. I am amazed to discover that publicly speaking about her trauma was the last of the rusty deadbolts to give way. Perhaps her husband's passing was the opening that gave her permission to tell her full story. Since Isaac had been so opposed to hearing about Ella's Holocaust past, and with Ella's singular focus on fitting in, causing no upset, and building her new life and family, it is not surprising that she would have buried her trauma. The move to Cape Town, and her husband's passing not long after, were the catalysts to unblocking and unlocking her whole self.

I began slowly.

I spoke to the Shoah Foundation[141] when I first arrived in Cape Town. I didn't really know anybody, I didn't know how to speak, and I never knew the purpose of it; I was just *hucking*[142]. I thought it was for my family and I had never really spoken much before, apart from

---

141 A non-profit organisation established by Steven Spielberg in 1994, a year after completing the movie *Schindler's List*. It creates audio-visual interviews with survivors and witnesses of the Holocaust (*Shoah* in Hebrew) and other genocides.
142 Yiddish for 'talking informally, rambling'.

the brief time at Hillel School in Benoni. I don't think that interview was of any value. I'm even ashamed of it.

It was Myra Osrin[143] who got me started properly. I could feel her sincerity.

So I spoke. Regularly. I talked to schools, and groups that came to the Holocaust Centre – tour groups, police, even to prison warders. I wasn't happy though; I knew they were comparing what I was saying to the tragedy that happened here [apartheid] and I had to explain the difference – some people would fall asleep and I could see that I wasn't getting through. So I decided I only wanted to talk to Jewish children because they can understand – they follow, they feel, they ask questions.

Myra arranged a big exhibition board with some of my photos to be put on display in the Holocaust Centre. I spoke about the photos on the board, I spoke about the fears, the tragedies, the horrors that befell us. A gentleman from Durban said, 'How can you bear to remember this? I'm sorry that I made you talk.' And I realised: I've got to talk! I owe it to the family I lost; I owe it to those who did not survive. We must not forget. We must keep on talking so that our children, our children's children, should know about it. I often say this to the kids: 'I don't think your children will ever meet a survivor, so you tell them that you yourself met a woman who went through these horrors and lived.'

Ella starts to rifle through a bumper folder that has been waiting patiently for its moment in the sun. Page after page of newsclips, some torn and yellowing, others crisp and neatly cut, spilling out of a plastic archive where they've been filed in no apparent chronology. Ella posing with a group of school children; Ella pictured with a dignitary; Ella at a communal commemoration event; Ella in conversation;

---

143 Myra is a doyenne of the Cape Town Jewish community, having led and served on numerous communal organisations. She is a great friend of Ella's and is the Founder of the Cape Town Holocaust & Genocide Centre.

Ella deep in thought; young Ella, old Ella, monochrome Ella, colourful Ella . . . every shade of Ella.

Ella has been busy.

I wrote a speech, with some help, to put my Holocaust experience into words, so that I would have something organised to say when I was asked to give a talk. This did help me, to have it written down, and I have some variations on this speech, depending on the event.

Ella then proceeds to read me one of her shorter speeches. She delivers it with practised aplomb and, although I've heard it, or slight variations on it, on other occasions, I feel deeply moved to be hearing these words against the backdrop of the many talking hours I've been privileged to share with Ella in interviews. And I am even more fiercely driven to write this book because no speech, however long, can encompass the stunning depth and detail of her full memoir.

As I said, Myra Osrin really got me started. And Stephen Smith – he's a non-Jewish professor, an amazing man who worked with Myra to help create Cape Town's Holocaust Centre. His father was a priest outside London and these Christian people built a Holocaust Centre on their premises. On one of my visits to London, I took the train to Nottingham; they waited for me with a car, took me out for the day, and of course they listened to my story. Stephen is still involved in Holocaust education – such a committed, unassuming type of person. These days he is in America; he's the director of a whole Holocaust enterprise there.

Here is a picture of me coming down the stairs at Marais Road Shul – this was for a talk I gave *erev*[144] Shabbat one time. And here is a flyer for a speech I gave at the shul's Rosh Hashanah learning session one year – *the bold headline, 'FEARLESS HERO: the triumph of faith', shouts above a picture of Ella robed in her* yom tov *finery.*

Here's another, from Herzlia High School – a lovely picture with the kids. And one with younger children from a primary school.

---

144 Hebrew: literal translation is 'evening/eve'; refers to the day before Shabbat or a Jewish holiday.

I've done quite a few interviews too, but nothing as extensive as these I'm doing with you.

Some years ago, around 2012, a Jewish woman came here from South America with a small team who were making a video. Her name was Elizabeth Kahn; I think her mother was a survivor. They came to film me as I lit candles for Shabbat and walked to shul all dressed up. I did feel like a celebrity, I suppose. But I don't know what happened to that film.

I was invited to events in Johannesburg and Pretoria . . . here is a photograph of me lighting a candle at a Yom HaShoah event, a clipping of a talk at the Cape Jewish Seniors Association, and something from the Friendship Forum – a group started by social workers for second-generation survivors. Look, this is a letter from a little girl in Grade 5. I have plenty of letters like this from children, plenty. And here's a picture from another shul; it says underneath: 'Remembering the destruction. Ella Blumenthal is one of the last survivors of the Warsaw Ghetto, Auschwitz, Majdanek and Bergen-Belsen . . . the gripping personal account of her horrifying ordeal.'

Now who is this? Sharon Ellwood: a Christian woman from Johannesburg who worked with the church to collect money for Israel and arrange tours there. She organised a big concert at Camps Bay School – that very pretty lady from the Zionist Federation in Johannesburg spoke – you know the one who was a model and businesswoman? Reeva Forman! Many people came and they collected a lot of money.

Some years ago I got a phone call from Moscow. It was coming up to the sixtieth anniversary of the liberation of Auschwitz and they invited me – all expenses paid – to come for a forum being organised by the Russians and the European Jewish Congress. The Russians had been the ones to liberate Auschwitz, so they wanted to put this together.

Now I'll tell you what I did. It was the biggest mistake in my life. Roma's granddaughter was getting married the week before this, in Israel. So instead of going directly to Warsaw, I went via Israel. Roma's granddaughter couldn't believe it when she saw me! Anyway the Shabbos afternoon I went to visit my old friend Guta Bankier and then, instead of going back to the hotel to rest, I walked to my late husband's niece – I was married in the yard of her parents' home and I was always very welcome. Of course I was walking since it was Shabbos – it was a lot of walking in Tel Aviv. By the time I left, it was already getting dark – this was winter, January – and the heavens opened. I had no money on me because of Shabbos so I could not get a taxi. I walked in the rain and arrived at the hotel soaking – you could wring out my clothes. Of course I got sick . . . but so sick that eventually the hotel ordered a doctor to come and see me. They took me by ambulance the next night to Ichilov Hospital where I spent a few days. My family sent Evy to bring me home eventually and I never made it to the Auschwitz event. Everything was organised and paid for – I even had to get a Polish visa because I never did get my citizenship reinstated – but I was a no-show at this important event because I was in hospital. I should have gone to Warsaw.

Alright, I don't think I'm going to show you any more of these things – we've got to get on with our work. I just thought we'll look through a little. *Nevertheless, Ella continues going through documents and photos, often muttering to herself.* I don't know why I've got this. Oh, this is the *chazzan* from Sandton Shul, and this is the *chazzan* that they brought from Israel – a Gerrer Chassid. Ohhhh, ohhh, *[paging through more]* . . . Okay, I must put this away now.

I'm enjoying watching Ella explore her pictorial history. I detect a growing sense of pride in those more imperceptible accomplishments: while it is obvious that Ella would be proud of her career, her children, the robust life she built from the ashes, I think she is only now becoming aware of her greatest achievement yet: her legacy of courage. Ella's strength reverberates like a sonic boom through all who hear her; she would never have been able to reach as far, or touch as many, if she hadn't been brave enough to talk. As she pages through posters, flyers, pamphlets, white papers with her name and photograph emblazoned across them, she sees for herself the fortitude in having survived the Holocaust, and the bravery in having spoken about having survived the Holocaust too.

Roma wrote a book called *Here There is No Why*. I told you about it. It was published by means of a grant from Yad Vashem. We decided to have a launch of the book in Cape Town, with me in Roma's place, since she could not be here. It was on Monday the 28th of April 2003 at an event to commemorate the sixtieth anniversary of the Warsaw Ghetto Uprising.

John Maytham, the radio personality, interviewed me at the Holocaust Centre. We laughed when we met because he was dressed in a black suit with a white shirt collar, and I was wearing the same. He is a very good interviewer.

We sold a lot of books – I think we even ran short – and I signed for Roma. People asked me why I did not write a book myself. At first I thought it's because I am not a talented writer like Roma, whose father was a well-known journalist and author. And I had no time to write books – I was busy with my family and my business. But in actual fact, I did have time because I was no longer working in the business, and my children were grown up. I could have someone write for me, like we are doing now. No, the real reason I could not write a book then is because I was not yet comfortable talking in public about my suffering. I was so used to keeping it all hidden, like my scar, as my husband's family had told me to; I was only just beginning to find my voice. The time was not right.

In 2000, I was invited to parliament by Andrew Feinstein, who was an MP. His mother, also a survivor, was there too. We were guests at a special discussion about the Stockholm Declaration[145] and its relevance in South Africa. We sat upstairs in the gallery with Myra Osrin from the Holocaust Centre.

---

145 In January 2000, Sweden hosted a forum on the Holocaust, attended by 46 countries. The forum concluded with the Stockholm Declaration, which committed the signatories to Holocaust commemoration and education, applying its all-important lessons about prejudice, racism and diversity.

This parliament discussion was a very important event for us. And the idea of the Stockholm Declaration. I am reminded of the World Gathering of Holocaust Survivors that took place in Jerusalem in 1981. Menachem Begin spoke, Elie Wiesel spoke, and I have a copy of the two important documents that were produced. The first is the 'Legacy of Survivors' – where we, the survivors, undertake to always honour and remember our fallen brethren:

> We take this oath! We take it in the shadow of flames whose tongues scar the soul of our people. We vow in the name of dead parents and children; we vow, with our sadness hidden, our faith renewed; we vow, we shall never let the sacred memory of our perished Six Million be scorned or erased . . . We take this oath! Vision becomes word, to be handed down from father to son, from mother to daughter, from generation to generation.[146]

And the second is the 'Pledge of Acceptance of the Second Generation', where our children – 'the generations born after the darkness' – pledge to remember, teach, tell, fight (anti-Semitism) and affirm their commitment to Israel and the Jewish people.

It was a huge gathering. People came from all over the world. Since then, I never attended anything of that scale, but the ideas were the same, even down here in our little South Africa: we must not forget. This is how Elie Wiesel put it in his speech:

> Let us pledge to one another our loyalty to Israel, our faith in friendship, our commitment to memory: we shall not give up, we shall not give in. It may be too late for the victims, and even for the survivors – but not for our children, nor for mankind. In an age tainted by violence, we must teach com-

---

[146] The full 'Legacy of Survivors' text and the 'Pledge of Acceptance' were read out at the closing ceremony of the World Gathering of Jewish Holocaust Survivors. Sheerit Hapleitah. https://sheerithapleitah.com/going-forward/. Last accessed 22/12/2022.

ing generations of the origins and consequences of violence; in a society of bigotry and indifference, we must tell our contemporaries that whatever the answer, it must grow out of human compassion and reflect man's relentless quest for justice and memory.

As the years passed, I spoke more and my profile grew: from being a silent observer at the support groups, to an occasional speaker at shuls or schools, to a guest of parliament and eventually the keynote speaker at the Yom HaShoah commemoration events.

Even a film. Do you know Jordy Sank? He is the son of the Sank family from Camps Bay – I know them well from that shul. Jordy made a documentary about my life.[147]

Speaking about the Holocaust has become a vital part of my life. I must do it for those who are no more with us. As Elie Wiesel said – we owe it to the dead. I do it for them.

By now I have spoken many times at Yom HaShoah events. Many times. But these days, in my late nineties, I don't think I will speak there any more. I can't . . . It's enough.

Now it is time for a book.

---

[147] Sanktuary Films' 2021 documentary about Ella, titled *I Am Here*, which premiered in Cape Town in December 2022, has received numerous awards and accolades. It depicts Ella's life story through a creative combination of recorded footage, interview material and dynamic 2D animation. The two projects (*I Am Here* and *I am Ella*) are not associated and the image used on the front cover, for both projects, was shot by Micha Serraf, owned by Sanktuary Films, and used by this book under license.

Chapter 15

Grandchildren

Our frenetic flip through the Rolodex of Ella's memory leads us here, to the present day and present people. Ella frequently bemoans the forgetfulness wrought by aging – if she has to cast around for anything more than a millisecond to recall a name or date, she is quick to berate herself and seems utterly indignant that her 96+-year-old brain would dare falter. I see no such evidence of memory failure. She always remembers the bothersome detail in the end, whether it is seconds, minutes or, only very occasionally, hours later. I, on the other hand, with my considerably younger brain, forget far more and far quicker than Ella does. And now that we're talking grandchildren, even great-grandchildren – none of whose names Ella ever forgets or confuses – I resort to a hastily-scribbled family tree which I pretend not to have to reference as often as I do.

I find Ella's memory recall staggering, especially because of her age and the sheer volume of memory. I wonder if this has something to do with the fact that so much of it stayed buried for so long. Rather than being clouded, diluted or erased by her years of silence, Ella's memories were neatly preserved, boxed up like fragile ornaments and stored where nothing could mar them. When she did start to talk about her past, she found that Roma's shared memories helped trigger her own, even claiming to have forgotten much of what Roma wrote about. But once the lid was lifted, and she took those first tentative looks inside, albeit already in her late 70s, memories emerged with all the crispness of her youth. If memory is a muscle, then Ella's

Grandchildren

suffered no atrophy with lack of use. If anything, it retained its elasticity and springs nimbly back and forth, even today, along this centenarian road.

ELLA:
My children got married, moved away, lived their own lives, and I became a grandmother. The feeling of having a grandchild is something else. After I've lost everything . . . to have my own family, my own children and children's children – it's something unbelievable *[tearful]*. Now I'm even having great-grandchildren, bless them. I'm urging my unmarried grandchildren to carry on our family and get married, have children, because I still want to see my family increase. It is truly amazing – that from me, only one survivor, came generations and a whole family.

My children are part of me, not outside of me; my blood flows in their veins and their blood in my veins. My grandchildren are of course different. Some of them grew up quite close by – like Alvin's children in Benoni when I was in Brakpan – and some without me being there as much or at all – like Norman and Henry's children. But no matter how far away, I have always connected with them, and my children always brought them to visit me. Of course, Evy's children are closest to me because they grew up with me in Cape Town; I think they feel the same towards me because their parents, Evy and Paul, are so close to me. Never mind a daughter, I would never believe that a son-in-law could be so devoted.

My other children are also very devoted to me, but of course they are far away and I don't expect to be looked after like a baby. I suppose most children are devoted to their parents, but there are some who have left this country and their parents are rotting in homes for the aged. Not me. I always have my children and grandchildren around; wherever they are in the world, they call and visit me often.

I talk to my children and grandchildren about the Holocaust, even more so in the last few years. They know all the details. Often, people will mix up the things that happened, like they will say I was first sent to Auschwitz and then to Majdanek, but my family knows exactly. Everyone should know the detail of what happened to us during the war.

It is at this point of writing that I am reminded of a seemingly pedestrian encounter that took place during one of our interviews at Ella's flat. And it is on reflection, now, that I appreciate just how extraordinary a moment it really was – or rather, how indicative it was of an extraordinary relationship:

Ella and I are deep in conversation. Tea has been poured, biscuits devoured, and carer Joan is out shopping. It's 4 pm. The closed bedroom door swings open and a bleary-eyed teenager emerges into the lounge. This is Jade, Evelyn's daughter. A warm smile spreads across Ella's face and she moves across the room to fuss over her granddaughter. 'Did you have a good rest, darling? Want something to drink? Eat? What can I get you?' Jade hugs her granny and says she is fine, needs nothing, and is going back to study. 'Thanks, Gran,' she says, 'I needed that.'

Ella explains that Jade is studying for her matric exams and sometimes comes over to work or relax. 'There is so much stress on these kids,' Ella complains. I marvel that, of all the possible respites, this teenager chooses her granny's flat, her Jewish cooking, and the warm embrace of the toughest woman she knows. Ella is safe harbour.

So now, as Ella's narrative seems to be wrapping up, segueing from the anecdotal to the philosophical, when I feel that I know Ella as well as I am ever going to within the confines of an interview environment, yet still not well enough, I reach out to her nearest – daughter Evelyn and granddaughter Jade – who know her best.

Although it is Evelyn who first called me about writing her mother's story, she has had very little to do with the process up to now, apart from liaising the best times for me to interview Ella. She strikes me as a much quieter, more reserved type than her rambunctious mother, never raising her voice any more than Ella's compromised hearing demands. During the Covid-19 lockdown, Ella moved in with Evelyn and Paul, and she lives there still, along with Jade who is now studying at university. This tribe – three generations of Blumenthal women – living under the same roof, is quite the power pack, and they move as such. I discuss scheduling interviews with Evelyn, Jade, maybe even Paul, and Evelyn instinctively arranges a joint discussion. Even though her mother's input is not required (on the contrary, I want to talk about Ella rather than with her), Evelyn ensures that our meeting won't clash with her mom's meals, rest times or scheduled visits from her many friends. She'd like her to be around, if not participating. She would also prefer to have Jade there too: blonde, studious, gentle Jade, whose complete adoration for her legendary grandmother is plain to see and whose appearance of fair-headed innocence belies the 'Warszawa-bred' craftiness she has inherited from Ella.

So this becomes a group interview, which gives me a welcome window into this unique family. For them, it is a well-worn dynamic. For me, it is pure entertainment. It is almost five years after my interviews with Ella began, and I finally understand what makes Ella's story so truly exceptional.

EVELYN:

We grew up knowing our mom was different, but maybe not always understanding why.

My parents were from Eastern Europe and other parents were locals, so that in itself made a difference. But on a deeper level, we just knew there was something sore there, something that needed to be protected.

There wasn't a specific moment that my mom told me she was a Holocaust survivor. I do remember, though, that she had a dressing table with a big mirror where she used to brush her hair, and I used to sit next to her when she got herself ready; I remember looking at the scar on her arm and asking: 'What's that?' There was also a scar on her thigh because she had had a skin graft. I must have been about four or five when I asked. She told me that she had been in a car accident and I thought, ooh – that's scary, picturing glass hitting her and cutting her arm and leg. I also remember seeing an old picture of a large group of people on her dressing table and asking who these people were and why didn't I have aunts or uncles or grannies or grandpas like everybody else.

In our home, I was definitely aware of an undercurrent of something, but I didn't know what. Sometimes, my mom used to cry out at night and it scared me. I'd hear her screaming and I remember running down the passage to her room.

'What's wrong,' I'd ask her, terrified.

'They're taking my children! They're taking my children!'

'But I'm right here, Mom. I'm here.'

Who would be taking me? Where? . . . That was before I really understood.

She still sometimes has these nightmares. I've got a monitor to her room and I can hear.

I was probably about 12 when she told me what had happened to her; my brothers already knew. She showed me who each person was on that dressing table picture and explained why they were no longer around.

From then, it became almost a topic of regular conversation within the family, a part of our daily existence. As a result, I think we all became super protective of my mom, more than is normal. Even my father was like that: we wanted to protect her from any further harm. To this day, I think everyone would agree that we are very protective of her, even overprotective. If something happens, this one phones this one and we all, as a family, get in on the discussion.

My immediate family was always close: my parents, my brothers and me. We discussed everything! Even once we were married. Let's say my brother's lawnmower broke, then the family would have a meeting about it. *Jade jumps in here in what will become regular commentary, to provide broader family context. She seems much older than her 22 years, adopting an objective stance from within the very nucleus in which she functions. 'Oh, that's the funniest – the Blumenthal Family Meetings. My parents have been married for, like, 30 plus years and even my dad is not invited. Me neither. Only actual Blumenthals. The siblings. The four of them have this weird relationship – they'll talk for hours and nothing will be decided. Say they have a decision to make about my gran, they'll talk and talk and talk – my mom says she must talk to Alvin, Alvin says he must talk to Norman, Norman says he must talk to my mom, and on it goes. It's amazing that they ever come to a conclusion.'*

Yes, I always do that – I defer to my brothers because they're older. But the lawnmower was back when my brother was living in Benoni. Now it's more accurate to say that any decision that has to do with my mom, we all have discussions about it. Growing up, we didn't have extended family that we were very close to. Of course there were my father's brothers, but we weren't attached to them in that warm, family way. My mother was the centre around which the whole family pivoted, including my father – he was quite happy to defer to her. She always had those qualities that you find in her now: sassy and smart, and very forthright. And as a mom: totally warm, loving, loyal, protective of all of us. I wouldn't say 'overprotective', but appropriately protective. She certainly wasn't neurotic. She'd say, 'Go out, come back 11, 12, whenever you want.' She trusted me. As a result, we hardly argued. *Jade again: 'I think the best way to put it is that she wanted the best for all her children. I remember you telling me, Mom, that when Norman was emigrating to Sydney, it was Bubbie, my grandfather, who was the one to say, "Don't leave, stay close . . ." But my gran said, "No. Go." Because she knew it was* ***best*** *for him to go and start his family there.'*

That's right. For me, there were never any limits put on anything: do whatever you want if you're happy doing it. That's why there were never harsh words because there was nothing for me to push back against. There was an expectation that we would do our best at everything, try hard and succeed. But she wasn't a strict disciplinarian, so when I say 'protective', I mean like a lioness over her cubs. *Jade pipes up again: 'Yes, that's definitely how the Blumenthals are. They're a clan and it's in their blood. If you cross one, you cross all. Like my dad, Paul – he is everyone's favourite because he is such a nice guy, so straightforward and honest. But I always joke: if he ever did something wrong, God forbid, they'd kill him, like one phone call, goodbye.' She and Evelyn burst out laughing. 'And my mom is like that with me. If someone does something to upset me, I might be over it but my mom is upset on my behalf.'*

So my mom had that relationship with me growing up and now I am reciprocating, it's in my DNA. I look after her not because I have to, or because I'm physically here. My brothers and I *all* look after her, in our own way, because that's just what we do. And we do overprotect her because of what's happened to her; we're very anxious about her not suffering. *'It's not only because of what happened to her,' says Jade. 'I think it's because you grew up with this dynamic of the tight-knit nuclear family. It's all you knew and that was normal. I think also for us, the grandchildren: we grew up with this Blumenthal dynamic and we don't know any different. As you get older and look at how friends interact with their families, you realise that perhaps what you always thought of as "normal" in your own family, is actually quite abnormal – or special – after all. Maybe "abnormal" is the wrong word, but it is extreme: the Blumenthal bond is very tight.'*

My mother is the least *faribeldik*[148] person, truly. She has the most incredible memory, but just does not hold a grudge or take offence. I'll give you an example.

She has always been religious and so my father's family used to come to our house in Brakpan for the *chaggim*[149]. It was Pesach, and

---

148 'Faribel': a Yiddish word meaning 'grievance/to insult or slight someone'. If you're 'faribeldik', you're prone to holding a grudge.
149 Hebrew for 'Jewish holidays/festivals'.

one of my uncles, who really liked his alcohol, asked for whiskey. He knew my mother wouldn't serve that because whiskey is not kosher for Passover, but he was pressing her buttons.

'I specially bought you this *Pesachdike*[150] brandy,' she said and showed him the bottle.

He took one look at it and said, 'I'm not drinking that, give me proper whiskey.'

'No, it's Pesach.'

'You know what—' now remember there is a whole table full of people, my father's brothers and their families, and he said in front of everyone: 'You know what, Ella, I don't like you and I've never liked you.'

I was a child and I thought, oh God, there's going to be a big argument now. But my mother, without skipping a beat, went over to him, gave him a big hug and said, 'Nonsense! I love you and I've always loved you. Don't be silly.'

I'm thinking, why did she do that after he was so insulting? It's her home, she has every right to keep it kosher. But what could he do in the face of that response? She just diffused the whole situation.

I said to her afterwards: 'How could you do that? He was so horrible.' And she was completely unfazed: 'Oh please, he always says things like that. I love him, he looks like my husband!' She simply wasn't insulted. I was insulted on her behalf! See? Not *faribeldik* at all.

My dad was the total opposite of my mom. He was quiet, serious, introverted, unsociable. *Jade teases: 'Like you, mom!'* He would be happiest on a Friday night if there was just one guest for Shabbat supper, or even if there weren't guests. He would stand up at about eight thirty or nine o'clock and say, 'Right, I'm going to bed because I have to open the shop in the morning,' and he'd just leave the table and go to bed and we would all just sit there. It's become

---

150 Kosher for Pesach (Passover).

a family joke now, so when my husband Paul wants to go to bed, he says, 'I have to open up the shop!'

My dad was very shy. On Saturdays he played bowls. He'd go home early from the shop and I had to take out his bowls outfit. Then he would take half a sedative tablet – because it made him anxious to deal with all the people at bowls. He was not a people's person. And he didn't like drinking beer. But everyone drank beer! So he said I must tell them to put sugar in his beer. Well, he couldn't manage even that one – when he got home, he said he couldn't walk and we had to carry him into the house. After just one beer.

He was very intelligent, and a big reader. His manner was very Germanic, a real disciplinarian. If you dropped your fork and made a bit of a noise at the table, you were in trouble. Or if he phoned his brothers, Sasha in particular (that's Jedidiah but everyone called him Sasha), we all had to sit quietly while he was speaking. Sasha became the de facto patriarch of my dad's side of the family, so we had to ask him everything. Like when I got into medicine, I had to go and ask Sasha, or if I wanted to get married to Paul, I had to go and ask Sasha what he thought. When I asked him about medicine, he told me he didn't think I should do it because I was a girl and how would I get married and have a family if I was studying. I did it anyway. But my father said I still had to go and ask.

On the contrary, my mom was so much fun. Even though she was incredibly busy with the business, you just knew she was there and would do anything for you. That was my feeling growing up: that she was behind us, life and soul. And I loved being with her. *'That's why I really wish I'd met Bubbie, because I feel like I'd understand you a lot better,' Jade says to Evelyn. 'He died before I was born and, from all the stories you've told me and from knowing Granny, I can't picture them together. If I ask Granny, "Did you find him good looking?", she's like, "He was a good man."'* I'll tell you what it was about them. He was good at things that she wasn't, and she was good at things that he wasn't. They were totally complementary. So, in the business they ran together, they were a perfect fit. Like if he had to do something that was confrontational and he was too scared to do it (which he often was), he'd say, 'Go call your mom.' And then she would come and do it without even blinking an eye. But when there were orders or accounts to be paid, he would take care of it because he was so precise and ordered, while she's very easily distracted. He was the one to wake us up in the morning for school; he'd get himself up at quarter to six and wake us at six.

We all had to help out in the shop. If my father told me to be in the shop at eight on Saturday morning and I arrived at five past eight, I was in the biggest trouble. How I got there was no one's business – it was far from the house and I couldn't drive so I had to walk, but that was my problem. If you chewed gum while you were working, there was hell to pay. If I had a sweet in my mouth while I was talking to a customer, hell to pay. In my school holidays, I once went to stay with Norman, who was already married and living in Johannesburg. I phoned my father to ask if I could stay one more night and he said, 'No, you have to come back, I need you.' So, I made my way back by train; it was an hour's journey. When I got home I asked what he needed me for. 'Oh, no, it's okay,' he said, but I was already home by then. He was just very particular.

On Sundays we did what they called the 'indexes', which was cashing up and writing everything down. All four of us had to work in the shop every Sunday morning – doctor (which Norman was by then) or not, you came, you helped, you contributed. If I learned one thing from my father, it was discipline.

My mom was the warm, cuddly one. If I was studying late, my mom would start baking at midnight, and then, at about two in the morning, we'd meet for tea and warm biscuits. When I was at medical school and living alone in a flat in Joburg, it was the night before an exam and I couldn't sleep. I phoned my mom at home in Brakpan, knowing she would answer even though it was the middle of the night. (Oh, by the way, my father never answered the phone. If he did, there was a problem. He would rather let the phone ring if my mother wasn't there. My mother did all the talking; he just read his paper on his chair and didn't say much.) So I called my mom and I'm like, 'I can't sleep, I'm writing this big exam, I'm so stressed . . .' Next thing I know, it's an hour later and she has driven through to come and be with me. She calmed me down and put me to bed and then drove back at six or seven the next morning to work. That's the sort of mom she was.

Mom isn't especially book-smart but she is very street-smart. Growing up, you just knew she was always one step ahead of the pack, like she's just got it. *'It's because she is a total schemer,' quips Jade. 'The way her mind works is very interesting. She can think around and ahead of things. That's why she tells me I'm from Warszawa, because I'm the same.'* Yes, she does love the subterfuge. She loves to go incognito: put on a big hat and sunglasses and think that no one will recognise her. And she doesn't do things the ordinary way; she is a very capable person and she's usually way ahead of everyone else. *Jade concurs: 'It's so funny: my parents recently went to Israel and I looked after Granny for a week. I spend a lot of time with her anyway, but that time it was just us two. The one day she says to me: "Now that your parents are away, I have to tell you: your dad, he is very much like this [puts her hand in an upright position and moves it in a straight line; shakes her head] – not good. But your mom . . ." [puts her hand in a diagonal position and snakes it along in a winding manner; nods her head]. She adores my dad, but he's not a schemer like she is!'* That's so true. She often says to Jade, 'You're Kaplan by name, but you're from Warsaw – you know how to go around things, because you're from Warszawa.'

She's been this way for as long as I can remember. I'm sure it's that capable, crafty nature that helped her survive the Holocaust. Like when I was five years old, my mother decided that I was wasting my time sitting at home with a nanny, I had to go to school. But I was too young to be eligible for government school and there was no Jewish pre-school in Brakpan. So she sent me to the convent school, which was private. They asked for my birth certificate and she told them, 'I'll bring it. I'll bring it.' But to me, she said, 'When they ask you, tell them you've reminded me. I'll bring it when I bring it.' Of course she never did give it to them and eventually they stopped asking. In Grade 2, I moved to the regular government school anyway. So, she beat the system.

Even in her old age, she doesn't stop. There she was a couple of years ago, lying in hospital where she'd been admitted for observation. She was having fainting episodes and needed to be checked out. So she's hooked up to the machines, resting in a hospital bed, when suddenly she says to me: 'Oy! I'm going to lose my gym membership!' Her gym offers discounted memberships but you have to clock in regularly to keep the access card active. So she's lying in ICU worrying about having to pay for a new card, or upgrade the membership, because being in hospital means she can't go swimming at the gym. As it happens, the gym has a branch in the same building as this hospital so she says: 'Evy, do me a favour: disconnect me. No one will know. We'll go down to the gym, we'll clock in, and we'll come back.' You see? She is always up to that sort of thing. Needless to say, I didn't take her, but it doesn't stop her scheming.

My mother is unique. And when you grow up with her, you don't necessarily realise how unusual she is. So for outsiders, or people coming into the family, it can take some getting used to. I'll tell you what happened to Paul, for instance, the first time he came to stay at the house in Brakpan.

Paul and I had just got married and the whole family gathered in Brakpan over a *yom tov*. Everyone was married already, there with their spouses, and Paul was a little nervous, understandably, since it was his first time staying over there. Anyway, you know my mom loves to swim. Well, she used to love swimming in our pool in Brakpan, but not necessarily with a costume on. Then she would get out and go straight to the shower.

We had one shower in that house. So, my mom gets out the pool without a costume and heads for the shower. The wall of the shower is misted and Paul's already in there, taking a shower. She opens the shower and he gets the shock of his life!

At this point, Ella has joined the conversation. She has woken from a nap and is sitting at the table with us, enjoying a cup of tea which Jade has expertly made and served to her with a couple of store-bought biscuits. Evelyn has clued her in to which story she is telling and Ella listens, facial expression giving away nothing. When Evelyn gets to the part about Paul getting a shock, Ella jumps in, the tiniest of smiles playing at the corner of her lips and, eyebrows raised, says: 'He covers himself like this [folds her arms in her lap] and I said to him: "Noooo, don't worry, I've seen it. I've got four specimens at home – three sons and a husband."' The rest of us dissolve into laughter and Ella simply shrugs. No big deal.

Paul was of course totally horrified. But she thought it was my brother in the shower, so she thought nothing of it! *Jade states the obvious – well, the obvious to me but clearly not to Blumenthal insiders: 'That in itself shows you how abnormal our family is: that Granny thought it was normal to get in the shower with her grown son!'*
  Well yes, but this is just how it was in our house . . . totally normal.
  Of course it is Ella who has the last word on this story, adding her singular spark to an already fiery conversation. While Evelyn started out this anecdote cautiously, saying she wasn't sure if it was appropriate material for the book, Ella concludes it by leaning over to me and asking: 'Nu? Why don't you put this in the book for a change?'

I can see how her strength might come across as tough or intimidating. I remember meeting someone at one of the first Kaplan dinners I went to when I started going out with Paul. We went to Paul's cousin for Shabbat supper and he asked me where I was from. When I told him Brakpan, he said, 'I know a lady there. I used to be a rep selling pantihose . . . There was a woman at the second shop on the main road. A difficult woman!' So I asked if the woman's name was Ella Blumenthal. 'Yes! That's the one! Such a difficult woman!' he said. 'I needed a whiskey every time I had to go sell her something!'

We laughed and he said that she's really not that bad. But there is no denying she is feisty and strong; everybody knew her to be that way and I guess people were a little scared of her. Years after we had left Brakpan and my parents sold the business, Alvin went back there. He met one of the workers from the furniture shop that had been next door to Lamb's. He said to Alvin: 'Where's Mrs Blum?' as they used to call her. 'Oooh but this town has gone down since she left. She was power!'

To me, to us, she is just the warm centre of everything. It's not that she was around all the time when we were kids or that she spoiled us with things. It's that when she was there, she was really there. We had Maude looking after us because my mom was busy running a big business. Even if she was not around physically, I still adored her. If I was sick, she would come straight home and take care of me. She never bought me a thing – we didn't have toys, she didn't believe in them. My brother and I shared one little metal cannon that we used to shoot a matchstick out of – that was the one toy we had. But she did spoil us with love.

I shift my focus to Jade who has been helping keep her mom on track. Jade's viewpoint, until now delivered in short sound bites as she keeps up her running commentary on Evelyn's perspective, is startlingly reflective. Although deeply ensconced in the family fold, Jade seems able to attain a certain psychological distance, imbuing her comments with objectivity and balance. I am eager to hear more about her experience of growing up with Ella.

JADE:
If you had to ask me to describe my gran in one word, I'd say 'cool', which is strange, I know, to describe an old lady that way. My friends call her a 'legend'.

Growing up, it was going to Granny's flat, sleeping over, making biscuits . . . standard, good memories. At the same time everyone's like 'Ah, what's it like growing up with *that* gran?' She's just my gran, you know, I don't see her as the icon she's known as. I mean, she is, I know she is, but she's also just my gran.

We used to go there Friday nights for Shabbos and I would usually sleep over. I'd often stay Saturday night too. One night, for some reason I couldn't sleep. I sleep next to her in the same bed *[she laughs]* so it's clearly a very close relationship. Anyway, she was fast asleep and I was wide awake, and I woke her at like 2 am, 'Gran,' I said, 'I can't sleep, I'm hungry.' And – I will never forget this – she was up in seconds! Like this *[clicks fingers]* she went from fast asleep to wide awake, voops off with the duvet, into the kitchen and the next thing I know we're having Israeli salad with literally, I kid you not, twenty pieces of toast. Like no toast is enough toast. Toast and butter and cheese and Israeli salad. At two in the morning.

Now it's Evelyn's turn to interject: *'That's just typical. And by the way, just to point out this business of sleeping in the bed with my mom: when you sleep at her place, you sleep in her bed, my brothers included. Even as adults. If my brother comes to visit, he sleeps in the bed – she has a big bed, two singles pushed together – and it's not even a question that you'll sleep there.'*

The funny thing is, I didn't know this wasn't normal. I grew up thinking it was totally normal to share your gran's bed. That's just how it has always been, for all of us.

We'd wake up on Sunday mornings very early, like six or seven, and we'd go to the gym to swim in the pool. That's where I learned the routine. She's quite particular that way *[laughs]*, the routine is very important. So you have your swim, then go into the bathroom to shower. Then you take off your costume and you've got to wring it out. She's not shy at all – she's walking around butt naked, like she has no problem. So you rinse your costume in water that is not-too-cold-not-too-warm, and then you wring it out. But if you wring it out incorrectly, it's very bad. There's a specific way. Then you have to hang your costume in a certain way so that it doesn't get saggy. Then comes the steam/sauna part. First you have to cream yourself with a lot of thick, pasty cream. I don't like the feeling of thick cream but no, you have to put it on. Then you go into the steam room, and then the sauna, and then you re-cream, and then you get dressed. And Gran goes, 'Ahh, don't you just feel amazing?'

Jade is chuckling and Evelyn adds: *'My friend told me a story about one time that she was in the sauna at the gym. She's lying there by herself and somebody puts their head in and says: "Excuse me, would you mind leaving now because someone wants to come in." So my friend says: "Why do I need to leave? Who wants to come in?" And the person replies: "It's Mrs Blumenthal."' My mother had sent Joan, her carer, to ask the woman to leave so that she could go through her whole routine. That's the kind of confidence she has.*

My gran, she rates herself, you know. She has this attitude about her and oozes confidence. That's what I want to emulate in my life – she is unapologetically herself.

So that was a big thing for all the grandchildren: on Sunday Granny would go swimming, then you'd come home and she would make these long sugar biscuits to have with tea. Or you'd have seventeen pieces of toast with butter. My mom is like, 'Don't eat bread, don't eat sugar, no carbs.' My gran eats whatever she wants. She loves biscuits, pasta, carbs . . . and who is the healthier one?

There was an interesting study by a psychologist looking at the difference between physical and mental strength; many of those who survived the Holocaust were not necessarily the strongest physically, but they had a mental toughness. Growing up with my gran, learning her personality, the way she operates, the way her mind works – I told you, a big schemer – I can see that mental strength. And people are drawn to her, like she's 'just got it'. She has the *it* factor.

Granny is the centre around which the family operates. *Evelyn* interjects: *'If there is something to be done, it goes to Granny first. You can ask all the grandchildren. Granny must give permission. Like if someone wants to get married, Granny has got to be in favour. It's different to how my uncle Sasha was for me because I wasn't close to him, I just did it because my father told me to. But my mom means everything to her children and grandchildren.'* Granny's words have a lot of power. Do you know that she gives me a blessing before every exam? And she knows exactly what I am writing and when. I've been studying for five years and she knows about every single exam. It's amazing, I'll tell her once, or maybe in a passing comment, and she'll remember. She keeps up with everything I'm doing. *Evelyn: 'She keeps up with all the grandchildren.'* Yes, all over the world. She'll FaceTime with all the grandchildren, and I've noticed that, when she speaks to you, she never says anything about herself. It's all about what's going on with you. 'You started a new job. How's that? How is your girlfriend? How is your boyfriend?' She lives for her children and grandchildren, that's what gives her happiness and joy . . . *'That's why she didn't need friends. Because we were it,'* adds Evelyn . . . and she pays attention because she cares. *'She is like this with everyone she meets. She asks them about themselves and makes a point of remembering; the hairdresser, the guy at the grocery store, the dermatologist. In fact one of the doctors who looked after her in hospital wrote to me recently. When he was on his rounds in the hospital, with twenty patients to see, my mom would stop him and ask about his family. I'd tell her: Mom, leave him, he's got other patients to look after, and he'd say, "No, no, it's fine, I'll sit a while." I told him recently that my mom reached 101 and he actually wrote me a note saying "Your mom made a huge impression on my life. Looking after her was a privilege. She is such a special person." This is just one example, but she's like this everywhere she goes.'*

The last year of my undergrad was very difficult. It was a tough year, and the odds were really stacked against me to pass at the end. But I did more than pass; I did fairly well. People ask me how I pulled through that. I believe one hundred per cent that it was the power of Granny's words.

I tell you, she gives the best advice – even better than my mom does. She's just so relatable and with it, even now at her age. She'll tell me information that I didn't even know and I'm like, 'How did you know that? Where did you read that?' And she'll say, 'I saw it on my phone.' She watches Mr Bean on YouTube late at night after everyone has gone to sleep, and she's reading Bill Browder[151] now – she loves business.

We were discussing Bitcoin the other day when she came in and asked what we were talking about. So my mom started explaining that there is this new type of currency blah blah blah. And my gran replies, 'I know what Bitcoin is!' – like all offended that we assume she doesn't! *Evelyn adds: 'I didn't think she would have a clue. But she says, "If you're talking about Bitcoin, why don't you just say so?" She wants to know what's going on in the world. She sits on her computer or checks her phone, she's not lazy to try.'*

She has so much insight and wisdom to offer, and people lean on her strength. She is so strong that when something traumatic does happen, she becomes a pillar for others. I've always been interested in how she was when her husband died. *Evelyn says: 'We were all worried when my dad got sick because she didn't let anyone else look after him and she was struggling because he was very disabled after the stroke. Then they came to Cape Town and he died soon after, and we thought she would go to pieces because they were so connected. But she was so strong – for herself and for everyone else.'* I think that's why people look to her in times of crisis.

The mentality she had back then in the war is the same mentality she has now. She loves life, she has a drive to live. She loves people, most of all. She is a true extrovert – she gets her energy from others. *Evelyn: 'She's the one dancing on the table at a wedding!'* My friends always tell me: 'Your gran is such a legend.' They came over one

---

151 British financier.

night and Gran took a look around and said: 'I want a tequila shot too! Pour one for me!' She's just a lot of fun to be around. *Evelyn points out that she is constantly getting requests from people to come and visit Ella. 'I have to stagger the visits or it'll be too much. Whoever meets her – young or old – wants to come over, sometimes to get a blessing but other times just to spend time with her.'*

I actually like it when my parents go away and it's just me and Granny. My mom is very anxious about my gran. When she is not here, it's somehow easier with my gran – we do things, we go out; she's fun to be with.

This is the first mention of a problematic characteristic I've picked up in our conversation – Jade's description of Evelyn as 'anxious', even if it is specifically about Ella. Through my questions to Evelyn and Jade, I have been mining for evidence of a pervasive negativity which I assume to be a natural consequence of having survived the Holocaust. In both the Holocaust generation (Ella), the second generation (her kids) and even the third (her grandkids), I'm looking for those tell-tale effects of having lived through, or been raised on, supreme suffering. Transgenerational trauma. But I'm not finding much – or nothing so significant as to contaminate the family way. I want to know about the psychological demons – in Ella herself, and the generations after her who might have inherited the residues of trauma. So I ask the question outright.

EVELYN:

My mom can't stand the smell of burning. She says it reminds her of burning flesh and the smell of burning feathers in the Warsaw ghetto. She also doesn't like you to waste anything. I always had to eat every morsel on my plate; I hated it, but I had to. And of course the nightmares, which she still gets.

She's also a big hoarder, won't throw anything away. I wonder if that's an after-effect of the Holocaust, a bit like the wastage thing. There was a cupboard in her kitchen where she kept every jar she ever used: peanut butter, jam, pickles . . . She's also fastidiously tidy.

But as far as anxiety, or over-protectiveness, or pessimism go – she is the absolute opposite. My mother is far from anxious and she is positive about everything. In fact, Brandon, my son-in-law who just joined the family a few years ago, always says he has never heard one negative thing come out of her mouth. Ever. Since he's known her. And he's right – she has always been that way.

She was in ICU with Covid-19. 'I'm going to be fine,' she says, 'I know it. I just know it.' Another time, in her early nineties, she fell and broke her hip so she had to have a hip replacement and then gall-bladder surgery straight after. She was really ill. It took three or four nurses to turn her in the bed. She said to me, 'Do you think I'll ever swim again?' And I'm thinking to myself, if she even walks again, I'll be so thankful – that's how ill she was. I swear to you, six weeks later, she was back in the pool. She has taught me such an important lesson about attitude and mindset. Medicine is medicine but a positive mind . . . that is true power.

If anything, the anxiety is more *about* her than *in* her. My siblings and I felt we needed to protect her from any further harm, and we formed a shield around her to do that. We were also very insular because we just had each other growing up. I, for one, have huge anxiety about her wellbeing. If something happens to her, I go to pieces. Yet she is not anxious about me in that way. Some time ago, I was very ill, for quite a while, and everyone asked me how she managed when I was sick. I remember lying in ICU and asking, 'Where's Granny?' Paul and my kids were all there and they said she was at the Holocaust Centre. I was glad; she didn't need to be at the hospital with me. The next thing, she totters in with her walking stick, and I'm like, 'How did you get here?' 'I was at the Holocaust Centre and I just asked someone for a lift,' she said. And she had no doubt that I would recover. 'You're going to be fine,' she reassured me. 'I just know it. I can see it.' She absolutely believes that she, that we, will get through.

So if you ask me what is different about my mom as a Holocaust survivor, I'd say it's that she is not what you imagine a survivor to be, emotionally. She has an utterly positive outlook on life.

Jade has an interesting view on how the generational transfer has worked in this family. 'My gran was the youngest, my mom was the youngest, I'm the youngest. I think there is an element of sameness in that thread: how my gran was with my mom, so my mom is with me – the warmth, the love, the protectiveness . . . for all their children. Not over-protectiveness. I never felt limited or suffocated by her manner. We're all very close, we speak all the time, and I can see my mom's anxiety for what it is – her fear around my gran.' It's true. I don't want her to hear this but my biggest anxiety . . . [Evelyn pauses and becomes visibly emotional], what pains me is . . . I know she's 101 now . . . my worst fear . . . I'm so terribly attached. That's the abnormal part. It's like a child, if something goes wrong with your child . . . Everyone worries about me for one day when— Evelyn is unable to even say the worst-case scenario out loud. Jade jumps in: 'We all have this strong attachment. My theory is that Granny knows that material things, where you are and what you do – all that can change in an instant. All you have is your family and your people. That's what you keep close.'

The more time I spend with these Blumenthal women, the more incredulous I feel at their descriptions of Ella and their family. Surely they were raised on a mother's milk of trauma? Where is the hand-wringing, guilt-laden, wide-eyed family dysfunction I'd been primed to see? Is this genuinely how they are? And if so, how did they manage to limit the fallout? Short of a psychologist's explanation, I need the input of an outsider – one who is close to this present dynamic but far from its genesis, one who may live this reality but is still surprised by it. I need to talk to Paul.

PAUL:

Evelyn and I have been married 33 years now. Among the siblings, I'm still an outsider in a sense but there came a point where I did feel more on the in.

Ella is very forthright. She was from the first moment I met her and she hasn't changed. I wasn't a great dresser back then – I'm still not *[chuckles]* – and I arrived to meet Evelyn's family for the first time. Right there, at the door to the house in Brakpan, Ella looked me up and down and said: 'Those pants . . . Give them away.' Not, 'Hi Paul, nice to meet you, how are you?' just that my pants were terrible. Admittedly they probably were – I was a poor engineer, arrived in my beat-up Mazda or something – but she said it straight out.

I soon realised, though, that this was a very warm family. I could see that straight away too. Their dad was a little standoffish, but Ella was very warm and I realised that she just says what's on her mind. *Evelyn jumps in to defend her mom: 'She doesn't mean it in a bad way. She thinks she is helping! She told the one rabbi after he gave his Shabbat speech: "It wasn't just me sleeping. Everyone was asleep! Why did you talk for so long? What you said for twenty minutes you could say in five." The rabbi came and told me this, but he also said: "She is the only one who was honest. And she is right!" He was actually grateful for the feedback. So you need to understand that she thinks she is helping, by being so forthright.'*

Ella is Ella. That incident with the shower in Brakpan: the fact that she stepped into the shower and got a shock because it was me and not one of her sons is shocking in itself! What is she doing climbing into the shower with her adult sons? I come from a very prim and proper family, and this house, this family, were so different. I just assumed it was a Brakpan thing! Within a few weeks, though, I realised that it's actually a Blumenthal thing.

It's not uncommon that children are closer to one parent, but in this family, the connection they have with their mom is in a higher gear. I didn't know their dad very well – he died soon after I joined the family. But their attachment to their mom is something different. They're very concerned about her welfare, almost – well maybe not pathological, but intense. When something even vaguely negative happens, they're all communicating and phoning, back and forth. It's always been like that, this overwhelming intensity with her welfare. Evelyn will admit that some of it is almost not rational, like even now, micromanaging Ella's meals. Daughters are often close to their moms but this almost crosses the boundary.

I don't know if you consider that intense attachment a negative outcome, but I see very few negative consequences of Ella surviving the Holocaust, and I think that's partly because she's got such a positive outlook. I would imagine that it could be different in other families where there was a more negative tone.

In their growing up, I don't get the impression that Ella was a doting mother who was present at every school function or whatever. She wasn't, she was focusing on the business. Yet it didn't affect the kids' attachment to her because they still felt very loved and they all feel very close. Perhaps it manifested in different ways; Evelyn's obviously the most protective, but they all have this incredible closeness. I don't think it's a negative thing.

Evelyn went to one of these talks with the second generation and so many people were crying and seemed to be emotionally scarred. I don't see scarring in this family. The only outward sign of it is the nightmares that Ella has. That's the only visible sign of the trauma.

We once asked a psychologist how Ella could be such a warm, loving mother coming from the trauma she endured. The answer is because she herself came from a loving home that was already established – she knew how to love. She knew what it was like to have a mother, a father, and siblings in a warm household. Even during the Holocaust, she functioned as more of a mother to Roma than an aunt. *Evelyn: 'She looked after Roma as she would – and did – look after her own children. Even when Roma came here to visit, she listened to whatever my mother said. If my mom said "sit" she sat. One time they were strolling along the beachfront and my mother was using a walker while Roma was walking quite ably. One of the members of Camps Bay Shul came up to them and asked if they were coming to shul on Shabbat. Now, to get to the shul is a bit of a walk and you have to go over some bumpy terrain through the park and the forest. My mother, with her walker, says to this* guy: "I'd like to come, but I don't know if she can make it" – pointing at Roma who was perfectly able.'

Paul's comment about Ella's own upbringing before the war makes me wonder how much Ella's particular response to the Holocaust has to do with her age when the war began. She was in her late teens, almost an adult and the youngest of seven siblings. She was old enough to have consciously observed and absorbed parental role modelling, attachment and values in ways that a much younger child could not. Paul, Evelyn and I discuss this idea and it's interesting to chart the differences in their own families and individual parents. Paul continues:

I'm sure research has been done on the impact of a survivor's pre-war background. Let's take Evelyn's father for example, who did not go through the Holocaust but who perhaps did not learn to love because he came to this country as a young orphan. So he always retained a bit of a distance because he did not grow up with a big, loving family. He was the quiet, orderly presence and Ella was the energetic, warm one.

I realised right from inception that Evelyn comes as a package with her mom. It was clear to see: Ella will be the priority, to this day. I have my own relationship with Ella now, though my nature is very different to others in the family. They say I have a low EQ, which I suppose I do *[laughs]*. I don't find anxiety useful; give me a problem, I'll find a solution – anxiety doesn't help, it just delays the solution. And I think we've established that Evelyn is the opposite. I wouldn't call them the patient types. But me? I've got to be! 'My mom adores Paul,' asserts Evelyn. 'And he contributes hugely to her life. If I've got to go out, he'll give her lunch or supper and sit with her for a chat. He nods and he listens. Alvin always marvels at that, tells Paul, "Jeez, you've got patience!"' It's interesting you know – my father will be 97 and, although close in age, Ella is so different to him because everything she does, she does with love and no strings attached. She doesn't buy toys and gifts – though she will say 'If you need something, go buy it on my account!' She gives the gifts of time and attention. She is the true matriarch of the family.

Ella's positive outlook is a major part of the story. She also has incredible faith.

Our own family's Jewish observance did not have much to do with Ella. Evelyn and I decided together to start keeping Shabbat, about fifteen years ago. We started slowly. We were enjoying it and decided we really liked being able to switch off on a Saturday. I suppose it has been a point of bonding for me with Ella – she likes to discuss things with me as I've learned more – but there has never been any pressure, and our kids must do what they like. *'It was the same for us growing up,' says Evelyn. 'My mom was the religious one – my father didn't have a clue; he got very into it because he believed in it through her. But she never put any pressure on me. We're the same with our kids.'* Jade reinforces this point and feels that this lack of pressure is the reason she has continued to embrace her Jewish observance: *'I don't remember much from before my parents were observant so all I really know is a strong sense of tradition. It was always important but at the same time they were never, ever pushy with me: do what you want to do, be respectful, but it's your life, your call. I think that's why I also saw value in it and thought it was cool,'* concludes Jade.

To me it seems that Ella's faith has always been a deeply personal thing, a treasure to which she has held fast throughout her life, anchored in her own childhood and religious family. Once again, the matter of her age at the start of the war is pertinent: she was old enough to have begun absorbing both the ritual and the meaning of Judaism before all the trappings of observance were stripped away, leaving her with just the beating heart of her own faith.

EVELYN:
One thing that has passed down to all of us is superstition. My mother is *very* superstitious. In fact, she mixes religion and superstition; growing up, I couldn't tell the difference. *Jade agrees: 'Yes, like lighting Shabbat candles on Friday night – that is one religious practice that Granny insists on, especially with Dani now that she is married, but because she feels it brings good luck.'* Oh there are lots of things, and it all comes down to the *ayin hora*[152]. When Dani was born, my mom made me put a red ribbon on the cot and the pram, to ward off the evil eye, and the first time I got my period, she slapped me through the face! I have no idea why.[153] She won't say the word 'cancer', instead she says *yenna meise* which in Yiddish means 'that thing'; she won't say it by name because of the *ayin hora*. And of course there is 'tu tu tu' on everything.[154] Oh, and if you sneeze, you get the whole song and dance. If you are eating a plate of food and moving the food around the plate, you must push it towards yourself, not away. *Ella is listening to all this and nodding. When asked why she does this she shrugs and says: 'I don't know, it's a* meshugas[155].' If I'm holding my arm up, you mustn't walk under the arm, you must go around, and then back. You can't step over the dog, you walk around it – and she'll make you do it again if you do it wrong!

---

[152] Hebrew, the evil eye. In Jewish superstition, the 'evil eye' is the negative energy that is created by drawing undue attention or flaunting blessings, which may attract the jealousy of others.

[153] There are many explanations for the old practice of 'the menstrual slap' but the one I remember hearing (though my own mother did not slap me at the time) was the sense that bringing blood to a daughter's cheek heralds a blessing for health and fertility, and a warning against improper sexual behaviour. Many Jewish women report having no idea why their mothers slapped them, so it seems to be a case of perpetuating tradition: my mother did it to me, her mother did it to her, so I must do it to you.

[154] The practice is to spit three times (or say 'tu tu tu' or 'pu pu pu') in response to something especially good or bad. The number three is significant mystically and the spitting is meant to protect one from the evil eye and prevent bad things from happening.

[155] Yiddish: crazy/foolish behaviour or ideas.

I myself do a lot of this stuff, often without thinking. Jade says: 'We all do! Like before my exam, I was getting dressed and not concentrating. I realised I had put my left shoe on first[156] and I was like "Oy, that's bad luck." For sure there are certain days which are mazeldika *days – like Tuesdays. If you're buying a house, do it on a Tuesday.' Paul intercepts here and points out: 'Well, that does actually come from the Torah,[157] but there you see how religion and superstition are mixed. I don't think Ella knows the real reasons behind any of these things.'* She's not very well versed in Jewish text or learning – she just does it and she remembers a lot so she bases it on what she remembers. I wouldn't say she is learned.

Jade makes an observation: 'I do think she is enjoying the religious stuff more as she gets older, though.' I think it's because her focus her whole life was on making a living and raising her family: her business and her children. After that, when she sold the business and the children were grown, she went back to her roots.

Superstitious or not my mom has incredible determination. *Paul nods: 'If she wants to get something done – or get something cheaper – nothing stands in her way. She simply doesn't take no for an answer.'* My brothers are also like that. We all remember December holidays. Mom would decide on the 24th of December that she wanted to go away. If anyone else phoned around to get us into a hotel, they'd be told they were full – it was Christmas Eve after all! Trust me, if my mom phoned, she'd get the whole family in. Sometimes we even drove to Durban, parked outside one of the fancy hotels, and waited while my mom went inside. She'd come back out, all sorted. I don't know how she did it.

Jade grins and asks: 'Have we told you about going grocery shop-

---

156 There are indeed Jewish laws about wearing shoes: when putting on shoes, the right shoe goes on first, then the left; when tying shoelaces, the left one is tied first.

157 In the first book of the bible, Genesis, which describes the creation of the world in seven days, God says 'And it was good' at the end of each day. But on Tuesdays and Fridays, God says 'And it was good' twice. So those two days are considered lucky days.

ping with Granny? There's a thing among the children and grandchildren: no one wants to go shopping with her.' Paul agrees: *'It's a twenty-minute exercise that will take two hours.'* She's got a guy for everything – a cucumber guy, a tomato guy, a pineapple guy. You can't just take what you see on display. There was a time that one of the overseas family came to Cape Town and agreed to take her to Checkers because no one else would. He would put things in the trolley and she'd say, 'No, you don't need this, take it out.' He put a watermelon in but then my mom decided that another woman's watermelon looked better. So she said, 'Watch this,' and she distracted the woman and swapped watermelons. She is naughty that way! *Jade knows the drill: 'If you're going to buy a liquid – milk or a cooldrink – she puts it on a flat surface and checks the levels. And you never take anything from the front row, oh no.'* You don't take what everybody else takes – that's why she's always 'got a guy': someone for the cucumber, someone for the pineapple. They all know her, and they keep the better stock for her. *'If you ever need help with a traffic ticket, go to Ella,'* says Paul. *'You can go to the traffic department yourself to have it reduced, but you'll spend all day there. Not Ella. She's got a guy . . .'* I don't know how she does it – I can take her to the traffic department or wherever but I'm not allowed to come in and see what she does or says. *'Well you know that if there is a queue, she'll go right to the front,'* Jade points out. That's right, she won't wait in line. At the traffic department – where there are always long queues – she went to renew her licence when she was about 90. One of the rabbis was waiting in the queue but she walked through the doors and straight to the front. She got everything done and waved to him on the way out. He was still standing and waiting! 'You should have asked me, I would have helped you,' she said!

I suppose it's one better than the story one of my patients told me: about how she (my patient) was at the grocery store and at the end of a long queue at the check-out. My mom went up to this patient of mine and handed her a bag, saying 'Do you mind just holding this?' When my patient got to the front, my mom came back and said, 'Okay, thanks,' and just stood in front of her. She had gone to do her own shopping and then came back to swoop in at the front!

'*I look at the reaction of people when Ella does stuff like this. She just gets away with it!*' marvels Paul. '*It's because she actually doesn't care what anyone else thinks of her,*' says Jade. '*She has charisma – she can sweet-talk anyone. And she knows everyone – she has her protectsia. Yet at the same time, she won't sugar-coat; anything that comes from her is the honest truth and sometimes it can be hard to hear. I never get a straight compliment from her – it's always back-handed; like if she says I look nice, it's probably because I didn't look nice the day before.*' It's true. I used to blow-dry my hair straight and she'd say, 'What have you done to your hair? You think you look nice, but you look like a witch.' *Jade explains: 'She's not actually insulting you; she's trying to do you a favour. She wants you to know that you must do your hair another way.'* But she can take what she dishes out! If you make a joke about her, or tell her something straight, she never gets offended, mainly because she doesn't care if you don't like what she likes. But she doesn't take offence and she doesn't expect others to either. People know that it's not coming from a bad place but sometimes I do feel I must apologise on her behalf. In hospital once, she said to her cardiologist, who was wearing a striped shirt: 'That shirt is terrible – you look like a farmer. Are you going to see other patients looking like that?' I was mortified and I was about to apologise to him, but he was in hysterics! He actually loved that! The next day, he came in a nice white shirt and she said: 'Today you look nice – I bet your wife dressed you!'

Old age certainly gives her more licence to be so candid, but she has always had an attitude. I guess it's refreshing. '*And she balances it with an incredible eye for detail,*' says Jade. '*I'll do something small – say my eyebrows – and no one else will notice a thing, but Granny will say: "You've done your eyes, very nice." And she really knows clothing too.*' That attitude, that confidence – that's my mom. She owns any room she walks into.

Grandchildren

As Paul takes his leave and my conversation with the family draws to a close, I feel an incongruous and unexpected lightness in Ella's story. Though I have always noticed, and commented on, Ella's sense of fun, I had not realised the extent to which it characterises her and is perhaps the very source of her courage. The family interview (into which other members periodically dipped for a few minutes in true Blumenthal style – Alvin on the phone from Sydney, Dani passing by the house) has allowed a whole other dimension of Ella, and by extension her Holocaust story, to unfurl. It feels much like a kid's expanding sponge toy – just add water to reveal the beautiful fullness of the creature. I want to know how we can capture this for others to enjoy and learn from – especially generations who may never get to meet Ella or a survivor.

JADE:

My gran rates herself. It's as simple as that.

She's got a very big presence, and she commands respect without ever having to raise her voice. Because she rates herself.

As I said to you before, I never saw her as anything special growing up. She's my gran. Hearing her stories, living with her – I don't know any different, and didn't understand how precious this person that I'm spending all this time with actually is.

When I got older, I went on the March of the Living, to Poland and Israel. That was an amazing, surreal experience, hard to explain. I had heard such detailed stories of the Holocaust and I had ideas of what to expect. But it wasn't quite what I was expecting or how I was expecting to feel. I had sadness, of course, but more than that was the feeling of triumph.

On the last day, we went to Majdanek – the camp where my gran was kept in a gas chamber and then let out. We had been to Auschwitz and the sheer size of it blew my mind – you can't even see the end. But a lot of it is replicas, and a lot is in ruins. In Majdanek, everything is original and intact. You walk through the camp and you get to the end and there's a huge dome of human ash. We stood around singing *Hatikvah*[158] and it was completely overwhelming. I had been FaceTiming with my family the whole way through the tour and I said to my mom: 'I can't actually wrap my head around the fact that Granny was actually *here*.' When you set foot in the gas chamber where she stood— All the stories I'd heard became more than stories; my gran's life became real to me. I have an even greater appreciation for her, what she went through, even though it is unfathomable. I touch her skin and I think: this skin, this physical body, was *there*!

In contrast to that, we spent a week in Israel and there I felt the sense of: wow, from just one person – my granny who is just my granny, who I sleep over at and spend time with and hang out and have fun with – from her comes my mom, my siblings, my uncles, my cousins . . . all of us! None of us would be alive if not for her.

When I came back home, I had a million and one questions, and that's why I'm so grateful that I went. People say you're too young to go to the camps in Poland when you're in Grade 11, but I don't see it that way. Why not go now when the generation of survivors is still around for you to come back and ask questions? They won't be here forever!

I think people who don't have the same direct connection with a survivor may feel they can't understand or connect to our Holocaust history as well as I can. But that is why this book, and stories like it, are so important. When the documentary *I Am Here* came out, a whole lot of us watched it together and I could see that my friends felt connected, even if it was just through me. My friends all know that my relationship with my gran is sacrosanct but they too can access her incredible gifts, as can anyone who meets her, or listens to her, or reads about her, because she is so willing and able to share them.

People are fascinated by my gran, even more so when they meet her. People have a perception of what someone who has gone through such trauma would be like; they might even feel apprehensive or

---

158 The national anthem of Israel; Hebrew for 'the hope'.

overwhelmed to meet a survivor. And then they come here and she's like, 'Let's have a tequila shot,' and all expectations are dispelled.

When you're young and immature, it's difficult to fully understand the importance of a story like my gran's. Every Jew has a link to the Holocaust, and every person has a link to World War II. As you get older, you realise the importance of connecting to your lineage and your heritage. The Holocaust is still in living memory – it's comparatively recent – and so its relevance is undeniable.

I do feel we have an obligation to preserve Holocaust memory and legacy, especially those who have a direct link, like my family. The stories live on through me. This is now my story to share, it's my legacy, it's my history, it's where I come from.

EVELYN:

Some years ago, my mom went to speak at an Afrikaans school, DF Malan, in Bellville. After her speech, all the high school children stood in line to hug her. She must have hugged a few hundred kids.

During the Covid lockdown, the school contacted me to say that they were changing their name and they had asked the students for commemorative ideas. The children wanted to dedicate a piece of the school garden to my mom – the Ella Blumenthal Garden – where they installed ten lights, each light for a decade of her life. They invited us to attend the garden ceremony.

It was in the middle of Covid but the event would be held outside, so we went. Paul and I took my mom there and she cut the ribbon and switched on the lights. The pupils formed a guard of honour and, as she walked down, everyone was clapping. The headmistress came to me afterwards to explain why they had chosen to do this now. She said that, during lockdown, the kids were really struggling, becoming so demotivated and depressed. When the teachers asked what they could do to help uplift them, the kids remembered my mom's talk from some time before and said, 'Call Ella, Ella is the one.' They felt that if she could endure what she had in her life, and still turn out to be a positive and inspiring person, then they could get through this too. If anyone could uplift them, it was Ella.

Chapter 16

No place for hate

I have been reading through Roma's book, even though Ella insists that she does not expect me to. I have found it to be a useful resource, particularly given my tendency to read very little around my subject while writing, apart from what the protagonist themselves recommends.

I'm led to consider, not for the first time, the issue of truth in memoir, or rather, accuracy. Is it naïve to assume that a memoir, particularly when it involves a subject as sensitive as the Holocaust, is accurate? I am not referring to the objectively verifiable details of historical record but rather the memory of the lived experience. It is here that we bump up against the soft edges of feeling, the rounded corners of individual perspective.

Ella and Roma are forever bonded by shared trauma, each woman central to the other's survival story. But two people's experience of the same event does not yield a carbon copy account. Each speaks or writes of it with her unique gaze, and the subjectivity of perspective makes it somehow inarguable. For Ella and her niece, any space between their particular vantage points is filled not with debate, or conformity or even an obligation to agree. It is filled only with love.

ELLA:
I was determined to do something with my life, I wanted to achieve something. I didn't want to have hatred for people, even Germans. I didn't want to grumble about giving up my life for my children or

work. I wanted to push away bitterness, get it out of me, and live a normal life. There is no place for hate, even with what I went through.

I still don't have my Polish citizenship back; the problem is my names and my passports. I am Rywka Blumenthal née Rothstein, not Frank; the Frank no longer exists. I've never changed it – I had no inclination. None of my husband's family knew the story of my name when I arrived in this country: that I was born Nechama Frank; that I travelled to Palestine under the assumed identity of my late niece, Rywka Rothstein; that everyone called me Hela and that my husband gave me the name Ella when I came to South Africa.

I had a British passport when I came here. When we got married, Palestine was still under British mandate, so my husband and I went to the British consulate. In order to travel to Johannesburg, I had to have a passport in the name of Blumenthal, born Rothstein. So I came here with a British passport with those names.

Over the years, I had many South African passports because we travelled a lot. When I was leaving Brakpan to come to Cape Town, I was clearing everything out and I destroyed the British passport too. I kept only one page with my picture and a stamp.

I renounced my Polish citizenship at the end of the war. It's not straightforward with me because I need documents to prove my birth name. I have copies from the telephone directory of Warsaw 1938/39 – you can see the name of my late father: Frank, Naftali, Targowa 55 and the phone number. I've also got a page from their banking account. The Jewish Institute in Warsaw gave me those documents. But I have not had any luck getting a Polish passport again.[159]

As for reparations and return of property, it's also a problem for me. I told you that my husband never wanted anything to do with the

---

159 As it stands now, the issue for Ella is not a lack of documentation proving her identity. It is the fact that, despite having been born in Poland, suffering persecution there and leaving against her will under traumatic circumstances, she remains ineligible for a Polish passport because she did not marry a Polish citizen.

Wiedergutmachungen. I did apply for some things though. First there was the property that my father owned in Poland. I did inquire. I got a note from the Claims Conference in New York and from the Jewish Board of Deputies that if you put in a claim by 1945, you can get it back, but if you didn't, then forget about it. You see with the one hand they give, and the other they take away. You recall that I went to that lawyer immediately after liberation when I returned to Warsaw on the train, but I had no money to give him so he never followed it up. Roma's son wrote to a lawyer in Poland some years ago and gave him all the details. In short, he says he checked up and there was no claim put in. And I had no record of having seen that lawyer nor did I follow up years afterwards. Who worried about property and money in 1945? I was alive. I wanted to see freedom, to live as a human being. I had my life and that is all that mattered.

I did have a file of papers to prove who I am, including an original letter from Dr Jack Penn who took out my tattoo. I had letters from witnesses who know me and a confirmation of my father's purchase of ten dunams[160] of land outside Warsaw. I gave all this, and a German version of my life story to a lady at the Board of Deputies but it was all lost!

Ella's tone is not one of regret or longing but rather of an officious irritation with herself, as if the outcome is more annoyance than anguish. This fits what I have come to appreciate about Ella: she does not stew. She strides forward, always forward, optimising her means and suffering neither fools nor sentimentality for very long. She ends every interview, every day, with wholehearted acceptance of herself and a deep sense of gratitude.

I remain Rywka Blumenthal née Rothstein, known as Ella, a South African.

I'm a woman of 96[161]. My children lost their father more than two decades ago. I myself don't realise that I'm 96 – I can't believe it.

---

160 A unit for measuring land (used in Israel): 1 dunam = 1000 m^2.
161 Ella's age in 2018, at the time of this particular interview.

I don't even want to tell Evy that I'm finding it more difficult to get up, move around. Maybe it's because I don't swim as much or do enough exercise. I must do better.

I am the way I am because of my past, yes, but also because of my personality – I'm superstitious, like many of us old Jews from *der heim*[162].

I don't allow my children to leave any food on their plate; they must finish everything off. And I don't like to throw food out; I take leftovers down to the people living on the street. Because I was starving once.

I don't like queues. You may think that is because of all the times we were forced to line up in the camps, but mostly I think it is because I am cheeky. I haven't got patience! I always try to jump and be in the front. You should take me with you when you need to apply for a car licence or a passport. I can get it done in a few minutes.

I use *chutzpah*[163] in place of fear. Evy reminded me about an incident that happened when she and Paul were away and I was staying over with their daughter Dani. We were lying in bed in the evening and talking, I think about school, and suddenly she jumped up and ran out of the bedroom because she heard a noise. I didn't hear anything. Dani got a terrible fright when she saw a man climbing through the bathroom window, one leg already over the elongated window frame. So what did I do? I shouted, 'I will shoot! Go away or I will shoot!' And he jumped out and ran away. The police came afterwards but the man was long gone.

I don't like counting, like if you want to know how many people are in the room – or at least, I never used to count people. This is not only from the camps, it is because of the *ayin hora*. When people asked me how many grandchildren I had, I'd say, 'Never mind.' My children I'd say four, yes, but grandchildren I wouldn't count. I've also never wanted to disclose my age; I'm afraid of *ayin hora* to say:

---

162 Yiddish for 'home', like 'back in the old country'.
163 Yiddish term meaning 'gutsy self-confidence, audacity'.

'Oh, she's still alive at this age.' But lately, it seems that my age is common knowledge. And I've also been talking more openly . . . after all, I've spoken about my age and the number of grandchildren with you.

I'm afraid of *ayin hora* because I still want to live. I love to see the world, I love to see life. I can't believe that I'm still here *[Ella is tearful now]*. For years I've been asking myself, 'How come I was chosen to survive? I was no better than anyone else, so why me?' A few years ago, I found an answer.

When I turned 90, the children decided to make it a memorable occasion. They came from Cape Town, Johannesburg, Australia, including most of my grandchildren; we were going to a private game reserve. Everyone began gathering in Johannesburg on the Thursday and on the Friday night we had the *seudah Shabbat* – I don't call it a regular Shabbat meal, like when people leave and they say 'Thank you for dinner.' It wasn't a dinner. It was a feast. *Seudah* means 'feast'.

Our feast was at Henry's place in Johannesburg. We sat at a big table and, when I looked around, I did something which I never used to do: I counted. Twenty-three. Including a couple of grandchildren who couldn't be there. I realised this is exactly what I lost. Twenty-three members of my immediate family and look – *HaShem* has given them back to me.

That was the reason that *HaShem* saved me.

Chapter 17

Faith and hope

My meetings with Ella are becoming less about the interview and more about the tea. Today, she insists on giving me some of the special biscotti baked by her granddaughter in Sydney and sent to Cape Town; when I protest that they are too precious for her to part with, she says: 'I share my life with you, I must share with you my biscuits.'

We decide to meet next at the Cape Town Holocaust & Genocide Centre where Ella's story has held prime position since the opening. She wants to show me the big exhibition board that Myra Osrin put together and, even though I have seen copies of all the photographs and documents she shared with the Centre, she wants me to see them in their official capacity as museum artefacts. My trusted transcriber, Carin Favis, joins us there. Carin has transcribed the interviews for most of my books. As is the way with transcription, she has spent many more hours than I have listening to my interviews. Although Carin always manages to find a personal and unique way to connect with the subjects' recorded words and experiences, she has found herself particularly moved by this project. She says she knew very little about the Holocaust before this and has certainly never met a survivor. Carin would like to break the professional barrier observed by her role and meet Ella in person.

It is a toasty day in March and the air-conditioned Centre offers a cool reprieve. I find Ella in the reception, having breezed through security and the main piazza like royalty. I introduce her to Carin *(whom she immediately refers to as 'darling') and we walk through time. Afterwards, we sit at the empty boardroom table, its mahogany as sombre as our mood after our survivor-led tour through parts of the museum, and Carin plies Ella with technical details to triple check her transcription accuracy. She throws out queries about spelling, place names, historical references, and Ella knocks back each one. Carin is visibly shaken by some of the detail and Ella reaches over to grab her arm, placing an always-manicured hand, lined with age and warm with affection, over Carin's trembling one. When she has reached the end of her list, Carin's ordinarily pale face is whiter than ever and she sets down her pen. She takes a deep breath, puts her other hand to her heart, and asks softly: 'But Ella . . . how can you still believe in God?'*

ELLA:

This is a question I am asked all the time. Why did I not lose my faith?

Not many survivors remained religious. I suppose I am one of the few. I know it might sound strange but I just felt that I'm not cross with *Ribono shel Olam*. How can I blame him? He's the ruler; that is the way he wanted it. Why I survived, why I was chosen . . . It was written that it should be this way. That is what I believed growing up and it is what I believe in still. People are shocked. 'You saw your parents, your brothers and sisters, murdered – how you can still believe God cares for you?' But I do. I can't be otherwise.

It's faith. It's hope. When you are in that terrible place, you just hope tomorrow will bring freedom. You've got to overcome it. You've got to live through it. You've got to carry on. In the Warsaw Ghetto, while we were hiding in that underground bunker of Mila 19, every night we climbed out just to breathe fresh air and feel alive, then crawled back in at dawn. And then, as the building was burning and we were suffocating, we chose not to follow the Jews who told us to follow them out; luckily, because the Germans had sent them in. Instead we held on to hope for a better tomorrow, so we found a place and we hid again – until somebody informed on us and we were found. And then, as we were marching to the *Umschlagplatz*, finally out in the open, we saw the sun, we saw the trees, we saw hope. Luckily our train did not go to Treblinka but instead to Majdanek, where I walked free of a gas chamber. And then Auschwitz, and then Bergen-Belsen. I had hope. I still had hope. It's amazing.

I know people respect me because I'm a survivor, but I say it wasn't me, it was *HaShem* above who saved me. It was meant to be that Roma and I survived – so our family shouldn't be completely wiped out, because from us, other generations came. Some families, you don't know what happened to them, you don't even know the names, because most of Europe's Jewish population was wiped out. I am here to remember those family members who died. As I told you, I keep the list of their names in the back of my *machzorim* so I can say each and every one during the *Yizkor* service, except for the name of my brother Luzer's wife – I just remember her face and I don't know her name. When I say *Kaddish*[164], I can't even mention her, but I can picture her.

At least now, new generations are blooming. Thank God, *Baruch HaShem*, for our country Israel. Had we had Israel before, this wouldn't have happened. It's like a mother: we've now got somewhere to go, somebody to defend us. Before, there was nobody; the whole world was standing and looking, not even taking notice of what was happening to us.

I want to repeat it to you and to myself now.

Eliezer (Luzer) and presumably his new wife, caught in an early round-up.

Then Sala, the wife of my brother Ephraim (Froim), went out

---

164 Jewish mourner's prayer.

to look for the maid and never came back.

Chaim (Heniek) left the ghetto with his wife and daughter and was killed somewhere near Lublin where he stayed with the farmer.

During the *kesl* in the Warsaw Ghetto, Froim got diarrhoea and the only thing that could help him was a bit of rice to bind the stomach. My father and my sister Golda were dispatched to me to get the rice; Roma followed them and they narrowly avoided getting caught. Froim, his children Ruth and Moishele, my mother and Roma's three siblings – all deported.

Yitzchak (Itche), the younger brother who got married in the ghetto, was deported after presenting himself with his new wife and the baby that was born in the bunker.

My sister Pola, with her husband Mietek, the Jewish policeman, sent to Treblinka.

Roma's mother, Golda, taken during the first small uprising when she came into the ghetto with her certificate for Palestine and the ghetto was closed off.

Only three remaining: my father, Roma, and me.

My father, sent to the gas chambers when we arrived at Majdanek.

Only Roma and me. *Ad hayom*[165].

You know what our downfall was? Families were lost because they tried to be together. Of course you wanted to struggle together, stay with one another, but this was the downfall. Roma's father left and he survived in Palestine. He tried to get my other brothers to go with him but they didn't want to leave the family. Roma too: when the others were sent to fetch the rice from me, she was meant to stay behind but she set out alone instead and eventually survived. And me: I don't know why I just knew that I needed to stay apart from the family even from quite early on. Everyone else tried to move, hide, live together. Most families were the same: they didn't want to part.

---

165 Hebrew: 'until today'.

Usually there is strength in numbers. But in the case of the Holocaust, it was better to divide and conquer, divide and survive.

You know what else killed us? Our wealth.

I told you that some people bribed the Nazis and were smuggled to Palestine, to Shanghai. Our family was well-to-do: we could have bought a bus and packed the whole family and travelled south to Romania while it was still free. But we never even thought of it because we had all our wealth around us. And this is what killed us. We were so attached to it, where could we take it? We could only take jewellery with us but no other goods, not the things that we kept selling and which we lived on. Eventually, we had to leave all of that anyway and our wealth was worthless.

A couple of years ago, I met a Polish man and he told me about a train of Jewish gold that the Nazis buried somewhere in the south of Poland. The Nazis collected all the silver and gold that victims brought with them to the camps and were forced to leave aside when they removed their clothing before the showers. Many people had valuables stitched into their clothes, just like I did. I also read on Facebook that in Auschwitz they found a cup with a false bottom; after 75 years it loosened up and inside they found jewellery. We are still finding things, *ad hayom*! And where did our wealth get us at the time? Nowhere. If anything, our wealth was our downfall too.

But faith, and hope, and belief in *HaShem* . . . those are things the Nazis could never take away. That is something we could bury deep inside where no SS soldier would ever find it. That is what saved us. That is what saved me. That is something I never lost.

Epilogue

At various points through our treasured hours together, Ella has marvelled at how easily she has been able to open up to me, at how much detail she has been able to remember during and between our interviews, and at how different our process has been from others in which she has been asked to participate. Perhaps it is because, like all big undertakings in life, 'the readiness is all' and, after 90-some years of processing her remarkable life, Ella was fully and finally ready to tell it.

Ella insists that our own connection is largely to thank, and I'm glad. Never one to mince words or skimp on either criticism or praise, she declares: 'You listen to me. I admire you because you understand my feelings – I think more than anybody else who has been with me since I was a little girl, *ad hayom*. I never see a reaction on you; you just absorb it . . . But I know it's in you, that it comes down and you understand. You feel with me, you go through it all with me. Am I right? You are just wonderful.' And then, lest we linger too long on the sentimental, she leans in and looks quizzically at my denim jacket with its patches of emblems and words: 'What does it say there? "Out of this world", "Chic", "Dream" . . . That's an interesting fabric. I'm sorry, I always take notice of clothes.'

Ever the textile merchant's daughter.

* * *

Soon after taking on the project to write Ella's story for the family, it became clear that to keep this 'in-house' would be to deny a larger

Epilogue

audience the gift of her legacy. I began to think about publication and to understand the book's most important mission: to reach the third generation – the likes of Ella's grandchildren, my children – and to keep reaching, to Ella's great-grandchildren and beyond. Reach. Touch. Ignite. Find the personal connection, get to know Ella and her story, tell it as if it were your own . . . as if you, yourself, were there.

Holocaust books number in their thousands: memoirs, novels, private histories, historical textbooks, all doing the important work of teaching history and perpetuating memory. In her book, Roma, who passed away on 29 January 2022, explored her own perspective of the experiences she and Ella shared. They lived parallel lives, yet their accounts are unique and personal. There is only one Rywka-Blumenthal-née-Rothstein-born-Nechama-Frank-aka-Hela-or-Ella. And her story, too, must be told.

While I never needed much convincing to seek mainstream publication of her story, nor doubted an audience's embrace or interest, Ella seemed more doubtful. We're about to wrap, and Ella makes a comment that rattles me:

'Do you think anyone will even be interested to read my story? Maybe they only want to know about my early background and what happened when the Nazis invaded Poland until the liberation. Maybe the rest – everything that happened after the war – is not important . . .'

As a witness who has listened, enthralled and amazed, not only at what Ella survived but also at how she embraced life with hope and positivity, I can hardly believe the thought has crossed her mind.

Ella once told me that the best of all her prepared speeches is the one about liberation. In actual fact, her entire life story is one of liberation. Freed from the Holocaust, she settled in a country where the concept is especially relevant, where the messages of resilience, tolerance and faith are keenly felt. So I call on Ella's own words, from this speech on liberation, to remind her that her *whole* life story, in all its 100+-year glory, matters and is meaningful to the rest of the world:

My name is Hela Blumenthal and I am a survivor.

I survived the horrors of the Warsaw Ghetto, the gas chambers of Majdanek, the depravity of Auschwitz and the utter hopelessness of Bergen-Belsen.

I lost 23 members of my immediate family, my parents, my brothers, my sisters, their spouses and eight nieces and nephews – the only other survivor being my eldest niece, Roma. But for me, while abnormal, this is not extraordinary.

That I went on to love, to talk, to write, to have toast and tea and to live my life – THAT is what is extraordinary.

Acknowledgements

ELLA:
There are many who have crossed my path in South Africa, the country I have called home for the last 75 years. I am grateful to everyone who has taken the time to hear my story, tell me theirs, spend a Shabbat or share a whiskey. This list of acknowledgements is not exhaustive. It mentions just some of the people who have given me strength to keep sharing my story and celebrating life after tragedy.

The first person I would like to acknowledge is Joanne Jowell, the creative and talented author of this account. In order to capture my journey, she recorded many hours of testimony. Even after the storytelling was complete, I was delighted to welcome Joanne into my home and we enjoyed our time talking, drinking tea and eating my famous biscuits.

Richard Freedman is an acclaimed local educator with a particular interest in the Holocaust. I have had a long and meaningful association with him for many years. He has spent valuable time reviewing the manuscript and has generously written the foreword to this book.

Myra Osrin is a founding member of the Cape Town Holocaust & Genocide Centre (CTHGC), a dedicated community stalwart and a wonderful friend. Her gentle encouragement and friendship over decades has given me strength to share my story and for this I will be eternally grateful. For my 100th birthday, Myra compiled a book of memories, chronicling my association with the CTHGC. This painstaking job is a demonstration of Myra's care and generosity.

On this note, I would like to acknowledge the CTHGC and its committed curators, educators and volunteers. It provides an impactful and inspired platform from which to portray the stories of Holocaust survivors such as myself, who have made South Africa their home. I have spent countless hours there speaking to guests, listening to talks and generally telling people how to run things!

I would also like to acknowledge Jordy Sank, the creator and director of the film *I Am Here*, who with Gabriella Blumberg, detailed my life story. As a teenager, Jordy heard me speak and was so moved that he vowed to capture my story in a movie. I am grateful that he has managed to do so in my lifetime. Although he now lives in Johannesburg with his wife and son, he remains a surrogate grandson and I am so proud of all his achievements in film and in life.

The Cape Town community has embraced me with open arms since I came to join my daughter Evelyn here in 1996. I have enjoyed countless Shabbat services at Marais Road and Camps Bay Synagogues, as well as in the homes of the welcoming, generous and tight-knit Cape Town Jewish community. I love to engage with people and am always keen to hear their stories. I would like to thank them for inviting me in to share mine and to listen to my opinion – even when it was not requested!

Last but certainly not least, my dear daughter Evelyn. She is my youngest child and only daughter. Since losing my dear husband, she has been my carer, confidante, cook and critic. It has been a privilege to spend this chapter of my life watching her children grow up and be a part of their journeys into adulthood. Since Covid-19, I have moved from Sea Point into her home where I have been lovingly cared for each and every day by Evelyn, her dear husband Paul and their children. Although there were many months where we could not leave home, I was grateful for the hours spent recounting memories, drinking tea and looking over the beautiful mountains of my adopted home, savouring each precious day.

* * *

Acknowledgements

JOANNE:

Some things in life are *beshert*, and if you've read this far, you'll also know that some things in life can only be described in Yiddish and are simply resistant to direct translation. Plainly put, *beshert* means 'destiny', but the term can be used for such lofty concepts as finding one's soulmate to such mundane incidents as missing the bus. Wherever it may sit on the continuum of *beshert*, I feel that this is a book I was destined, and blessed, to write.

As far as the destiny part goes, I explored my personal connection to the Holocaust in the Author's note where I described 'seeing myself' in the Warsaw Ghetto Boy photograph. As for the blessing part, it is only now that the book is written that I can fully appreciate this great fortune and give thanks to those who bestowed it.

To the *baleboste*, Ella, this book's source, muse, gravitational pull and light relief: you are the very definition of 'unique'. Writing your story has been an incomparable honour. I only hope my efforts do you justice and find your favour. *Biz hundert un tsvantsik.*

To Ella's *kinderlach* Norman, Alvin, Henry and Evelyn, and the *tatalehs* and *mamalehs* all over the world: thank you for initiating and supporting my visits with your mother/grandmother. You appreciate what a gem you have in your midst, so thank you for sharing her. Evy, Paul and Jade – your insights dispersed Ella's ray of light into its many facets and helped me understand why this Holocaust story is such a shining beacon of positivity.

To the *mayven*, Richard Freedman: you approached the review of this book as a gifted educator and historian and the text is so much richer for your input. The great joy of working with you is not only in your extensive knowledge of Holocaust history, but also in your deep well of feeling for Ella, her generation, and their stories.

To Ella's many friends and admirers, particularly the beloved *macha* Myra Osrin, whose grace and brilliance has infused the Cape Town Jewish community for decades: thank you for your friendship (and ready provision of treasures from your trove of photographs).

To the many institutions that talk *tachlis*, online and in situ – The

Holocaust & Genocide Centres of Cape Town, Johannesburg, Washington DC and more; Yad Vashem; the museums of the concentration camps and significant historical sites; testimony collections such as The USC Shoah Foundation: thank you for the unfettered access to the material of memory. These ready resources make research on the Holocaust freely available, enabling us to learn from history, preserve memory and build tolerance.

To Jordy Sank and Gabriella Blumberg of Sanktuary Films, masters of *spiel*-making: we are bound by our love and respect for our protagonist. Thank you for supporting the book version of Ella's story to share a platform with your documentary masterpiece, *I Am Here*. They are beautiful complements of one another, and I hope we can grow both viewers and readers alike.

Thanks cannot be overstated to the *menschen* of the book, behind the book, at NB Publishers:

Na'eemah Masoet championed *I am Ella*, donned a *Yiddishe kop* with such sensitivity, and quelled the rising panic of looming deadlines with the salve: 'I've got you. Don't worry . . .'; never has a book-baby felt so safe.

Gillian Warren-Brown edited *I am Ella*, donned a *Yiddishe kop* as if she had a Masters in Semitic Languages and Jewish Culture, and was the perfect architect to my draftsperson.

Kathleen Sutton proofread, Anna Tanneberger indexed, Nazli Jacobs arranged, Mike Cruywagen covered and Jean Pieters publicised *I am Ella*: I doubt that a single umlaut, pixel or schmooze opportunity got by you talented folk. To you, to us all, I hope this book brings *nachas* and *glick*. *Alevai amen!*

If there is anyone who *kleibs nachas* from my books as much as, if not more than, any *Yiddishe mama*, it is transcriber Carin Favis. Thank you for the unique filter you bring to our projects and your tender treatment of difficult topics. On this occasion, you're a character-in-writing too!

Acknowledgements

To my personal *Kvetch, Kibbitz & Koch* Department – the talking girls, the walking girls, the somewhere-it's-five-o-clocking girls . . . Gila, Talya, Lauren, Stacy, Debra, Tami, Jeanne, Kim G and gang: without you there would be no sanity, ever.

To the S*chlep & Fress* Team – Charity, Ephy and Arnold: you look after us all and ensure that my intravenous line to Seattle Coffee Company (not-so-subtle shout out) is well flushed. Thank you!

Actually, the schlep award should go to Sharon and Mark: though no Amazon parcel may be too bulky and no request from your nephews too outlandish, no visit can come soon enough. Thank you for always being my people.

To Shirlee, whose brave heart teaches us so much and overflows with love and ginger biscuits: *zei gezunt*.

To Richard, CTO, COO, captain of our ship, and my soul's *beshert*: as it began, so may it continue.

To Tristan, steadfast *Michael*, my starboard seraph;

Phoenix, golden *Uriel*, the angel before me;

and Maxx, bold *Gavriel*, my cherub portside . . .

For you three I give thanks every minute of every day (except at 5 am on gala days). It is to you that the legacy of Ella, and our people, is passed. It is on you that the mantle of responsibility – to honour memory, to embrace life, to build humanity – now falls. Wear it well.

To my Papa, Cecil, the very definition of a *mensch*: in addition to thanking you for all that you are, mean, and do, I'd love to take this opportunity to shower you with Yiddish blessings. Ironically, and amusingly, Yiddish is more famed for its curses and, while I love that we share a deep appreciation for etymology and languages as colourful as Yiddish, I will refrain from trying to invert those curses to serve my purpose. Instead, I wish *gezunt zolstu zein*, and more than that, *a gezunt af dein kop, a lebn af dayn kop!*

In loving memory of my very own *Yiddishe mama*, Phyllis – she is now, as she always was, the angel right behind me.

Selective glossary

ad hayom	Hebrew: until today
ayin hora	Hebrew: the evil eye
Baruch HaShem	Hebrew: blessed be God, thank God
brocha	Hebrew: blessing
chazzan	Hebrew: cantor
cholent	Traditional Jewish stew simmered overnight and eaten on Shabbat day
daven	Yiddish: pray
Eretz Yisrael	Hebrew: Land of Israel
frum	Yiddish: very religious
gefilte fish	Yiddish: stuffed fish – a traditional Jewish appetiser made from a poached mixture of ground deboned fish
goldene medine	Yiddish: golden state, for South Africa's association with the precious metal
goy	Biblical Hebrew: nation Modern Hebrew/Yiddish: gentile (non-Jew)
Grossaktion	German: 'Great Action'; Nazi code name for mass deportation of Jews of the Warsaw Ghetto, starting July 1942

Selective glossary

Judenrat	German: Jewish Council – responsible for administering Jewish affairs in the ghettos
kesl	Yiddish: cauldron
kibbutz (plural – kibbutzim)	Collective, voluntary communities in Israel, traditionally agriculturally based
kiddush	Hebrew: sanctify; Jewish blessings recited before meals on holy days
kleine	German/Yiddish: small
Kommando	German: labour group in the concentration camp
links	German: left
lokshen	Flat egg noodles in Jewish food
machzor (plural – machzorim)	Prayer book used on some special Jewish holidays
mazeldik	Yiddish: bringing good fortune, a good luck charm
mensch (plural – menschen)	German/Yiddish: human; a person of integrity
mezuzah	Hebrew: small box placed on the right-hand doorposts of Jewish homes containing parchment inscribed with Torah verses
mikvah	A bath used for ritual immersion in Judaism
mitzvah	Hebrew: commandment or good deed
Obersturmführer	German: assault/storm unit leader, a Nazi paramilitary rank
pension	European term for a boarding house
protectsia	Hebrew: using connections to your advantage
rechts	German: right

Ribono shel Olam	Hebrew: Master of the Universe
schnell	German: quick
sechel	Yiddish/Hebrew: wit, intelligence, common sense
sefarim	Hebrew (plural): books
sefer Torah	Hebrew: handwritten Torah scroll
sheitel	A wig worn by married Orthodox Jewish women
Shoah	Hebrew: Holocaust
shtiebel	Yiddish: 'little house' or 'little room'; a place used for communal Jewish prayer and gathering, more informal than a synagogue
Sonderkommando	Groups of Jewish prisoners forced to dispose of remains from the gas chambers and crematoria of the death camps
tallit	Jewish prayer shawl
Umschlagplatz	German: collection point; holding areas where Jews were assembled and sent to the camps
Warszawa	Polish: Warsaw
Wiedergutmachung (plural -en)	German: reparation
yeshiva (plural – yeshivot)	An Orthodox Jewish college or seminary
Yizkor	Jewish memorial service
yom tov	Hebrew: a good day, referring to a Jewish holiday
zemirot	Jewish hymns and songs, most famously those sung around the table during Shabbat and holidays

Index

A

Agudas Yisroel 51, 73, 156, 162, 163, 164, 165, 166, 185, 186
   Paris 75
Aliyah Bet 182
Alvin (Ella's second son, Elchanan) 160, 204, 206
   advocate and stockbroker 220
   Alvin's children 231
   conscription 216
   emigrates to Sydney 217
   makes arrangments for Isaac 218
   marries Debbi 217
   sells the business 217
amenorrhea 104, 116
Angel of Death 111
Anielewicz, Mordechai 86
appendectomy, Ella has to have an 53–54
armbands 60, 64, 74, 145
Auschwitz 110–135, 139, 140, 142, 145, 148, 149, 150, 152, 154, 155, 167, 168, 170, 171, 193, 199, 219, 226, 232, 259, 269, 271, 274
   bound for 109
   Kommandants arrive in Bergen-Belsen 138
   leaving 136–137
   March of the Living 8
   sixtieth anniversary of the liberation of 225
Auschwitz-Birkenau 139

B

bank accounts frozen 47
Bankier, Guta 127, 128, 129, 226
Bankier, Lena (Mrs Helene Maria 'Lena' Lakomy née Bankier) 127–129
Bauer, Yehuda (historian) 60, 74
Bekleidungskammer 119, 120, 121, 132, 168–170
Benoni 204, 217, 218, 221, 223, 231, 235
   Jewish school Hillel 209
   school invites Ella and Roma to speak 221
Bergen-Belsen 136–143, 145, 148, 149, 150, 151, 152, 153, 155, 156, 157, 162, 200, 225, 269, 274
Betar (Revisionist Zionist youth movement) 213

Biała Lubelskie, farm area outside Warsaw 155
Bialystok 127
Birkenau 8, 127
Block 25 of gas chamber 114, 131
Blockalteste (blokowa in Polish) 113, 115, 117, 131, 132
Blocksperre 130
Blösche, Josef, SS 7
Blumenthal
   dynamic 236, 251, 258
   Ella's testimony 274
   Family Meetings 235
   Identity papers 263
   Lamb's 242
   three generations of women 233, 250
Blumenthal, Adolf (Ella's brother-in-law in Johannesburg) 202, 209
   Cora (Adolf's daughter) 209
Blumenthal, Ella 1, 2, 3, 4, 11, 63, 198
   confidence 245
   Holocaust survivor testimony 222
   Johannesburg and Pretoria Yom HaShoah events 225
Blumenthal, Isaac (Ella's husband) 30, 190–194, 197, 201, 202, 204, 205, 208, 209, 210, 217–219, 222
   passes away 218–219
   suffers a stroke 217
Blumenthal, Jedidiah (Sasha) Ella's brother-in-law 201, 211, 213, 238
Blumenthal, Julius (Ella's father-in-law) 203
Bordeaux (apartment block) 15, 16, 62
   Ella moves in 218
Brakpan 170, 206, 208, 210–212, 216–218, 221, 222, 231, 236, 239–243, 251, 263
   shul 209, 217
Brenthurst Primary School 209
Brukowa Street 25, 26
Bryanston 194

Buchenwald 192
Bundists 186

C

Camps Bay 17, 229
   School 225
   Shul 17, 252
Cape Jewish Seniors Association 225
Cape Town's Gardens Synagogue 44
CD Lamb 206, 207, 208. *See also Lamb's*
Celle, outside Auschwitz 149
Chavatzelet (Ella schooldays) 35, 36, 127, 139
Chernobyl *rebbe* 191
Ciechocinek (health spa) 40
Claims Conference in New York 264
Cohens from OK Bazaars 202
collaborators 71, 73, 94
Continental Lingerie 205
Covid-19 3, 10, 233, 249, 261
cuisine 15, 22, 29–36, 30, 106, 125, 186, 210, 280, 281, 282
Cuthberts 216
Czechoslovakia 45, 113, 132
Czerniaków, Adam 49, 71, 72, 73, 74

D

Danka (fellow-inmate from Auschwitz, meet-up in Johannesburg) 219
death camp arrival 101–102
death marches 139
Deena (Ella's great-granddaughter) 11
deportation of family, except Ella, her father and Roma 69–70
Donan, Abe 204
Dos Judisze Togblat 50

E

Edelman, Marek 75
Egypt 94, 141, 196, 202
Ella
   currency trading 176
   family leave their home when the bombing starts 46
   finds out her brother Heniek was shot 118
   gets enteritis 118
   gets typhus 117
   last in Warsaw – Ella, her father, Roma and Golda 70
   Warsaw address – Targowa 55 263
   wedding 192–193
Ella Blumenthal Garden 261
Ellwood, Sharon 225
Entlausung 126
European Jewish Congress 225
Eveleigh, Silla 194
Evy – Evelyn (Chava) Ella's daughter 4, 5, 11, 17, 34, 35, 154, 177, 198, 210–213, 216–218, 220, 226, 231–233, 236, 238, 241–248, 250–254, 265
   at Wits medical school 216
   birth 211
   growing up in Brakpan 212
   marries Paul Kaplan 217
   Paul 154, 217, 218, 231, 233, 236, 238, 241, 242, 249, 250, 251, 253, 255, 256, 257, 258, 261, 265

F

Feinstein, Andrew 227
Fernebok, Gina 171
fir forests 37
Forman, Reeva 225
Frank, Anne (author of the diary) 42
Frank, Chava (Ella's Mother) 22
Frankel, Rabbi Yitzchak Yedidya 192–193
   daughter Chaya Ita (friend of Ella) 192
Frank, Hans, SS man in charge of Nazi-occupied Poland 42
Frank, Hela (Ella's name in Poland) 20, 129, 151, 153, 162
Frank, Naftali and Chava (Ella's parents) 26, 153
   donated family Torah to local *shtiebel* 26
Frank, Naftali (Ella's father) 17, 56, 203, 263, 270
   arrival at Majdanek and murder 101–102
Freedman, Richard 2, 46, 170
Friedberg, Edna 5
Friendship Forum 225
Froim (Ephraim) Ella's eldest brother 19, 23, 46, 55, 56, 57, 66, 69, 70, 189, 190, 208, 269, 270
   father-in-law Rabbi Noach Mendelsohn 23
   Froim's wedding 23–24
   wife Sala 66

G

gas chamber, inside the 107–108
Genia (Ella's eldest sister) 19
German industrialists 76
Gęsia Street 12 46, 55, 56, 65, 66, 67, 83, 91
Gestapo HQ Warsaw 77
ghetto
   food rations 59
   fur confiscated 68
   hiding in our flat 68
   making a living 68–69
   meshuggenah Rubinstein 58
   on fire 96
   start of the 56–61
   wedding in the 65–66
Golda (Ella's sister and Roma's mother) 13, 25, 39, 48, 50, 55, 59, 68, 191, 270
   attempted but failed rescue 82
   attempts to see Dr Hillel Seidman 77
   deceived by religious man 78–79
   dilemma with visa to Palestine 77
   Golda and Roma's narrow escape 69–70
   Golda deported 77–78, 82
   narrow escape 69–70
   owns a clothing business 43
   youngest daughters disappear and return 66–67

Index

Goldman, Dr (performed Ella's appendectomy) 53, 54
Greece, Jews from 125
Grochów (suburb outside Warsaw) 153, 154
Grossaktion (round-ups) 75, 78, 124, 280
Grzybowska 26 (building of the Judenrat) 74
Gypsy camp, Auschwitz 125

H

Haifa 166, 186
Harrows, Ella's first job in Johannesburg 205
Helena (daughter of the washerwoman) 27
Heniek (Chaim) Ella's dancing brother/ Henry/ Henrik Frankowski 19, 39, 41, 42, 54, 66, 118, 150, 154, 208, 269
Henry Errol (Chaim Ephraim) Ella's third son 14, 208, 209, 220
   at Wits (accountancy) 216
   conscription 216
   growing up in Brakpan 213
   marries Fran 217
Herbers from Greatermans 202
Herzlia High School 224
hideout in the ghetto, creating a 83–84
Hillel (Jewish school in Benoni) 209, 213, 223
Holocaust Centre 223, 224, 227, 249
Holocaust Heroes Award 129
Holocaust Remembrance Day. 3, 8
hospital of the nuns 54

I

Internierungslager 138, 139
Israel 148, 177, 186, 187, 190, 192, 194, 197, 199, 200, 201, 202, 211, 212, 221, 225, 226, 228, 240, 259, 260, 264, 269, 280, 281
Israeli army 201
Itche (Avraham Yitzchak) Ella's brother 19, 270
   has a baby 69
   in-laws 55, 56
   wedding in the ghetto 150

J

Jacobson brothers (Harrows) 205
Jade (Evelyn's daughter/Ella's granddaughter) 11, 232
Jaffa, stuck in 193
Janów ghetto 66, 118, 154
Jeppe Street 197
jewellery sewn into our clothing 78
Jewish Board of Deputies 264
Jewish Brigade Group of the British Army 162
Jewish committee 152, 162
Jewish council formed in Warsaw 48, 68, 71, 77, 281
Jewish daily paper *Dos Judisze Togblat* 50
Jewish Fighting Organisation (Żydowska Organizacja Bojowa, ŻOB) 86, 89
Jewish Herald 201
Jewish Historical Institute 72, 111
Jewish police 61, 66, 67, 71, 73, 74, 92, 93, 270

Jewish Quarter, on Gęsia Ulitsa 46
Jewish Underground 73, 94, 95
Jews who converted to Christianity 53
Joan (Ella's carer) 16, 39, 62, 63, 232, 245
Johannesburg Dress 201, 204
Johannesburg Holocaust survivors clubs 220
Joint Distribution Committee 148, 162, 165, 172, 176
Judenrat 48, 49, 59, 61, 71, 73, 74, 75, 92, 94, 281
   census 49
Jüdischer Ordnungsdienst 61

K

Kahan, Bronka (Ella's schoolfriend) 139
Kahn, Elizabeth 225
Kalwaria, Góra 166
Kanada 119, 129
Karski, Jan 200
kesl, time of the 70, 93
ketubah 193–194
Kierbedź Bridge 39
Kirson, Levitt 207
Kohen 20, 52
kohnhellerki 59
Kommandos 104, 114
Korczak, Janusz 72
Kordeckiego 153–154
Kramer, Josef 139, 145
Krankimel, Mr 165
Krausz, Don 220
Kupiecka Street 19
Kursi Pirka 24

L

Lager ruhig 130
Lakomy, Helene Maria 'Lena' (née Bankier) 129
Lamb, Charles Dickson 206, 207
Lamb's 207, 208, 216, 220, 243
Latvians 61, 65, 70, 98, 199, 202, 203
Lau, Yisrael Meir 192
Legacy of Survivors 228
Levin, David 148, 149
Libau, Latvia 202
Lichterman, Miriam 222
Lipova 7 101
Lithuanians 70, 199, 210
Lodz 18, 23, 48, 53, 66, 189
   ghetto 189
Lower Houghton 197, 201, 203
Lublin 66, 89, 101, 118, 155, 269
Lutrin, Mrs (elocution teacher) 197
Luzer (Eliezer) Ella's brother 19, 20, 33, 43, 65, 103, 269

M

Majdanek 6, 100, 101, 102, 103, 104, 109, 110, 111, 112, 126, 142, 148, 150, 225, 232, 259, 269, 270, 274
Majerowicz, Mr 158, 160, 162, 163, 165
Mala attempts to escape 122–123

Mandela, Nelson 6, 201
Mané-Katz, Emmanuel (French artist) 175
Maquis (French Resistance) 158, 163
Marais Road Synagogue 16, 224
March of the Living 8, 259
market, camp 132–133
Marysia (Ella's school friend) 35, 53, 100
Maude (child minder) 243
Maytham, John 227
Mendelsohn, Rabbi Noach (Sala's father) 23
Mengele, Josef 111, 117
Mila 19 80–99, 133, 268
Miladys 208, 217
Mincer (mayor of Johannesburg) 206
Moishe Moishele (Ella's nephew/Froim's son) 66, 85, 87, 97, 134, 270
Moishe the baker 85
Mulka (boy who used to take Ella out in Palestine) 187, 189

N

Naftali haKohen 193–194
Naftali Yehudah (Norman Julius) Ella's eldest son 203, 206
   becomes a gynaecologist 220
   bris 203–204
   conscription 215
   emigrates to Sydney, Australia 217
   Lorin (Ella's grandchild from Norman) 217
   maries Caron 217
   robe for *bris* 211
   Wits medical school 216
Nahalat Yitzhak Cemetery 202
Nathan, Gary 17
Nazi collaborators 92
Nazi proxies 73
Nechama bat Naftali haKohen (Ella's Hebrew names, nickname Chumele) 20, 193, 263
Norman, Maude 207, 208
Nożyk Synagogue 154

O

Osrin, Myra 223, 224, 227, 267
Oświęcim 150
Otwock 17, 37

P

Palestine 30, 52, 54, 75, 76, 77, 128, 138, 139, 148, 150, 151, 156, 162, 164, 166, 168, 173, 177, 178, 180, 181, 182, 184–194, 195, 197, 202, 221, 263, 270, 271
Palmietfontein Airport 197
Paris 162–167, 169–182
   Ella's employment 174–177
Parish, Jan 118, 155
Park Hotel 189
Paula (friend in Paris) 178
Penn, Dr Jack 199, 264

Petah Tikva 190, 191
Pledge of Acceptance of the Second Generation 228
Pletzl – the Jewish quarter in the 4th arrondissement of Paris 165, 170
Poland 8, 17, 42, 43, 45, 46, 47, 49, 51, 60, 61, 64, 73, 98, 99, 111, 113, 128, 136, 149, 151, 154, 158, 166, 188, 189, 199, 200, 216, 220, 259, 260, 263, 264, 271, 273
Pola (Perel) Ella's sister 20, 26, 37, 53, 67, 69, 76, 79, 82, 83, 90, 91, 92, 93, 127, 128, 162, 270
   boyfriend 53
   disappearance 93
   gets married 92
   narrow escape 82
   Pola stayed and nursed me to health 53
Polish Home Army 86
Polish Underground 46, 88, 95, 123
politische Teilung 129
Poniatów 82
Poniatowski Bridge 39
Praga (smaller portion of Warsaw) 17, 19, 39, 53, 54, 91, 92, 152, 158, 172, 212
Prague 113
Pressburger, Mietek (husband of Pola, Ella's sister) 53, 67, 92, 93, 270
   Jewish policeman 67–68
Pricowa, Mrs ('Mrs Price') 152–153, 154
protectsia 121, 257, 281
public gatherings forbidden 47
Puff, der 121

Q

quarantine 53

R

Rachel Getz, Dr 203
Rami (Roma's fourth child) 177, 212
Reitzer, Vera 220
Resistance 88, 95
Revisionist Party 201, 213
Ringelblum, Dr Emanuel 72
River Bug 49, 50
Roma Rothstein (Ella's niece) 13, 25, 30, 37, 38, 46, 55, 131, 151, 153
   at death camp 103
   book on Holocaust 227
   Ella helps Roma get a job under a roof 119
   gets typhus 117
   hears she has a visa for Palestine 76–77
   husband Shlomo 185, 187, 188, 192
   in Paris 128
   leaves for Palestine 166–168
   life in the *Bekleidungskammer* 121
   little sisters disappear and return 66–67
   makes a promise 106
   narrow escape 69–70, 270
   school in the ghetto 58

Index

visits Brakpan 211
wedding preparations 188
Roosevelt, President of the United States 200
Rosensaft, Josef 151
Rothstein (Rotsztajn), Samuel (Shmuel) Golda's husband, Roma's father, Ella's brother-in-law), writer 54, 55, 56, 73, 74, 75, 79, 151, 156, 158, 180, 181, 187, 189, 191, 192
   gets visas for wife and four children 76
   leaves for Palestine 51
   urged to leave by Ella's father 52
   warns us to try and run 50
Rubenstein, beggar in the ghetto 58
Russia 49, 59, 138, 141, 199
   liberators of Auschwitz 225
Russian man who saved Ella 137–138
Ruth (Froim's daughter, Ella's niece) 66, 270
Rydz-Śmigły, Edward 46
Rywka-Blumenthal-née-Rothstein-born-Nechama-Frank-aka-Hela-or-Ella 273
Rywka Rothstein (Roma's sister) 181, 185, 191, 193, 263

S

Sala (Froim's wife) 22, 23, 66, 107, 269
Scheiße Kommando 104
Schenirer, Sarah 36
Schwartzmann, Paula 171
Seidman, Dr Hillel 73, 74, 75, 77, 156, 158, 164, 166
Shapiro, Goldie 210
Shapiro, Mr 189, 206
shoemakers, first relatives who disappeared 48
skating 22, 35, 43, 212
Slovakian girls 113
Smith, Stephen 224
Sneh, Simcha 162, 163, 165, 173, 178, 180, 181
Sonderkommando 121, 142, 282
Springs 204
SS men at the ghetto restaurant 59–60
Stockholm Declaration 227, 228
Strafkommando 130
Stroop, Jürgen 7, 98–99
swimming 38–40, 244–245
   in the Wisla River 212
Szeroka Street 25, 26
Szeryński, Józef 72–73, 93, 94

T

Targowa Street (Ella's father's shop) 18–19
Tel Aviv 151, 181, 185, 187, 190, 192, 202, 226
Torstein, Marcel 172, 173
transgenerational trauma 248
Trawniki 82

Treblinka 6, 61, 66, 72, 75, 78, 81, 87, 88, 89, 93, 96, 101, 113, 269, 270
tuberculosis 37, 105
typhoid fever 53
typhus 56, 125

U

Ukrainians 61, 65, 67, 70, 82
Umschlagplatz 60, 69, 70, 78, 82, 89, 92, 96, 98, 269, 282
   little girls escape 67–68
Underground 46, 59, 73, 76, 78, 81, 86, 87, 88, 94, 95, 123, 187
   Ella goes 69
United Nations Relief Rehabilitation Administration (UNRRA) 157
uprising, first Jewish 78

V

valuables buried at death's door 103
Vistula River (Wisla) 17, 39, 49

W

Warman family 163, 164, 175, 185
Warsaw/Warszawa 13, 17, 40, 60, 133, 233, 240, 282
   final liquidation of Ghetto 99
   Ghetto: the Stroop Report 99
   Ghetto Uprising 6, 19, 75, 78, 86, 98, 227
   Jewish Historical Institute 72
   Synagogue 99
Weiss, Ellie and Clara 137, 149
Werterfassung 69
West, Maude 209
Wiedergutmachung 220, 264, 282
Wiesel, Elie 5, 228, 229
Women's Zionist Organisation 221
World Gathering of Holocaust Survivors 228

Z

Zgierz (town outside Lodz) 23
Ziemba, Luzer 19
   wife and daughters at the death camp 103
Zille, Helen 44
Zionism 186
Zionist conference in Basel 180
Zionist Federation 156, 225
Z – story of Mr Z in Paris 174–178

About the author

Photographer: Carli Smith

With an academic background in English and Psychology, and a brief but formative stint in management consulting, JOANNE JOWELL began writing professionally at age 28.

Her first book, *Managing the Quarterlife Crisis: Facing life's choices in your 20s and 30s*, was published in 2003. Over the course of a Masters degree in Creative Writing and numerous subsequent books, Joanne has created a signature style of creative non-fiction that examines the multiple voices that collide in any single life story, and sets the author as character too, voicing the reader's thoughts and exploring our own access points to a story which, at first glance, may seem entirely different to our own. In this way, Joanne explores our shared humanity and celebrates the extraordinary lives of ordinary people.

Joanne's bestselling biographies include *On the Other Side of Shame: An Extraordinary Account of Adoption and Reunion* and *Zephany: Two mothers, one daughter. An astonishing true story*.

She lives in Cape Town, South Africa with her husband, three children and an ever-evolving menagerie. *I am Ella* is her seventh book.

www.ingramcontent.com/pod-product-compliance
Lightning Source LLC
Chambersburg PA
CBHW031314160426
43196CB00007B/524